PRINCIPLES OF HOSPITALITY AND TOURISM MANAGEMENT

PRINCIPLES OF HOSPITALITYAND TOURISM MANAGEMENT

B.K.KOCHHAR

CYBER TECH PUBLICATIONS
4264/3, Ansari Road, Daryaganj, New Delhi-110002 (India)
Ph.: 011-23244078, 011-43559448 Fax: 011-23280028
E-Mail: cyberpublicationsdelhi@yahoo.com
Website: www.cybertechpublications.com

PRINCIPLES OF HOSPITALITY AND TOURISM MANAGEMENT

B.K.KOCHHAR

First Edition 2011

Published by :

G.S. Rawat for **Cyber Tech Publications**
4264/3, Ansari Road, Daryaganj, New Delhi-110002 (India)
Ph.: 011-23244078, 011-43559448 Fax: 011-23280028
E-Mail: cyberpublicationsdelhi@yahoo.com
Website: www.cybertechpublications.com

CONTENTS

Preface

Tourism is travel for recreational or leisure purposes. The World Tourism Organization defines *tourists* as people who "travel to and stay in places outside their usual environment for more than twenty-four (24) hours and not more than one consecutive year for leisure, business and other purposes not related to the exercise of an activity remunerated from within the place visited". Tourism has become a popular global leisure activity. In 2007, there were over 903 million international tourist arrivals, with a growth of 6.6% as compared to 2006. International tourist receipts were USD 856 billion in 2007.

Despite the uncertainties in the global economy, international tourist arrivals during the first four months of 2008 followed a similar growth trend than the same period in 2007. However, as a result of the economic crisis of 2008, international travel demand suffered a strong slowdown beginning in June 2008, with growth in international tourism arrivals worldwide falling to 2% during the boreal summer months, while growth from January to April 2008 had reached an average 5.7% compared to its 2007 level. Growth from 2006 to 2007 was only 3.7%, as total international tourism arrivals from January to August were 641 million tourists, up from 618 million in the same period in 2007.

Tourism is vital for many countries, such as the U.A.E, Egypt, Greece and Thailand, and many island nations, such as The Bahamas, Fiji, Maldives and the Seychelles, due to the large intake of money for businesses with their goods and services and the opportunity for employment in the service industries associated with tourism.

—*Author*

Preface

1

Tourism and Management

INTRODUCTION

The United Nations classified three forms of tourism in 1994, in its "Recommendations on Tourism Statistics: Domestic tourism", which involves residents of the given country traveling only within this country; Inbound tourism, involving non-residents traveling in the given country; and Outbound tourism, involving residents traveling in another country. The UN also derived different categories of tourism by combining the three basic forms of tourism: Internal tourism, which comprises domestic tourism and inbound tourism; National tourism, which comprises domestic tourism and outbound tourism; and International tourism, which consists of inbound tourism and outbound tourism. *Intrabound tourism* is a term coined by the Korea Tourism Organization and widely accepted in Korea. Intrabound tourism differs from domestic tourism in that the former encompasses policymaking and implementation of national tourism policies. Hunziker and Krapf, in 1941, defined tourism as people who travel "the sum of the phenomena and relationships arising from the travel and stay of non-residents, insofar as they do not lead to permanent residence and are not connected with any earning activity." In 1976, the Tourism Society of England's definition was: "Tourism is the temporary, short-term movement of people to destination outside the places where they normally live and work and their activities during the stay at each destination. It includes movements for all purposes." In 1981, the International Association of Scientific

Experts in Tourism defined tourism in terms of particular activities selected by choice and undertaken outside the home.

Recently, the tourism industry has shifted from the promotion of inbound tourism to the promotion of intrabound tourism, because many countries are experiencing tough competition for inbound tourists. Some national policymakers have shifted their priority to the promotion of intrabound tourism to contribute to the local economy. Examples of such campaigns include: "See America" in the United States; "Truly Asia" in Malaysia; "Get Going Canada" in Canada; "Peru. Live the Legend" in Peru; "Wow Philippines" in the Philippines; "Uniquely Singapore" in Singapore; "100% Pure·New Zealand" in New Zealand; "Amazing Thailand" in Thailand; "Incredible India" in India; and "The Hidden Charm" in Vietnam.

Tourism is travel for recreational or leisure purposes. The World Tourism Organization defines **tourists** as people who "travel to and stay in places outside their usual environment for more than twenty-four (24) hours and not more than one consecutive year for leisure, business and other purposes not related to the exercise of an activity remunerated from within the place visited". Tourism has become a popular global leisure activity. In 2007, there were over 903 million international tourist arrivals, with a growth of 6.6% as compared to 2006. International tourist receipts were USD 856 billion in 2007.

Despite the uncertainties in the global economy, international tourist arrivals during the first four months of 2008 followed a similar growth trend than the same period in 2007.

However, as a result of the economic crisis of 2008, international travel demand suffered a strong slowdown beginning in June 2008, with growth in international tourism arrivals worldwide falling to 2% during the boreal summer months, while growth from January to April 2008 had reached an average 5.7% compared to its 2007 level. Growth from 2006 to 2007 was only 3.7%, as total international tourism arrivals from January to August were 641 million tourists, up from 618 million in the same period in 2007.

Tourism is vital for many countries, such as the U.A.E, Egypt, Greece and Thailand, and many island nations, such as

The Bahamas, Fiji, Maldives and the Seychelles, due to the large intake of money for businesses with their goods and services and the opportunity for employment in the service industries associated with tourism. These service industries include transportation services, such as airlines, cruise ships and taxis, hospitality services, such as accommodations, including hotels and resorts, and entertainment venues, such as amusement parks, casinos, shopping malls, the various music venues and the theatre.

SUSTAINABLE TOURISM

"Sustainable tourism is envisaged as leading to management of all resources in such a way that economic, social and aesthetic needs can be fulfilled while maintaining cultural integrity, essential ecological processes, biological diversity and life support systems." (World Tourism Organization)

Sustainable development implies "meeting the needs of the present without compromising the ability of future generations to meet their own needs" (World Commission on Environment and Development, 1987).

MEDICAL TOURISM

When there is a significant price difference between countries for a given medical procedure, particularly in Southeast Asia, India, Eastern Europe and where there are different regulatory regimes, in relation to particular medical procedures (e.g. dentistry), travelling to take advantage of the price or regulatory differences is often referred to as "medical tourism".

EDUCATIONAL TOURISM

Educational tourism developed, because of the growing popularity of teaching and learning of knowledge and the enhancing of technical competency outside of the classroom environment. In educational tourism, the main focus of the tour or leisure activity includes visiting another country to learn about the culture, such as in Student Exchange Programs and Study Tours, or to work and apply skills learned inside the classroom in a different environment, such as in the International Practicum Training Program.

OTHER DEVELOPMENTS

Creative Tourism

Creative tourism has existed as a form of cultural tourism, since the early beginnings of **tourism** itself. Its European roots date back to the time of the Grand Tour, which saw the sons of aristocratic families traveling for the purpose of mostly interactive, educational experiences. More recently, creative tourism has been given its own name by Crispin Raymond and Greg Richards, who as members of the Association for Tourism and Leisure Education (ATLAS), have directed a number of projects for the European Commission, including cultural and crafts tourism, known as sustainable tourism. They have defined "creative tourism" as tourism related to the active participation of travelers in the culture of the host community, through interactive workshops and informal learning experiences.

Meanwhile, the concept of creative tourism has been picked up by high-profile organizations such as UNESCO, who through the Creative Cities Network, have endorsed creative tourism as an engaged, authentic experience that promotes an active understanding of the specific cultural features of a place.

More recently, creative tourism has gained popularity as a form of cultural tourism, drawing on active participation by travelers in the culture of the host communities they visit. Several countries offer examples of this type of tourism development, including the United Kingdom, the Bahamas, Jamaica, Spain, Italy and New Zealand.

Dark Tourism

One emerging area of special interest tourism has been identified by Lennon and Foley (2000) as "dark" tourism. This type of tourism involves visits to "dark" sites, such as battlegrounds, scenes of horrific crimes or acts of genocide, for example: concentration camps.

Dark tourism poses severe ethical and moral dilemmas: should these sites be available for visitation and, if so, what should the nature of the publicity involved be. Dark tourism remains a small niche market, driven by varied motivations, such as mourning, remembrance, macabre curiosity or even entertainment. Its early origins are rooted in fairgrounds and medieval fairs.

Growth

The World Tourism Organization (UNWTO) forecasts that international tourism will continue growing at the average annual rate of 4 %. By 2020 Europe will remain the most popular destination, but its share will drop from 60% in 1995 to 46%. Long-haul will grow slightly faster than intraregional travel and by 2020 its share will increase from 18% in 1995 to 24%. With the advent of e-commerce, tourism products have become one of the most traded items on the internet. Tourism products and services have been made available through intermediaries, although tourism providers (hotels, airlines, etc.) can sell their services directly. This has put pressure on intermediaries from both on-line and traditional shops.

It has been suggested there is a strong correlation between Tourism expenditure per capita and the degree to which countries play in the global context.

Not only as a result of the important economic contribution of the tourism industry, but also as an indicator of the degree of confidence with which global citizens leverage the resources of the globe for the benefit of their local economies. This is why any projections of growth in tourism may serve as an indication of the relative influence that each country will exercise in the future.

Space tourism is expected to "take off" in the first quarter of the 21st century, although compared with traditional destinations the number of tourists in orbit will remain low until technologies such as a space elevator make space travel cheap.

Technological improvement is likely to make possible airship hotels, based either on solar-powered airplanes or large dirigibles. Underwater hotels, such as Hydropolis, expected to open in Dubai in 2009, will be built. On the ocean, tourists will be welcomed by ever larger cruise ships and perhaps floating cities.

Latest Trends

As a result of the economic crisis of 2008, international arrivals suffered a strong slowdown beginning in June 2008. Growth from 2007 to 2008 was only 3.7% during the first eight months of 2008.

The Asian and Pacific markets were affected and Europe stagnated during the boreal summer months, while the Americas performed better, reducing their expansion rate but keeping a 6% growth from January to August 2008. Only the Middle East continued its rapid growth during the same period, reaching a 17% growth as compared to the same period in 2007. This slowdown on international tourism demand was also reflected in the air transport industry, with a negative growth in September 2008 and a 3.3% growth in passenger traffic through September.

The hotel industry also reports a slowdown, as room occupancy continues to decline. As the global economic situation deteriorated dramatically during September and October as a result of the global financial crisis, growth of international tourism is expected to slow even further for the remaining of 2008, and this slowdown in demand growth is forecasted to continue into 2009 as recession has already hit most of the top spender countries, with long-haul travel expected to be the most affected by the economic crisis.

However, some travel destinations have experienced growth during hard economic times, drawing on low costs of living, accessibility, and friendly immigration laws permitting tourists to stay for extended periods of time. Recession tourism, a phrase coined by Matt Landau in his research about Panama, has evolved as an alternative escape option for nervous crisis-goers in 2009.

Negative Impacts

Tourism is the issue that nearly every city faces. It is worldwide and a threat to beaches, famous landmarks, holy areas and also resorts. Attracting a high volume of tourists can have negative impacts, such as the impact of 33 million tourists a year on the city of New York, or the potential to impact fragile environments negatively, or the impact of the December 26,

2004 tsunami on the tourists themselves. The environment can be affected negatively by cruise ship pollution in many ways, including ballast water discharge, and by pollution from aircraft.

WORLD TOURISM STATISTICS AND RANKINGS

Most Visited Countries

The World Tourism Organization reports the following ten countries as the most visited in 2007 by number of international travelers. When compared to 2006, Ukraine entered the top ten list, surpassing Russia, Austria and Mexico. Most of the top visited countries continue to be on the European continent.

Rank	Country	UNWTO Regional Market	International tourist arrivals (2007)	International tourist arrivals (2006)
1	France	Europe	81.9 million	79.1 million
2	Spain	Europe	59.2 million	58.5 million
3	United States	North America	56.0 million	51.1 million
4	China	Asia	54.7 million	49.6 million
5	Italy	Europe	43.7 million	41.1 million
6	United Kingdom	Europe	30.7 million	30.7 million
7	Germany	Europe	24.4 million	23.6 million
8	Ukraine	Europe	23.1 million	18.9 million
9	Turkey	Europe	22.2 million	18.9 million
10	Mexico	North America	21.4 million	21.4 million

International Tourism Receipts

International tourist receipts were USD 96.7 billion in 2007, up from USD 85.7 billion in 2006. When the export value of international passenger travel receipts is accounted for, total receipts in 2007 reached a record of USD 1.02 trillion or 3 billion a day.

The World Tourism Organization reports the following countries as the top ten tourism earners for the year 2007. It is noticeable that most of them are on the European continent, but the United States continues to be the top earner.

Rank	Country	UNWTO Regional Market	International Tourism Receipts (2007)	International Tourism Receipts (2006)
1	United States	North America	$96.7 billion	$85.7 billion
2	Spain	Europe	$57.8 billion	$51.1 billion
3	France	Europe	$54.2 billion	$46.3 billion
4	Italy	Europe	$42.7 billion	$38.1 billion
5	China	Asia	$41.9 billion	$33,9 billion
6	United Kingdom	Europe	$37.6 billion	$33.7 billion
7	Germany	Europe	$36.0 billion	$32.8 billion
8	Australia	Oceania	$22.2 billion	$17.8 billion
9	Austria	Europe	$18.9 billion	$16.6 billion
10	Turkey	Europe	$18.5 billion	$16.9 billion

International Tourism Top Spenders

The World Tourism Organization reports the following countries as the top ten biggest spenders on international tourism for the year 2007. For the fifth year in a row, German tourists continue as the top spenders. A study by Dresdner Bank forecasts that for 2008, Germans and Europeans, in general, will continue to be the top spenders, because of the strength of the Euro against the United States dollar, with strong demand for the U.S. in favor of other destinations.

Rank	Country	UNWTO Regional Market	International Tourism Expenditures (2007)	International Tourism Expenditures (2006)
1	Germany	Europe	$82.9 billion	$73.9 billion
2	United States	North America	$76.2 billion	$72.1 billion
3	United Kingdom	Europe	$72.3 billion	$63.1 billion
4	France	Europe	$36.7 billion	$31.2 billion
5	China	Asia	$29.8 billion	$24.3 billion
6	Italy	Europe	$27.3 billion	$23.1 billion
7	Japan	Asia	$26.5 billion	$26.9 billion
8	Canada	North America	$24.8 billion	$20.5 billion
9	Russia	Europe	$22.3 billion	$18.2 billion
10	South Korea	Asia	$20.9 billion	$18.9 billion

History

Wealthy people have always traveled to distant parts of the world, to see great buildings, works of art, learn new languages, experience new cultures and to taste different cuisines. Long ago, at the time of the Roman Republic, places such as Baiae, were popular coastal resorts for the rich. The word *tourism* was used by 1811 and *tourist* by 1840. In 1936, the League of Nations defined *foreign tourist* as "someone travelling abroad for at least twenty-four hours". Its successor, the United Nations, amended this definition in 1945, by including a maximum stay of six months.

Leisure Travel

Leisure travel was associated with the Industrial Revolution in the United Kingdom – the first European country to promote leisure time to the increasing industrial population. Initially, this applied to the owners of the machinery of production, the economic oligarchy, the factory owners and the traders. These comprised the new middle class. Cox & Kings was the first official travel company to be formed in 1758.

The British origin of this new industry is reflected in many place names. In Nice, France, one of the first and best-established holiday resorts on the French Riviera, the long esplanade along the seafront is known to this day as the *Promenade des Anglais*; in many other historic resorts in continental Europe, old, well-established palace hotels have names like the *Hotel Bristol*, the *Hotel Carlton* or the *Hotel Majestic* – reflecting the dominance of English customers. Many leisure-oriented tourists travel to the tropics, both in the summer and winter. Places often visited are: Cuba, the Dominican Republic, Thailand, North Queensland in Australia and Florida in the United States.

Winter Tourism

Major ski resorts are located in the various, mainland European countries, Canada, the United States, Australia, New Zealand, Japan, Korea, Chile and Argentina.

Mass Tourism

Mass tourism could only have developed with the improvements in technology, allowing the transport of large numbers of people in a short space of time to places of leisure interest, so that greater numbers of people began to enjoy the benefits of leisure time.

In the United States, the first great seaside resort, in the European style, was Atlantic City, New Jersey and Long Island, New York. In continental Europe, early resorts included: Ostend, popularized by the people of Brussels; Boulogne-sur-Mer (Pas-de-Calais) and Deauville (Calvados) for the Parisians; and Heiligendamm, founded in 1797, as the first seaside resort at the Baltic Sea.

Adjectival Tourisms

Adjectival tourism refers to the numerous niche or specialty travel forms of tourism that have emerged over the years, each with its own adjective. Many of these have come into common use by the tourism industry and academics. Others are emerging concepts that may or may not gain popular usage. Examples of the more common niche tourism markets include:

1. Culinary tourism
2. Dark tourism
3. Disaster tourism
4. Ecotourism
5. Heritage tourism
6. LGBT tourism
7. Medical tourism
8. Nautical tourism
9. Sex tourism
10. Space tourism
11. War tourism

Recent Developments

There has been an upmarket trend in the tourism over the last few decades, especially in Europe, where international travel for short breaks is common. Tourists have higher levels of disposable income and greater leisure time and they are also better-educated and have more sophisticated tastes. There is now a demand for a better quality products, which has resulted in a fragmenting of the mass market for beach vacations; people want more specialised versions, such as Club 18-30, quieter resorts, family-oriented holidays or niche market-targeted destination hotels. The developments in technology and transport infrastructure, such as jumbo jets, low-cost airlines and more accessible airports have made many types of tourism more affordable. There have also been changes in lifestyle, such as retiree-age people who sustain year round tourism. This is facilitated by internet sales of tourism products. Some sites have now started to offer dynamic packaging, in which an inclusive price is quoted for a tailor-made package requested by the customer upon impulse.

Thousands of lives were lost and many tourists died. This, together with the vast clean-up operation in place, has stopped or severely hampered tourism to the area. The terms *tourism* and *travel* are sometimes used interchangeably. In this context, travel has a similar definition to tourism, but implies a more purposeful journey.

The terms *tourism* and *tourist* are sometimes used pejoratively, to imply a shallow interest in the cultures or locations visited by tourists. There have been a few setbacks in tourism, such as the September 11 attacks and terrorist threats to tourist destinations, such as in Bali and several European cities. Also, on December 26, 2004, a tsunami, caused by the 2004 Indian Ocean earthquake, hit the Asian countries on the Indian Ocean, including the Maldives.

TOURISM AND MANAGEMENT

Many chains recognize the importance of brand loyalty to guests and have expanded the range of lodging options offered under one corporate name to include a full range of hotels from limited-service, economy-type hotels to luxury inns. The hotel industry has become dominated by a few large national hotel chains.

To the traveler, familiar chain establishments represent dependability and quality at predictable rates. While these national corporations own some of the hotels, many properties are independently owned but affiliated with a chain through a franchise agreement or management contract. As part of a chain, individual hotels can participate in the company's national reservations service or incentive program, thereby appearing to belong to a larger enterprise.

For those who prefer more personalized service and a unique experience, *boutique hotels* are becoming more popular. These smaller hotels are generally found in urban locations and provide patrons good service and more distinctive décor and food selection. While there are nationwide RV parks and campgrounds, most small lodging establishments are individually owned and operated by a single owner, who may employ a small staff to help operate the business. The lodging industry is moving towards more limited-service properties mostly in suburban, residential, or commercial neighborhoods, often siting hotels near popular restaurants. Many full-service properties are limiting or quitting the food service business altogether, choosing to contract out their food service operations to third party restaurateurs, including long-term arrangements with chain restaurant operators. Urban business and entertainment districts are providing a greater mix of lodging options to appeal to a wider range of travelers.

Increased competition among establishments in this industry has spurred many independently owned and operated hotels and other lodging places to join national or international reservation systems. This allows travelers to make multiple reservations for lodging, airlines, and car rentals with one telephone call or Internet search. Nearly all hotel chains and many independent lodging facilities operate online reservation systems through the Internet or maintain websites that allow individuals to book rooms. Online marketing of properties is so popular with guests that many hotels promote themselves with elaborate websites and allow people to investigate availability and rates.

NATURE OF THE HOTEL INDUSTRY

The hotels and motels comprise the majority of establishments in this industry and are generally classified as offering either full-service or limited service. Full-service properties offer a variety of services for their guests, but they almost always include at least one or more restaurant and beverage service options—from coffee bars and lunch counters to cocktail lounges and formal restaurants. They also usually provide room service. Larger full-service properties usually have a variety of retail shops on the premises, such as gift boutiques, newsstands, and drug and cosmetics counters, some of which may be geared to an exclusive clientele. Additionally, a number of full-service hotels offer guests access to laundry and valet services, swimming pools, beauty salons, and fitness centers or health spas. A small, but growing, number of luxury hotel chains also manage condominium units in combination with their transient rooms, providing both hotel guests and condominium owners with access to the same services and amenities. People travel for a variety of reasons, including for vacations, business, and visits to friends and relatives. For many of these travelers, hotels and other accommodations will be where they stay while out of town. For others, hotels may be more than just a place to stay, but destinations in themselves. Resort hotels and casino hotels, for example, offer a variety of activities to keep travelers and families occupied for much of their stay.

Goods and services. Hotels and other accommodations are as different as the many family and business travelers they accommodate. The industry includes all types of lodging, from luxurious 5-star hotels to youth hostels and RV parks. While many provide simply a place to spend the night, others cater to longer stays by providing food service, recreational activities, and meeting rooms. In 2006, approximately 62,000 establishments provided overnight accommodations to suit many different needs and budgets.

The largest hotels often have banquet rooms, exhibit halls, and spacious ballrooms to accommodate conventions, business meetings, wedding receptions, and other social gatherings. Conventions and business meetings are major sources of revenue for these properties. Some commercial hotels are known as conference hotels—fully self-contained entities specifically designed for large-scale meetings. They provide physical fitness and recreational facilities for meeting attendees, in addition to state-of-the-art audiovisual and technical equipment, a business center, and banquet services.

Limited-service hotels are free-standing properties that do not have on-site restaurants or most other amenities that must be provided by a staff other than the front desk or housekeeping. They usually offer continental breakfasts, vending machines or small packaged items, Internet access, and sometimes unattended game rooms or swimming pools in addition to daily housekeeping services. The numbers of limited-service properties have been growing. These properties are not as costly to build and maintain. They appeal to budget-conscious family vacationers and travelers who are willing to sacrifice amenities for lower room prices.

Hotels can also be categorized based on a distinguishing feature or service provided by the hotel. *Conference hotels* provide meeting and banquet rooms, and usually food service, to large groups of people. *Resort hotels* offer luxurious surroundings with a variety of recreational facilities, such as swimming pools, golf courses, tennis courts, game rooms, and health spas, as well as planned social activities and entertainment.

Resorts typically are located in vacation destinations or near natural settings, such as mountains, seashores, theme parks, or other attractions. As a result, the business of many resorts fluctuates with the season. Some resort hotels and motels provide additional convention and conference facilities to encourage customers to combine business with pleasure. During the off season, many of these establishments solicit conventions, sales meetings, and incentive tours to fill their otherwise empty rooms; some resorts even close for the off-season.

Extended-stay hotels typically provide rooms or suites with fully equipped kitchens, entertainment systems, office space with computer and telephone lines, fitness centers, and other amenities. Typically, guests use these hotels for a minimum of 5 consecutive nights often while on an extended work assignment or lengthy vacation or family visit. *All-suite hotels* offer a living room or sitting room in addition to a bedroom.

Casino hotels combine both lodging and legalized gaming on the same premises. Along with the typical services provided by most full-service hotels, casino hotels also contain casinos where patrons can wager at table games, play slot machines, and make other bets. Some casino hotels also contain conference and convention facilities.

In addition to hotels, *bed-and-breakfast inns, recreational vehicle (RV) parks, campgrounds,* and *rooming and boarding houses* provide lodging for overnight guests and are included in this industry. *Bed-and-breakfast inns* provide short-term lodging in private homes or small buildings converted for this purpose and are characterized by highly personalized service and inclusion of breakfast in the room rate. Their appeal is quaintness, with unusual service and decor.

RV parks and campgrounds cater to people who enjoy recreational camping at moderate prices. Some parks and campgrounds provide service stations, general stores, shower and toilet facilities, and coin-operated laundries. While some are designed for overnight travelers only, others are for vacationers who stay longer. Some camps provide accommodations, such as cabins and fixed campsites, and other amenities, such as food services, recreational facilities and equipment, and organized recreational activities. Examples of these overnight camps include children's camps, family vacation camps, hunting and fishing camps, and outdoor adventure retreats that offer trail riding, white-water rafting, hiking, fishing, game hunting, and similar activities.

Other short-term lodging facilities in this industry include *guesthouses,* or small cottages located on the same property as a main residence, and *youth hostels*—dormitory-style hotels with few frills, occupied mainly by students traveling on limited budgets. Also included are *rooming and boarding houses,* such as fraternity houses, sorority houses, off-campus dormitories, and workers' camps. These establishments provide temporary or longer term accommodations that may serve as a principal residence for the period of occupancy. These establishments also may provide services such as housekeeping, meals, and laundry services.

WORKING CONDITIONS

Hours. Because hotels are open around the clock, employees frequently work varying shifts or variable schedules. Employees who work the late shift generally receive additional compensation. Many employees enjoy the opportunity to work part-time, nights or evenings, or other schedules that fit their availability for work and the hotel's needs. Hotel managers and many department supervisors may work regularly assigned schedules, but they also routinely work longer hours than scheduled, especially during peak travel times or when multiple events are scheduled. Also, they may be called in to work on short notice in the event of an emergency or to cover a position. Those who are self-employed, often owner-operators of small inns, camp sites, or RV parks, tend to work long hours and often live at the establishment or nearby.

Office and administrative support workers generally work scheduled hours in an office setting, meeting with guests, clients, and hotel staff. Their work can become hectic processing orders and invoices, dealing with demanding guests, or servicing requests that require a quick turnaround, but job hazards typically are limited to muscle and eye strain common to working with computers and office equipment.

Computer specialists, information technology and audiovisual technicians who are employed mostly by larger convention hotels typically maintain standard hours servicing the property's websites and computer and communications networks. However, they often work long hours setting up and testing equipment for events that require their services.

Work environment. Work in hotels and other accommodations can be demanding and hectic. Hotel staffs provide a variety of services to guests and must do so efficiently, courteously, and accurately.

They must maintain a pleasant demeanor even during times of stress or when dealing with an impatient or irate guest. Alternately, work at slower times, such as the off-season or overnight periods, can seem slow and tiresome. Still, hotel workers must be ready to provide guests and visitors with gracious customer service at any hour.

Food preparation and food service workers in hotels must withstand the strain of working during busy periods and being on their feet for many hours. Kitchen workers lift heavy pots and kettles and work near hot ovens and grills. Job hazards include slips and falls, cuts, and burns, but injuries are seldom serious. Food service workers often carry heavy trays of food, dishes, and glassware. Many of these workers work part time, including evenings, weekends, and holidays.

In 2006, work-related injuries and illnesses averaged 5.8 for every 100 full-time workers in hotels and other accommodations, compared with 4.4 for workers throughout private industry. Work hazards include burns from hot equipment, sprained muscles and wrenched backs from heavy lifting, and falls on wet floors.

EMPLOYMENT

Hotels and other accommodations provided 1.8 million wage and salary jobs in 2006. In addition, there were about 40,000 self-employed and unpaid family workers in the industry, who worked in bed-and-breakfast inns, camps, and small inns and hotels.

Employment is concentrated in cities and resort areas. Compared with establishments in other industries, hotels and other accommodations tend to be small. About 75 percent employed fewer than 20 workers and 55 percent employed fewer than 10 (chart). As a result, lodging establishments offer opportunities for those who are interested in owning and running their own business. Although establishments tend to be small, the majority of jobs are in larger hotels with more than 100 employees.

Hotels and other lodging places often provide first jobs to many new entrants to the labor force. In 2006, about 17 percent of the workers were younger than age 25, compared with about 14 percent across all industries.

INDUSTRY OCCUPATIONS

Workers in these occupations usually learn their skills on the job. Postsecondary education is not required for most entry-level positions; however, college training may be helpful for advancement in some of the occupations. For those in administrative support—mainly hotel desk clerks—and service occupations, positive personality traits and a customer-service orientation may be more important than formal schooling. The vast majority of workers in this industry—more than 4 out of 5 in 2006—were employed in service and office and administrative support occupations. Traits most important for success in the hotels and other accommodations industry are good communication skills; the ability to get along with people in stressful situations; a neat, clean appearance; and a pleasant manner.

Service occupations. Service workers are by far the largest occupational group in the industry, accounting for 65 percent of the industry's employment. Most service jobs are in housekeeping occupations—including *building cleaning workers, maids and housekeeping cleaners*, and *janitors and cleaners*—and in food preparation and serving jobs—including *chefs and head cooks, waiters and waitresses, bartenders, fast food and counter workers*, and various other kitchen and dining room workers. The industry also employs many *baggage porters and bellhops, gaming services workers*, and *grounds maintenance workers.*

Workers in cleaning and housekeeping occupations ensure that the lodging facility is clean and in good condition for the comfort and safety of guests. *Maids and housekeeping cleaners* clean lobbies, halls, guestrooms, and bathrooms. They make sure that guests not only have clean rooms, but have all the necessary furnishings and supplies. They change sheets and towels, vacuum carpets, dust furniture, empty wastebaskets, and mop bathroom floors. In larger hotels, the housekeeping staff may include assistant housekeepers, floor supervisors, housekeepers, and executive housekeepers. *Janitors* help with the cleaning of the public areas of the facility, empty trash, and perform minor maintenance work.

Workers in the various *food preparation and serving* occupations deal with customers in the dining room or at a service counter. *Waiters and waitresses* take customers' orders, serve meals, and prepare checks. In smaller establishments, they often set tables, escort guests to their seats, accept payment, and clear tables. In larger restaurants, some of these tasks are assigned to other workers.

Hosts and hostesses welcome guests, show them to their tables, and give them menus. *Bartenders* fill beverage orders for customers seated at the bar or from waiters and waitresses who serve patrons at tables. *Dining room and cafeteria attendants* and *bartender helpers* assist waiters, waitresses, and bartenders by clearing, cleaning, and setting up tables, replenishing supplies at the bar, and keeping the serving areas stocked with linens, tableware, and other supplies. *Fast food and counter workers* take orders and serve food at fast-food counters and in coffee shops; they also may operate the cash register.

Chefs, cooks and food preparation workers prepare food in the kitchen. Larger hotels employ chefs and cooks who specialize in the preparation of many different kinds of food. They may have titles such as salad chef, grill chef, or pastry chef. Individual chefs may oversee the day-to-day operations of different kitchens in a hotel, such as a fine-dining full-service restaurant, a casual or counter-service establishment, or banquet operations. Chef positions generally are attained after years of experience and, sometimes, formal training, including apprenticeships. Larger establishments also employ *executive chefs* and *food and beverage directors* who plan menus, purchase food, and supervise kitchen personnel for all of the kitchens in the property. *Food preparation workers* shred lettuce for salads, cut up food for cooking, and perform simple cooking steps under the direction of the chef or head cook. Beginners may advance to more skilled food preparation jobs with experience or specialized culinary training.

Many full-service hotels employ a uniformed staff to assist arriving and departing guests. *Baggage porters and bellhops* carry bags and escort guests to their rooms. *Concierges* arrange special or personal services for guests. They may take messages, arrange for babysitting, make restaurant reservations, provide directions, arrange for or give advice on entertainment and local attractions, and monitor requests for housekeeping and maintenance. *Doorkeepers* help guests into and out of their cars, summon taxis, and carry baggage into the hotel lobby.

Hotels also employ the largest percentage of *gaming services* workers because much of gaming takes place in casino hotels. Some gaming services positions are associated with oversight and direction—supervision, surveillance, and investigation—while others involve working with the games or patrons themselves, by tending the slot machines, handling money, writing and running tickets, dealing cards, and performing related duties.

The industry also employs a large number of *recreation and fitness workers*. At resort hotels and at vacation and recreational camps, recreation workers organize and conduct recreation activities for guests and campers.

Camp counselors lead and instruct children and teenagers in outdoor-oriented forms of recreation, such as swimming, hiking, horseback riding, and camping. In addition, counselors at vacation and resident camps also provide guidance and supervise daily living and general socialization. Other types of campgrounds may employ trail guides for activities such as hiking, hunting, and fishing.

Office and administrative support occupations. These positions accounted for 19 percent of the jobs in hotels and other accommodations in 2006. Hotel desk clerks, bookkeeping and accounting clerks, and switchboard operators ensure that the front office operates smoothly. *Hotel, motel, and resort desk clerks* process reservations and guests' registrations and checkouts, monitor arrivals and departures, handle complaints, and receive and forward mail. The duties of hotel desk clerks depend on the size of the facility. In smaller lodging places, one clerk or a manager may do everything. In larger hotels, a larger staff divides the duties among several types of clerks.

Management, business, and financial operations occupations. Hotels and other lodging places employ many different types of managers to direct and coordinate the activities of the front office, kitchen, dining room, and other departments, such as housekeeping, accounting, personnel, purchasing, publicity, sales, security and maintenance. *Lodging managers*, typically the general manager and assistant managers, make decisions that affect the general operations of the hotel, including setting room rates, establishing credit policy, and having ultimate responsibility for resolving problems. In smaller establishments, lodging managers also may perform many of the front-office clerical tasks. In the smallest establishments, the owners—sometimes a family team—do all the work necessary to operate the business.

Other managers are responsible for different phases of hotel operations. For example, *food and beverage managers* oversee restaurants, lounges, and catering or banquet operations. *Rooms managers* look after reservations and occupancy levels to ensure proper room assignments and authorize discounts, special rates, or promotions. Large hotels, especially those with conference centers, use an executive committee structure to improve departmental communications and coordinate activities. Other managers who may serve on a hotel's executive committee include *public relations* or *sales managers, human resource directors, executive housekeepers,* and *heads of hotel security.*

Other occupations. Hotels and other accommodations employ a variety of workers found in many other industries. *General maintenance and repair workers* fix leaky faucets, do some painting and carpentry, make sure that heating and air-conditioning equipment works properly, mow lawns, and exterminate pests. The industry also employs cashiers, accountants, personnel workers, and entertainers. As properties acquire and use more sophisticated computer systems, they employ more *computer specialists* to help maintain these systems as well as the hotel's website, and computer connections for guests. Also, many additional workers inside a hotel may work for other companies under contract to the hotel or may provide personal or retail services directly to hotel guests from space rented by the hotel. This group includes guards and security officers, barbers, cosmetologists, fitness trainers and aerobics instructors, valets, gardeners, and parking attendants.

Training and Advancement

Most large hotel properties employ persons in occupations that require a wide range of skills and experience. Most entry-level jobs require little or no previous training; basic tasks usually can be learned in a short time. Lodging managers and many department heads conversely usually require some formal training or years of hospitality industry experience, or both. All positions though require employees to maintain a customer-service orientation. Yet, almost all workers in the hotel and other accommodations industry undergo some on-the-job training provided under the supervision of an experienced employee or manager to acclimate new employees to any unique characteristics of the property or the local area.

Hotel managers and owners recognize the importance of personal service and attention to guests; so they look for persons with positive personality traits and good communication skills when filling many guest services positions, such as desk clerk and host and hostess positions. Many hotel managers place a greater emphasis on customer service skills while providing specialized training in other skill areas, such as computer technology and software. Vocational courses and apprenticeship programs in food preparation, catering, and hotel and restaurant management, offered through restaurant and lodging associations and trade unions, provide training opportunities. Programs range in length from a few months to several years.

Service workers. Most service workers need only a high school diploma or equivalent to get hired, but some can be hired with even less. Some entry-level jobs are filled by students looking for part-time or seasonal work. Most hotels, particularly the chain hotels, have some formal training sessions for new employees that may include video or on-line training. Advancement opportunities for service workers in the hotel industry vary widely.

Some workers, such as housekeepers and janitors, generally have few opportunities for advancement. In large properties, some may advance to supervisory positions. Advancement opportunities for chefs and cooks are better than those for most other service occupations. Cooks often advance to chef or to supervisory and management positions, such as executive chef, restaurant manager, or food service manager. Hotel desk clerks sometimes advance to supervisory or managerial front-office positions.

Promotional opportunities often are greatest for those who are willing to take on a new assignment in a different department. Advancement for those who excel at customer service and demonstrate a willingness to learn front-office jobs can serve as a steppingstone to jobs in public relations, advertising, sales, and management.

Management, business, and financial operations occupations. Many hotels fill first-level manager positions by promoting staff from within—particularly those with good communication skills, a solid educational background, tact, loyalty, and a capacity to endure hard work and long hours. People with these qualities still advance to manager jobs but, more recently, lodging chains have primarily been hiring persons with 4-year college degrees in the liberal arts or other fields and starting them in assistant manager or management trainee positions. Bachelor's and Master's degree programs in hotel, restaurant, and hospitality management provide the strongest background for a career as a hotel manager, with nearly 150 colleges and universities offering such programs. Graduates of these programs are highly sought by employers in this industry, because of their familiarity with technical issues and their ability to learn related skills quickly. Eventually, they may advance to a top management position in a hotel or a corporate management position in a large chain operation. Upper management positions, such as general manager, food service manager, or sales manager, generally require considerable formal training and job experience. Some department managers, executive housekeepers, and executive chefs, generally require some specialized training and extensive on-the-job experience. To advance to positions with more responsibilities, lodging managers frequently change employers or relocate within a chain to a property in another area.

Office and administrative support occupations. For office and administrative support workers, advancement opportunities in the hotel industry vary widely. These occupations offer excellent entry-level job prospects and can serve as a steppingstone to jobs in hospitality, public relations, advertising, sales, and management.

Outlook

The hotels and other accommodations industry is expected to provide many new jobs over the 2006-16 period. New hotel construction and steady strength in the business and international travel segments will create job opportunities in an array of occupations in this industry.

Employment change. Wage and salary employment in hotels and other accommodations is expected to increase by 14 percent, compared with 11 percent growth projected for all industries combined. Travel and tourism, having rebounded since the recession following 9/11, is expected to continue growing and result in a greater need for transient rooms. All segments of the hotel market are expected to see increases in the number of rooms, but the greatest number of rooms coming on line will be in limited service hotels that do not provide food service. Many of these newer hotels are being built in the suburbs where a growing population is increasingly based and a base of business establishments is being developed.

Employment outlook varies somewhat by service class of hotel and occupation. Growth of full-service hotels, casino hotels, and the small, but burgeoning, luxury hotel market that specializes in personal service will cause employment of lodging managers to grow much faster than the average. The accelerating trend toward chain-affiliated hotels should provide managers with opportunities for advancement into general manager positions, manager jobs at larger and busier properties, and corporate administrative jobs.

Opportunities should be more limited for self-employed managers or owners of small lodging places, such as bed-and-breakfast inns, because of the competition from long-established chains as they move into new markets once friendly to the quainter properties. Job opportunities at outdoor recreation and RV parks should grow as RVs and driving vacations gain popularity in the United States. Also, gaming services and gaming manager occupations should grow as more casino hotels are built.

Employment of hotel, motel, and resort desk clerks is expected to grow faster than some other occupations in the industry in part because the growing numbers of limited-service hotels still require desk clerks. Employment of waiters and waitresses will grow more slowly—reflecting the increasing number of hotels and other accommodations that either do not offer full-service restaurants or contract them out to other food service establishments.

Job prospects. Although most of the hotels opening over the next decade will be limited service hotels, most of the job openings will arise in full-service hotels, including convention, casino, and resort hotels, because they employ the most workers.

Limited-service properties do not operate restaurants, or lounges; therefore, these establishments offer a narrower range of employment opportunities; however, the streamlined organizational structure offers a faster route to the general manager level for those more interested in running or owning their own hotel. Job opportunities will be concentrated in the largest hotel occupations, such as building cleaning workers and hotel, motel, and resort desk clerks. These workers are found in all types of hotels and accommodations, from the limited service economy hotels to posh casino hotels. They also are important to the growing luxury hotel segment that emphasizes personal service.

Some occupations in this industry have relatively high numbers of workers who leave their jobs and must be replaced. Many young people and those looking only for seasonal or part-time work, and not a career, take food service and clerical jobs that require little or no previous training. To attract and retain workers, the hotel and other accommodations industry is placing more emphasis on training and retaining employees. Therefore, job opportunities in this industry should be plentiful for first-time jobseekers and people with limited skills.

Earnings

Industry earnings. Earnings in hotels and other accommodations generally are much lower than the average for all industries. In 2006, average earnings for all nonsupervisory workers in this industry were $353 a week, compared with $533 a week, for workers throughout private industry. Many workers in this industry earn the Federal minimum wage of $5.85 an hour or less, if tips are included as a substantial part of earnings. Workers in these lower paying occupations will see their future earnings increase on a phased-in basis to $7.25 per hour by 2009. Some States have laws that establish a higher minimum wage.

Food and beverage service workers, as well as hosts and hostesses, maids and housekeeping cleaners, concierges, and baggage porters and bellhops, derive their earnings from a combination of hourly earnings and customer tips. Waiters and waitresses often derive the majority of their earnings from tips, which vary greatly depending on menu prices and the volume of customers served. Many employers also provide free meals and furnish uniforms. Food service personnel may receive extra pay for working at banquets and on other special occasions. In general, workers with the greatest skills, such as restaurant cooks, have the highest earnings, and workers who receive tips have the lowest.

Salaries of lodging managers are dependent upon the size and sales volume of the establishment and their specific duties and responsibilities. Managers may earn bonuses ranging up to 50 percent of their basic salary. In addition, they may be furnished with meals, parking, laundry, and other services, and sometimes on-site lodging for themselves and their families. Some hotels offer profit-sharing plans, tuition reimbursement, and other benefits to their employees.

Benefits and union membership. About 10 percent of the workers in hotels and other accommodations are union members or are covered by union contracts, compared with 13 percent of workers in all industries combined.

TOURISM & DESTINATION MANAGEMENT

Managing tourism destinations is an important part of controlling tourism's environmental impacts. Destination management can include land use planning, business permits and zoning controls, environmental and other regulations, business association initiatives, and a host of other techniques to shape the development and daily operation of tourism-related activities.

The term "destination" refers broadly to an area where tourism is a relatively important activity and where the economy may be significantly influenced by tourism revenues. Destination management is complicated by the fact that a single, recognizable destination may include several municipalities, provinces, or other government entities-in island environments it may be the entire country.

Participating governance structures led by local authorities, with the involvement of local NGOs, community and indigenous representatives, academia, and local chambers of commerce, make up what are known as "Destination Management Organizations" (DMOs). Often DMOs take the form of local tourism boards, councils, or development organizations. The network of local tourism businesses (hotels, attractions, transportation services, service providers such as guides and equipment rentals, restaurants, etc.) are also a significant part of a destination.

Destination Management Approach

The needs, expectations and anticipated benefits of tourism vary greatly from one destination to the next, and there is certainly no "one size fits all" approach to destination management. As local communities living in regions with tourism potential develop a vision for what kind of tourism they want to facilitate, a comprehensive planning framework such as Local Agenda 21 has proved useful and is being used more and more often. Promoting sustainable tourism within Local Agenda 21 processes is a way to strengthen local stewardship of the environment.

Cities and Tourism

Cities to Absorb Growth in World Tourism: International tourist arrivals in 1995 were 563 million and are expected to reach 1.6 billion by the year 2020. These forecasts use a conservative growth rate of 4.3% and 6.7% respectively; less than the current growth rate. They do not include any domestic tourism which can readily be anticipated to equal the international. It is obvious that most of this increase will have to be absorbed by cities.

World Tourism Organisation: The most recent trends and forecasting studies by the World Tourism Organisation indicate that cities will continue to be in high demand by tourists of all sorts, and the problems associated with the handling of these tourists will have to be more systematically tackled by all parties concerned.

Cities face, therefore, a double challenge.

Firstly, they have to be able to respond to the expectations and needs of the growing numbers of tourists who are attracted to their rich and varied array of cultural, business, entertainment, shopping, sports and other attractions; furthermore, they need to continuously renovate and improve such facilities in order to maintain their share in the competitive tourism market and the benefits resulting from it.

Secondly, cities have to ensure that tourism is developed and managed in such a way that it benefits the resident population, does not contribute to the deterioration of the urban environment but rather to its enhancement, and does not become a financial burden to the local authority. Some of the key stakeholders in urban tourism include: Private Sector i.e. airlines, hotel chain operators and owners, tour operators, credit card companies, tourist attraction operators (theme parks, events etc.), real estate agencies;

- Public Sector i.e. city managers (from the historic city to the seaside resort), transportation planners, bus and train operators, information departments, economic development agencies, national parks, national tourist organisations;
- Touristic Institutions i.e. museums, art galleries, historic facilities (e.g. the national trust) and educational organisations.

There are three key dimensions of tourism in cities and urban areas:

- Products-the anticipated changes necessary from tourist attraction providers; theme parks, operators of events (sports, shows, fairs), museums and hotels. What are their plans, how do they respond to the anticipated growth?
- Information-How does a city make itself more tourist friendly? What are the information systems available to tourists? How do tour operators deal with this growing demand? How to accumulate information on customer preferences and requirement, seasonal changes, age groups etc.? How to develop enduring attractions which will provide sustainable development? What information does the city provide in order to attract tourist attraction providers?
- Impacts-economic and development opportunities as well as the impact of tourism growth on sustainable develop-

ment, transportation, cultural and environmental, social and economic aspects.

Environmental Management System and Eco-Tourism

Since the introduction of Agenda 21, the hospitality sector has adopted numerous strategies, approaches and measures in response to the challenge of sustainable development. These include:

- Environmental management systems and tools
- Education, awareness creation, training and information dissemination
- Voluntary initiatives
- Multi-stakeholder communication and consultation
- Environmental reporting
- Implementation of the Rio principles

The sector has particularly used environmental management systems and tools to demonstrate committment to an environmentally friendly work ethic. Many multinational and independent hotel companies have introduced environmental management practices at the property level. Ideally, the framework for this involves defining an environmental policy and building a management system to measure environmental impacts and compliance with the policy and local regulations, as well as documenting the system's performance for inspection and auditing purposes. Such environmental management systems (EMS) help businesses to evaluate, manage and reduce their negative environmental impacts by providing a methodology to integrate environment management into business operations in a systematic manner.

A NEW ARENA FOR CAREER BUILDING

Tourism and its related business activities belong to the most important sectors of the economies worldwide. Surprisingly this is widely underestimated because the complexity of tourism does not allow its quantitative perception and its real economic relevance. For this reason it has not been realized thoroughly that the tourism industry is the biggest employer in the world, and will continue to be despite the actual recession due to terrorism and other turbulences that have disturbed the peaceful environment of travellers.

Universities and training institutions recognized the needs of the prosperous tourism industry and have been developing qualification programmes on different levels and differentiations of focus. But they have been followers of the industry's demand rather than strategic planners aiming at an anticipated goal of management competence.

How to Support the Industry

Today it is necessary for universities and other institutions involved to be more entrepreneurial and more strategy orientated. They have to assess the actual tourism industry with its needs and demands for management excellence to enable themselves to design and implement curricula for programmes which guarantee the output of appropriate graduates.

The Growing Needs: In cooperation with the industry, universities must look ahead and try to get an imagination of the prospective development. Management skills are changing permanently, refreshing them is a continuous necessity. Tourism management is no exception. The industry is becoming more and more global. Global players are dominating the market while local partners depend on them, on their strategies and preferences. Management and operations for all people involved have become more sophisticated and challenging over the years.

Competition between tour operators, hotel chains, destinations, airlines, agencies etc. is fierce. At this stage industry needs excellent management competence, but where to recruit this excellence?

Negligence and Ignorance of Academics: The underestimation of the tourism business has been shared by universities for long. Similar to the century-long fight of business administration and management for recognition by the academic community, tourism management in many cases is not recognized as a serious subject. This irrational perception of tourism business with its relation to leisure and travel is still influencing the choice made by students today in the programmes provided by universities and other institutes. Such programmes don't appeal to male students because they don't consider tourism as a reasonable career opportunity. They prefer courses in general business administration and management, however for the tight labour market they cannot avoid the tourism industry as an employer later on.

What they lack in this case is a sound qualification in tourism management. This can only partly be compensated by learning on the job, what does not fulfill the career expectations of young managers and does not meet the requirements for differentiation of human resource departments as well. Additional qualification is a must. Is this qualification provided by an MBA?

Additional Qualification

An MBA is not an appropriate means for compensating the lack of compentence as long as the MBA is merely seen as an introduction to general management. Graduates of business studies got this introduction and much more in their four years degree course. Such an introduction is appropriate for those whose first academic degree was engineering, informatics, architecture etc., but not for graduates of business studies. For them the core subject of an additional qualification must be related to the specific industry or to the management function they are in respectively they want to acquire.

An elective focused on their speciality, as it is offered in many MBA programmes, does in no way fulfill the requirements. They must get the opportunity to dig deeper into their core skills (e.g. marketing or HRM) but now related to their business (e.g. global marketing in tourism) respectively to their function (e.g. staffing of subsidiaries abroad). A master of science is not the right answer to the respective demand because it is not regarded as an award of excellence in management but rather as a sign of academic excellence and a step to the PhD.

The Specialist MBA: Only a Specialist MBA is the adequate solution, an MBA in tourism or in international tourism management. Such a specialized programme would overcome the problem and results in multiple demand. Are there constraints to the implementation of a specialist tourism MBA?

A Contradiction in Terms?: In the traditional academic perspective, the MBA is by definition a broad qualification in general management. Specialities can only be electives, which should never dodge the breadth of business orientation intended. From this point of view the Specialist MBA is a contradiction in terms. But this traditional perspective to an MBA is being pushed back by the market forces. And it is not reasonable to withstand this development. Further specialisation has to be achieved by Specialist MBA programmes.

Higher Management Career: Since the MBA became the brand of highest academic award of managers it cannot be denied that this award is appreciated not only by managers whose first academic education was different to business administration and management.

Should the MBA shop be closed for those who got their first degree in business administration and management and who covered almost all the subjects of the MBA syllabus so that they cannot be motivated to get an MBA in terms of a mere general introduction to business and management? Should they waive on an MBA degree, the highest appropriate practice orientated academic award for their career?

The MBA became a mark of distinction for academics in business. Therefore it must be accessible for all who want to add a specialized qualification to their first academic degree. For graduates in business administration this can only be something apart from general business management: it has to be a Specialist MBA. In such a case the entry requirement for all should be equal, a degree in a business related subject.

A Pragmatic Solution: It has to be acknowledged that the additional skills which an engineer gains by an MBA course (Type 1) deserves the same award like the additional qualification of a business graduate who gets an MBA with the specialization in international marketing or information systems (Type 2). The quality and the rating of the two types of MBAs achieve the same levels, only the qualifications differ.

Universities should not assume that the business world would not be able to identify the difference between the variety of MBAs. The Specialist MBA is improving the possibility to differentiate and to select the candidates who are fitting best into the needs of the employers.

Specialist MBA in Tourism Management

Taking all those factors into account it is only a logical consequence to create Specialist MBAs focusing on tourism management, to equip the tourism industry with highly skilled management staff. But how to dot hat? The tourism business is known for its complexity and its international dimension. An MBA specialised on tourism or international tourism cannot cover everything. Therefore even the design of this industry related Specialist MBA remains general, covering the most important basic skills required by the tourism industry.

What Tourism Management Means: The touristic product is a bundle of offered components. Many industries are brought together in a system of relationships. Their capability of interaction and cooperation in the respective environments determines the economic success of each of them. Management of the different elements in various scopes of tourism needs highly developed skills to cope with the challenges of a business which is volatile and constantly influenced by the changes of travel motivations of tourists and the trends in society or by natural disasters and political developments. Managers in the tourism business need-more than in other scopes of business-the awareness of the complexity of interrelationships of the players and a sensibility for changes in demands and environments. They need the skills to adjust the business to these respective changes. That requires strategic thinking, creativity, intercultural competence, skills of communication and leadership, the capability of self-learning and the stimulation of organizational learning as well as knowledge management.

Specialist MBA in International Tourism Management: An MBA in international tourism management with about 600 hours of class presence therefore should include the following subjects of different weight:

- The phenomenon of tourism and its systems
- Economics of tourism and its industries

- Environments of tourism
- Tourism demand
- International and global tourism management
- Culture and cross-cultural management
- Tourism marketing
- Marketing research in tourism
- Strategic planning in tourism
- Business policy and ethics
- Specific management functions in tourism (e.g. HRM, financial management, operations management, strategic quality management)
- Management of international projects
- E-tourism
- Communication and negotiation

An MBA in international tourism management is inevitably a real necessity. This need is pushed by the industry that is constantly affected not only by the economic changes but also by other phenomena surrounding them. It is therefore a rational move to be taken by the learning institutions to develop such a programme to accommodate this need-rather than to reject this demand.

The market requires Specialist MBAs. It is the logic of the general trends of more specialization driven by the concentration process in particular. Universities have to design qualification programmes which support these requirements as far as academic responsibility allows. By offering Specialist MBAs universities don´t loose their virtues. Their interest should only be to secure transparency of what is offered and which award is delivered. It is possible to avoid confusion by clear information on the respective type of MBA. So universities are contributing to the needs of employers and ambitious young managers by the differentiation of awards, which are not differing in quality but only in its specific qualification.

The Specialist MBA in international tourism management will provide the prospective candidates with the competitive advantage of securing a career in the respective industry.

SUPPORT IN FINANCIAL ECONOMY

The tourism industry generates substantial economic benefits to both host countries and tourists' home countries. Especially in developing countries, one of the primary motivations for a region to promote itself as a tourism destination is the expected economic improvement. As with other impacts, this massive economic development brings along both positive and negative consequences.

In this chapter we would talk about

* Negative economic impacts from tourism
* How tourism can contribute to economic development

According to the World Tourism Organization, 698 million people traveled to a foreign country in 2000, spending more US$ 478 billion. International tourism receipts combined with passenger transport currently total more than US$ 575 billion-making tourism the world's number one export earner, ahead of automotive products, chemicals, petroleum and food.

NEGATIVE IMPACTS

There are many hidden costs to tourism, which can have unfavorable economic effects on the host community. Often rich countries are better able to profit from tourism than poor ones. Whereas the least developed countries have the most urgent need for income, employment and general rise of the standard of living by means of tourism, they are least able to realize these benefits. Among the reasons for this are large-scale transfer of tourism revenues out of the host country and exclusion of local businesses and products.

Leakage

The direct income for an area is the amount of tourist expenditure that remains locally after taxes, profits, and wages are paid outside the area and after imports are purchased; these subtracted amounts are called leakage. In most all-inclusive package tours, about 80% of travelers' expenditures go to the airlines, hotels and other international companies (who often have their headquarters in the travelers' home countries), and not to local businesses or workers. In addition, significant amounts of income actually retained at destination level can leave again through leakage. A study of tourism 'leakage' in Thailand estimated that 70% of all money spent by tourists ended up leaving Thailand (via foreign-owned tour operators, airlines, hotels, imported drinks and food, etc.). Estimates for other Third World countries range from 80% in the Caribbean to 40% in India.

Of each US$ 100 spent on a vacation tour by a tourist from a developed country, only around US$ 5 actually stays in a developing-country destination's economy. The figure below shows how the leakage happens.

There are two main ways that leakage occurs:

Import Leakage: This commonly occurs when tourists demand standards of equipment, food, and other products that the host country cannot supply. Especially in less-developed countries, food and drinks must often be imported, since local products are not up to the hotel's (i.e. tourist's) standards or the country simply doesn't have a supplying industry. Much of the income from tourism expenditures leaves the country again to pay for these imports.

The average import-related leakage for most developing countries today is between 40% and 50% of gross tourism earnings for small economies and between 10% and 20% for most advanced and diversified economies, according to UNCTAD.

Even in developed regions, local producers are often unable to supply the tourism industry appropriately even if good will is present: the 64-room hotel "Kaiser im Tirol" in Austria, an award-winning leader in sustainable practices, cannot find organic food suppliers in the local farming networks in the appropriate quantity, quality and reliability, as production cycles and processes are not compatible with its needs.

Export Leakage: Multinational corporations and large foreign businesses have a substantial share in the import leakage. Often, especially in poor developing destinations, they are the only ones that possess the necessary capital to invest in the construction of tourism infrastructure and facilities. As a consequence of this, an export leakage arises when overseas investors who finance the resorts and hotels take their profits back to their country of origin.

A 1996 UN report evaluating the contribution of tourism to national income, gross levels of incomes or gross foreign exchange, found that net earnings of tourism, after deductions were made for all necessary foreign exchange expenditures, were much more significant for the industry. This report found significant leakage associated with: (a) imports of materials and equipment for construction; (b) imports of consumer goods, particularly food and drinks; (c) repatriation of profits earned by foreign investors; (d) overseas promotional expenditures and (e) amortization of external debt incurred in the development of hotels and resorts. The impact of the leakage varied greatly across countries, depending on the structure of the economy and the tourism industry. From the data presented in this study on the Caribbean, St. Lucia had a foreign exchange leakage rate of 56% from its gross tourism receipts, Aruba had 41%, Antigua and Barbuda 25% and Jamaica 40%.

Economic Enclave Tourism

Local businesses often see their chances to earn income from tourists severely reduced by the creation of "all-inclusive" vacation packages. When tourists remain for their entire stay at the same cruise ship or resort, which provides everything they need and where they will make all their expenditures, not much opportunity is left for local people to profit from tourism. The Organization of American States (OAS) carried out a survey of Jamaica's tourist industry that looked at the role of the all-inclusives compared to other types of accommodation. It found that 'All-inclusive hotels generate the largest amount of revenue but their impact on the economy is smaller per dollar of revenue than other accommodation subsectors.'

It also concluded that all-inclusives imported more, and employed fewer people per dollar of revenue than other hotels. This information confirms the concern of those who have argued that all-inclusives have a smaller trickle-down effect on local economies. The cruise ship industry provides another example of economic enclave tourism. Non-river cruises carried some 8.7 million international passengers in 1999. On many ships, especially in the Caribbean (the world's most popular cruise destination with 44.5% of cruise passengers), guests are encouraged to spend most of their time and money on board, and opportunities to spend in some ports are closely managed and restricted.

Other Negative Impacts

Infrastructure Cost

Tourism development can cost the local government and local taxpayers a great deal of money. Developers may want the government to improve the airport, roads and other infrastructure, and possibly to provide tax breaks and other financial advantages, which are costly activities for the government. Public resources spent on subsidized infrastructure or tax breaks may reduce government investment in other critical areas such as education and health.

Price Hikes

Increasing demand for basic services and goods from tourists will often cause price hikes that negatively affect local residents whose income does not increase proportionately. A San Francisco State University study of Belize found that, as a consequence of tourism development, the prices for locals increased by 8%.

Tourism development and the related rise in real estate demand may dramatically increase building costs and land values. Not only does this make it more difficult for local people, especially in developing countries, to meet their basic daily needs, it can also result in a dominance by outsiders in land markets and in-migration that erodes economic opportunities for the locals, eventually disempowering residents. In Costa Rica, close to 65% of the hotels belong to foreigners. Long-term tourists living in second homes, and the so-called amenity migrants (wealthy or retired people and liberal professionals moving to attractive destinations in order to enjoy the atmosphere and peaceful rhythms of life) cause price hikes in their new homes if their numbers attain a certain critical mass.

Economic Dependence of the Local Community on Tourism

Diversification in an economy is a sign of health, however if a country or region becomes dependent for its economic survival upon one industry, it can put major stress upon this industry as well as the people involved to perform well. Many countries, especially developing countries with little ability to explore other resources, have embraced tourism as a way to boost the economy.

In the Gambia, for instance, 30% of the workforce depends directly or indirectly on tourism. In small island developing states, percentages can range from 83% in the Maldives to 21% in the Seychelles and 34% in Jamaica, according to the WTO. Over-reliance on tourism, especially mass tourism, carries significant risks to tourism-dependent economies.

Economic recession and the impacts of natural disasters such as tropical storms and cyclones as well as changing tourism patterns can have a devastating effect on the local tourism sector. Malta has only 380,000 residents, but received 1.2 million tourists in 1999.

As 25% of GDP (and indirectly 40%), tourism generated more than $650 million in foreign exchange earnings. Malta's high dependence on tourism and a limited number of export products makes its trade performance vulnerable to shifts in international demand.

Seasonal Character of Jobs

The seasonal character of the tourism industry creates economic problems for destinations that are heavily dependent on it. Problems that seasonal workers face include job (and therefore income) insecurity, usually with no guarantee of employment from one season to the next, difficulties in getting training, employment-related medical benefits, and recognition of their experience, and unsatisfactory housing and working conditions.

Other Industrial Impacts

Economic crises, like the Asian crisis that hit Thailand, Malaysia and Indonesia a few years ago, can be devastating to inbound tourism flows. The financial turmoil triggered a sharp fall in tourism flows to affected countries during 1997 and 1998. In the Philippines, the crisis and the temporary closure of Philippine Airlines affected inbound arrivals significantly as there was a decline of almost 3.3% in 1998.

CONTRIBUTION OF TOURISM IN ECONOMIC CONSERVATION

The main positive economic impacts of tourism relate to foreign exchange earnings, contributions to government revenues, and generation of employment and business opportunities.

Foreign Exchange Earnings

Tourism expenditures and the export and import of related goods and services generate income to the host economy and can stimulate the investment necessary to finance growth in other economic sectors. Some countries seek to accelerate this growth by requiring visitors to bring in a certain amount of foreign currency for each day of their stay and do not allow them to take it out of the country again at the end of the trip. An important indicator of the role of international tourism is its generation of foreign exchange earnings. Tourism is one of the top five export categories for as many as 83% of countries and is a main source of foreign exchange earnings for at least 38% of countries.

Contribution to Government Revenues

Government revenues from the tourism sector can be categorized as direct and indirect contributions. Direct contributions are generated by taxes on incomes from tourism employment and tourism businesses, and by direct levies on tourists such as departure taxes. Indirect contributions are those originated from taxes and duties levied on goods and services supplied to tourists. The United States National Park Service estimates that the 273 million visits to American national parks in 1993 generated direct and indirect expenditures of US$ 10 billion and 200,000 jobs. When visits to land managed by other agencies, and to state, local, and privately-managed parks, are added, parks were estimated to bring around US$ 22 billion annually to the US economy. These expenditures also generate significant tax revenues for the government.

The World Travel and Tourism Council estimates that travel and tourism's direct, indirect, and personal tax contribution worldwide was over US$ 800 billion in 1998-a figure it expects to double by 2010.

Employment Opportunities

The rapid expansion of international tourism has led to significant employment creation. For example, the hotel accommodation sector alone provided around 11.3 million jobs worldwide in 1995. Tourism can generate jobs directly through hotels, restaurants, nightclubs, taxis, and souvenir sales, and indirectly through the supply of goods and services needed by tourism-related businesses. According to the WTO, tourism supports some 7% of the world's workers.

Infrastructural Stimulation

Tourism can induce the local government to make infrastructure improvements such as better water and sewage systems, roads, electricity, telephone and public transport networks, all of which can improve the quality of life for residents as well as facilitate tourism.

Contribution to Local Economies

Tourism can be a significant, even essential, part of the local economy. As the environment is a basic component of the tourism industry's assets, tourism revenues are often used to measure the economic value of protected areas. For example, Dorrigo National Park in New South Wales, Australia, has been estimated to contribute 7% of gross regional output and 8.4% of regional employment. The importance of tourism to local economies can also be illustrated by the impacts when it is disrupted: the catastrophic 1997 floods that closed Yosemite National Park in California cause locally severe economic losses to the areas around the park. In the most heavily impacted county, Mariposa County, 1997 personal income was reduced by an estimated US$1,159 per capita (US$18 million for the entire county)-a 6.6% decline. The county was also estimated to have lost US$1.67 million in county occupancy and sales tax revenues, and 956 jobs, a significant number in a county of fewer than 16,000 residents.

There are other local revenues that are not easily quantified, as not all tourist expenditures are formally registered in the macro-economic statistics. Money is earned from tourism through informal employment such as street vendors, informal guides, rickshaw drivers, etc. The positive side of informal or unreported employment is that the money is returned to the local economy, and has a great multiplier effect as it is spent over and over again. The World Travel and Tourism Council estimates that tourism generates an indirect contribution equal to 100% of direct tourism expenditures.

For those remaining destitute residents in the Cape Town, Waterfront area, many of whom seem to subsist largely from soliciting money from tourists, life is made incredibly difficult by the harsh treatment doled out by nearly everyone they come into contact with. In one instance, while I was eating with our group in a café in the area, one ragged local man came to the door and, in plain view of all the patrons, the manager opened the door and yelled at the man "go away and don't ever come here again!". The man was most likely there to ask the patrons for money, and, as it could potentially disrupt business, I am not entirely surprised by the manager's reaction. It is the structural dynamic the example demonstrates that is most appalling: with most residents already priced out of the area, the most common remaining residents I encountered lived in various stages of destitution and had to resort to humiliating acts to get by. (Another cause of local resident displacement is the growing trend of ecotourism. Ecotourists want to see so-called 'unspoiled' nature.

This, of course, does not include people. However, communities reside in many areas that might make excellent ecotourist havens. This conflict of interest is increasingly leading to confrontations between the developers who envision their own Kruger Park (which itself, as Herman mentioned, displaced former inhabitants in its development) and the people, often indigenous, who reside on the land. Not surprisingly, with the all-powerful tourist lobby in their corner, the developers are not encountering much trouble.

Earlier this year, in an effort to clear the area for an ecotourism venture, 250 residents of the Ambulong shore village in the Philippines were evicted from their homes. As they had refused to leave earlier, the eviction was violent: police attacked the village, wounding many inhabitants and demolishing 24 houses. While the people have pledged to continue the fight for their homes, the outlook is clearly not good.

In Bangladesh over 1000 families of the Khasi and Garoare indigenous groups face eviction from their tribal land for development of a park. In Brazil two villages near the resort town of Fortaleza have gone to court to show that a real estate agency that forced them off their lands to build an "ecological resort" broke the law. In Africa, more recent examples than Kruger include the Masai in East Africa and the Bushmen of Botswana. (Mail & Guardian June, 2002). Even when the indigenous peoples themselves propose to start ecotourism, as the Botswana Bushmen did, governments, as occurred in the Botswana case, often refuse to relinquish their potential earnings to the residents. (Mail & Guardian June, 2002)

Tourism also plays a significant role in the continuing economic subordination and dependency of the third world upon the core nations. The first world has a long tradition of forcing first world ideology and concepts upon drastically different third world countries, often their former colonies.

One example if the first world (WTO/IMF)'s forcing of globalization and neo-liberal policies upon the third world instead of encouraging more third world appropriate concepts like localization. Another example is that by forcing third world economies to be based upon precarious and unpredictable exports (i.e. coffee and bananas) the first world effectively inhibits autonomous growth in the third world countries.

Tourism is a similarly unpredictable and fluctuating business and is entirely dependent on, essentially, entertaining visitors from outside the country. Thus, tourist based third-world economies become both dependent on, and subordinate to, tourists. This comes at the expense of fostering more organic, autonomous and lasting growth.

The result is the perpetuation of a structure in which strong, industrialized countries are able to impose terms of trade to their advantage upon weaker states. Within this broader perspective of relationships, the first world tourist visiting a third world tourist based economy is akin to a colonizer both visiting, and perpetuating the domination of, a colony.

This dependency in a tourist economy manifests itself in the subordination of the people, culture and structures of the society to tourist interests. If a third world country wants and IMF loan, it must demonstrate its compliance with the IMF's interests. The tourist/service relationship is, in some ways, a microcosm of this exchange. If a third world tourist economy wants tourist money, it must be sensitive to tourist interests.

In this sense, tourism is a form of domination and of the master/servant dynamic tracing its lineage to the colonial era. I could sense this dynamic in many instances on our trip. Nearly everyone staying at the Breakwater Inn were white tourists.

However, the staff, especially the cleaning and maintenance crew, was composed almost entirely of local blacks who had to serve us everyday, clean up after us, and ultimately treat us as if we were somehow above them. The people who would transport our luggage were like our servants, as well as the unseen maids at all the hotels we stayed at.

The hundreds of vendors we encountered on the trip were entirely dependent on tourists, and many of them utilized, either by choice or desperation, that same master/servant dynamic. Often they would say things to me like "oh please sir, please buy something, I will never forget you, and my family will always remember you." I heard variations of that pitch throughout our trip from vendors of all kinds.

It seems that many tourists either consciously or unconsciously fulfill their 'master' role. I often encountered tourists treating vendors, staff and other employees with shocking rudeness and almost scornful disregard. Professor McCall drew my attention to one tourist becoming enraged at the black cooking staff for giving him what he called ¾ of an egg, as opposed to the whole egg he expected. On the return flight a member of the safari groups sitting near me verbally assaulted a stewardess when she said that she would need to take his suitcase to a storage compartment on the plane as the overhead bins were overflowing.

The tourist, after arguing with her about why she had no right to move his suitcase anywhere, on the plane or off, then yelled, as if to accuse the entire staff of being inept and corrupt, that "If anything and I mean anything is missing from that suitcase, there will be hell to pay!". These examples add to the countless instances I can recall throughout my experience of encountering stereotypically "angry tourists". They seem to consistently be appealing to a sense that they deserve better than everyone else, and are entitled to utter subservience.

To this end, I have come to accept that I, like all tourists in a third world country, could, and probably often do, symbolize arrogance, oppression and the subservience of much of the country's people. In South Africa I often did feel people holding variations of this view of me, and I understand why they did. Several people said that they resented me, and people like me, who came to their country. Others mentioned my arrogance, which I am sure I do have to some extent, as well as the collective arrogance of the first world.

With the spread and intervention of capitalism into Third World societies, tourism has also had the effect of turning Third World places, landscapes and people into commodities. Essentially tourists consume elements of a vacation in the same way as we consume other objects or commodities.

This is perhaps most obviously evident in the packaging of African culture, history and imagery into convenient souvenirs sold by vendors throughout the tourist enclaves. Another example is the play we saw, entitled "African Footsteps" which commoditized African history into a sanitized, tourist-pleasing, and overly simplistic package to be bought and consumed by tourists eager to move onto the next item. Trips to the country are sold as a package, but it is more importantly the country itself that is being transformed, along with its uniqueness, people, and cultural heritage, to be sold as a commodity to the golden hordes of tourists.

In the vein of commoditizing is the 'otherness' that is fostered by the separateness of tourism interactions with the local peoples and surroundings. Tourists, like the first world they come from, have come to view the core and periphery nations as a situation of 'us' and 'them', 'them' being the societies outside the first world which are variably defined by ideas of simplicity, disease, barbarism, instability, poverty and as generally problematic. Much tourism entrenches this sense of 'otherness.'

For instance, the township tours (link to chapter on township tours) we went on consisted of driving through people's communities in buses, stopping occasionally to look around while guarded by police, perhaps asking a few questions (if the people are lucky) and then gathering to get back on the bus from whence we came, never to be seen again. We were, however, preceding, and will be followed by, a never-ending string of the same buses unloading the same people. Only the faces will really change, but even they won't change too drastically. Eventually it will just blend into a blur of otherness. Now I imagine if that was my community, if that backyard our bus pulled up in was my backyard.

If I had busses stopping in front of my house to momentarily let out peering faces and cameras who would peruse my driveway before getting back onto their bus. Then, a day later, another bus, and then another, and another. I would feel on display, like a commodity being captured in the visitors' cameras and taken away. Above all, I would feel like I was 'other'.

The yearning of first-world tourists to venture to third-world locales is a kind of postmodern reaction to a certain meaninglessness and dissatisfaction with modern life. One backlash against the post-industrial complex is the desire to return to the purity of pre-modern life and to experience the supposed authenticity of 'unspoiled' land, people and environments. As the continuing existence of any people or environment entirely unaffected by humans is nearly impossible, fabrications are necessary to satiate this yearning.

Professor Wittenberg, in his introduction to Kruger Park, spoke at length about the desire of those who created the park to maintain a place where, in this case white men, could go to reconnect with pure nature and experience what their forefathers lived in, re-creating such lost rites of passage as "the first hunt".

Kruger, however, is not a real, natural habitat. It is an artificially maintained semblance of a time long past. This also holds true for the Zulu cultural village many of us went to see. It utilizes the desire to see pure indigenous cultures, but is in fact, no more than a reenactment of a lifestyle long since altered by the very societies of many who now come to gaze at the sights.

These things are not real, they remain in a romanticized vision of "untouched" land and peoples that exists today only as a fantasy in the mind of tourists. It is a mentality that encourages the "disneyizing" of culture and of environments, creating some romanticized fantasy rather than grappling with the modern day reality and conflicts of the places.

The vision of "untouched" "virgin" land and peoples has a long history in the collective Western thought, tracing back to the mythologized colonial voyages and stories of explorers pushing to the frontier. For instance, as we drove through the Kruger terrain I wanted to imagine going to the area for the first time, I even remarked to Herman "imagine what it would have been like for the first voyagers coming to this area....how incredible and desperately hard it must have been". He then noted about the high death rate for them, but I was already drifting off into imaging how breathtaking it must have been to see these lands for the first time, yearning to have that experience as well. I had not realized it, but the efficacy of that idealized story had firmly enraptured my mind as well. This seems due, in large part, to the historical education I received.

I was taught far more about the Indians of the 1700's in American high school than about the Indians of today. Additionally, I was bombarded with the supposedly heroic tales of explorers like Columbus and Magellan who first witnessed untouched people and lands. Few seem to care about, or have any desire to face, the complex, often difficult realities facing modern indigenous peoples or the crises facing many remaining tracts of actual wilderness. They would rather see a reenactment of a lifestyle long passed, or an artificially idyllic, maintained nature preserve, and leave with their preconceptions intact than have to deal with the often ugly and difficult reality. Tourists, after all, are not there to feel conflicted and are not paying to feel guilt; they want it to be simple, romantic, and easy to deal with.

In spite of all these problems, it must be noted that in many instances, utilization of third world tourism comes at a cost of less than many alternatives. For some areas, such as small islands, tourism is often the most viable means by which to develop the economy. Furthermore, given the desperate economic state of many third world countries, with unemployment often in double digits, it must be considered that there may be little choice other than tourism. While the jobs in the tourism market are mostly low-paying and unskilled, any job is better than none. Clearly, this does not excuse the multiplicity of problems endemic to third world tourism. Yet, it is often this lack of better economic alternative that leads countries to accept them. Thus, the goal must be to ensure that no country is in a position to need tourism to survive.

Tourism is, by many metrics, the world's largest industry. It has become a permanent part of the modern global economy and is only becoming more widespread. However, the third world tourism industry is obligated to address the multitude of aforesaid problems before it can become an equitable form of development. This will require the creation of alternate forms of tourism that truly benefit the majority of a country's residents as much, if not more, than the incoming tourists. Until then, third world tourism will continue to serve as a perpetuation of the colonial legacy, providing enjoyable exploration for tourists and festering exploitation for locals.

2

Planning and Stretagies of Tourism Development

INTRODUCTION

Plans for a firm can be made at several different levels. At the corporate level, the management considers the objectives of the firm as a whole. For example, Microsoft may want seek to grow by providing high quality software, hardware, and services to consumers. To achieve this goal, the firm may be willing to invest aggressively.

Plans can also be made at the business unit level. For example, although Microsoft is best known for its operating systems and applications software, the firm also provides Internet access and makes video games. Different managers will have responsibilities for different areas, and goals may best be made by those closest to the business area being considered. It is also more practical to hold managers accountable for performance if the plan is being made at a more specific level. Boeing has both commercial aircraft and defense divisions. Each is run by different managers, although there is some overlap in technology between the two. Therefore, plans are needed both at the corporate and at the business levels.

Occasionally, plans will be made at the functional level, to allow managers to specialize and to increase managerial accountability. Marketing, for example, may be charged with increasing awareness of Microsoft game consoles to 55% of the U.S. population or to increase the number of units of Microsoft

Office sold. Finance may be charged with raising a given amount of capital at a given cost. Manufacturing may be charged with decreasing production costs by 5%.

The firm needs to identify the business it is in. Here, a balance must be made so that the firm's scope is not defined too narrowly or too broadly. A firm may define its goal very narrowly and then miss opportunities in the market place. For example, if Dell were to define itself only as a computer company, it might miss an opportunity to branch into PDAs or Internet service. Thus, they might instead define themselves as a provider of "information solutions."

LEVELS OF PLANNING AND STRATEGIES

A company should not define itself too broadly, however, since this may result in loss of focus. For example, a manufacturer of baking soda should probably not see itself as a manufacturer of all types of chemicals. Sometimes, companies can define themselves in terms of a customer need. For example, 3M sees itself as being in the business of making products whose surfaces are bonded together. This accounts for both Post-It notes and computer disks. A firm's mission should generally include a discussion of the customers served (e.g., Wal-Mart and Nordstrom's serve different groups), the kind of technology involved, and the markets served.

Several issues are involved in selecting target customers. We will consider these in more detail within the context of segmentation, but for now, the firm needs to consider issues such as:

- The size of various market segments;
- How well these segments are being served by existing firms;
- Changes in the market-e.g., growth of segments or change in technology;
- How the firm should be positioned, or seen by customers. For example, Wal-Mart positions itself as providing value in retailing, while Nordstrom's defines itself more in terms of high levels of customer service.

The Boston Consulting Group (BCG) matrix provides a firm an opportunity to assess how well its business units work together. Each business unit is evaluated in terms of two factors: market share and the growth prospects in the market. Generally, the larger a firm's share, the stronger its position, and the greater the growth in a market, the better future possibilities. Four combinations emerge:

- A star represents a business unit that has a high share in a growing market. For example, Motorola has a large share in the rapidly growing market for cellular phones.
- A question mark results when a unit has a small share in a rapidly growing market. The firm's position, then, is not as strong as it would have been had its market share been greater, but there is an opportunity to grow. For example, Hewlett-Packard has a small share of the digital camera market, but this is a very rapidly growing market.
- A cash cow results when a firm has a large share in a market that is not growing, and may even be shrinking. Brother has a large share of the typewriter market.
- A dog results when a business unit has a small share in a market that is not growing. This is generally a somewhat unattractive situation, although dogs can still be profitable in the short run. For example, Smith Corona how has a small share of the typewriter market.

Firms are usually best of with a portfolio that has a balance of firms in each category. The cash cows tend to generate cash but require little future investment. On the other hand, stars generate some cash, but even more cash is needed to invest in the future-for research and development, marketing campaigns, and building new manufacturing facilities.

Therefore, a firm may take excess cash from the cash cow and divert it to the star. For example, Brother could "harvest" its profits from typewriters and invest this in the unit making color laser printers, which will need the cash to grow. If a firm has cash cows that generate a lot of cash, this may be used to try to improve the market share of a question mark. A firm that has a number of promising stars in its portfolio may be in serious trouble if it does not have any cash cows to support it. If it is about to run out of cash-regardless of how profitable it is-is becomes vulnerable as a takeover target from a firm that has the cash to continue running it.

A SWOT ("Strengths, Opportunities, Weaknesses, and Threats") analysis is used to help the firm identify effective strategies. Successful firms such as Microsoft have certain strengths. Microsoft, for example, has a great deal of technology, a huge staff of very talented engineers, a great deal of experience in designing software, a very large market share, a well respected brand name, and a great deal of cash. Microsoft also has some weaknesses, however:

The game console and MSN units are currently running at a loss, and MSN has been unable to achieve desired levels of growth. Firms may face opportunities in the current market. Microsoft, for example, may have the opportunity to take advantage of its brand name to enter into the hardware market. Microsoft may also become a trusted source of consumer services. Microsoft currently faces several threats, including the weak economy. Because fewer new computers are bough during a recession, fewer operating systems and software packages.

Rather than merely listing strengths, weaknesses, opportunities, and threats, a SWOT analysis should suggest how the firm may use its strengths and opportunities to overcome weaknesses and threats. Decisions should also be made as to how resources should be allocated. For example, Microsoft could either decide to put more resources into MSN or to abandon this unit entirely. Microsoft has a great deal of cash ready to spend, so the option to put resources toward MSN is available. Microsoft will also need to see how threats can be addressed. The firm can earn political good will by engaging in charitable acts, which it has money available to fund. For example, Microsoft has donated software and computers to schools. It can forego temporary profits by reducing prices temporarily to increase demand, or can "hold out" by maintaining current prices while not selling as many units.

Criteria for effective marketing plans. Marketing plans should meet several criteria:

- The plan must be specific enough so that it can be implemented and communicated to people in the firm. "Improving profitability" is usually too vague, but increasing net profits by 5%, increasing market share by 10%, gaining distribution in 2,000 more stores, and reducing manufacturing costs by 2% are all specific.
- The plan must be measurable so that one can see if it has been achieved. The above plans involve specific numbers.
- The goal must be achievable or realistic. Plans that are unrealistic may result in poor use of resources or lowered morale within the firm.
- The goals must be consistent. For example, a firm cannot ordinarily simultaneously plan improve product features, increase profits, and reduce prices.

Consumer Behaviour

Consumer behavior involves the psychological processes that consumers go through in recognizing needs, finding ways to solve these needs, making purchase decisions (e.g., whether or not to purchase a product and, if so, which brand and where), interpret information, make plans, and implement these plans (e.g., by engaging in comparison shopping or actually purchasing a product).

Sources of influence on the consumer. The consumer faces numerous sources of influence. Often, we take cultural influences for granted, but they are significant. An American will usually not bargain with a store owner. This, however, is a common practice in much of the World. Physical factors also influence our behavior. We are more likely to buy a soft drink when we are thirsty, for example, and food manufacturers have found that it is more effective to advertise their products on the radio in the late afternoon when people are getting hungry. A person's self-image will also tend to influence what he or she will buy-an upwardly mobile manager may buy a flashy car to project an image of success. Social factors also influence what the consumers buy-often, consumers seek to imitate others whom they admire, and may buy the same brands. The social environment can include both the mainstream culture (e.g.,

Americans are more likely to have corn flakes or ham and eggs for breakfast than to have rice, which is preferred in many Asian countries) and a subculture (e.g., rap music often appeals to a segment within the population that seeks to distinguish itself from the mainstream population). Thus, sneaker manufacturers are eager to have their products worn by admired athletes. Finally, consumer behavior is influenced by learning-you try a hamburger and learn that it satisfies your hunger and tastes good, and the next time you are hungry, you may consider another hamburger.

Consumer choices are often influenced dramatically by values. Some consumers, for example, seek to "fit in with the crowd" and would like to own a car as similar as possible to that of the neighbor. Others, on the other hand, want to stand out. In the consumption context, then, a consumer may choose to spend a great deal of money on buying and maintaining neat and professional attire, not because he or she is particularly interested in that appearance for its own sake, but rather because this will help the consumer be successful in his or her career.

Subculture often significantly influences the consumer. There are several potential ways that a society can be divided up. Some consumers are highly influenced by their ethnic origin. In some areas in Los Angeles, shopkeepers may transact all their business in a language of the predominant immigration patterns into the neighborhood-e.g., Spanish or Korean in some parts of downtown and Chinese in parts of the San Gabriel Valley. Virtual pets at first spread in the U.S. through Asian-American teenagers. Only after a while did the product diffuse into other ethnic groups. Occasionally, religious groups will influence consumers' behavior, usually because a religion may set certain standards-e.g., some religions do not allow the consumption of alcohol, while others may disapprove of charging interest. The fact that many Americans spend a great deal of time with members of their religious groups in churches, synagogues, and mosques implies that members have a great deal of influence on each other. People in similar age groups also tend to have more influence on each other. This is particularly evident in the spread of fashion. Social status may also have some influence, as people may tend to emulate others in similar occupations or neighborhoods.

One way to look at social influence is though "reference groups"-people against which one compares oneself. Thus, a consumer may notice that all his friends are wearing a special kind of jeans and may expect to be ostracized if he or she chooses to wear a different brand. Interestingly, however, one may also hold dissociative reference groups-people that one would not want to be compared to. For example, Cadillac has an image problem in being associated with older consumers, who are not considered "hip" enough by younger, upwardly mobile consumers that the firm would like to target. Thus, Cadillac ran the campaign "It's not your father's car."

Family may influence the consumer's choices a great deal. Research has shown, for example, that there is a tendency for adult children to use the same brands that their parents used over time. In many cases, these brand choices are made without much conscious thought.

In marketing jargon, a consumer problem refers to a "discrepancy" between the "ideal" situation and reality. Thus, problems can range greatly in severity. One problem, for example, is that you are hungry. The problem is easily solved by eating. Other problems can be significantly more severe-for example, a consumer is scared that he will be rejected by his wife because he is growing bald. Note that problems can be solved in more than one way. Baldness could be addressed by obtaining a wig, medical treatment, buying a fancy car (as an alternative way to achieve attractiveness), or some other creative way. One model of consumer decision making involves several steps. The first one is problem recognition-you realize that something is not as it should be. Perhaps, for example, your car is getting more difficult to start and is not accelerating well. The second step is information search-what are some alternative ways of solving the problem? You might buy a new car, buy a used car, take your car in for repair, ride the bus, ride a taxi, or ride a skateboard to work. The third step involves evaluation of alternatives.

A skateboard is inexpensive, but may be ill-suited for long distances and for rainy days. Finally, we have the purchase stage, and sometimes a post-purchase stage (e.g., you return a product to the store because you did not find it satisfactory). In reality, people may go back and forth between the stages. For example, a person may resume alternative identification during while evaluating already known alternatives. Consumer involvement will tend to vary dramatically depending on the type of product. In general, consumer involvement will be higher for products that are very expensive (e.g., a home, a car) or are highly significant in the consumer's life in some other way (e.g., a word processing program or acne medication).

It is important to consider the consumer's motivation for buying products. To achieve this goal, we can use the Means-End chain, wherein we consider a logical progression of consequences of product use that eventually lead to desired end benefit. Thus, for example, a consumer may see that a car has a large engine, leading to fast acceleration, leading to a feeling of performance, leading to a feeling of power, which ultimately improves the consumer's self-esteem. A handgun may aim bullets with precision, which enables the user to kill an intruder, which means that the intruder will not be able to harm the consumer's family, which achieves the desired end-state of security. In advertising, it is important to portray the desired end-states. Focusing on the large motor will do less good than portraying a successful person driving the car.

Information search and decision making. Consumers engage in both internal and external information search. Internal search involves the consumer identifying alternatives from his or her memory. For certain low involvement products, it is very important that marketing programs achieve "top of mind" awareness. For example, few people will search the Yellow Pages for fast food restaurants; thus, the consumer must be able to retrieve one's restaurant from memory before it will be considered. For high involvement products, consumers are more likely to use an external search. Before buying a car, for example, the consumer may ask friends' opinions, read reviews in Consumer Reports, consult several web sites, and visit several dealerships. Thus, firms that make products that are selected predominantly through external search must invest in having information available to the consumer in need-e.g., through brochures, web sites, or news coverage.

A compensatory decision involves the consumer "trading off" good and bad attributes of a product. For example, a car may have a low price and good gas mileage but slow acceleration. If the price is sufficiently inexpensive and gas efficient, the consumer may then select it over a car with better acceleration that costs more and uses more gas. Occasionally, a decision will involve a non-compensatory strategy. For example, a parent may reject all soft drinks that contain artificial sweeteners. Here, other good features such as taste and low calories cannot overcome this one "non-negotiable" attribute.

The amount of effort a consumer puts into searching depends on a number of factors such as the market (how many competitors are there, and how great are differences between brands expected to be?), product characteristics (how important is this product? How complex is the product? How obvious are indications of quality?), consumer characteristics (how interested is a consumer, generally, in analyzing product characteristics and making the best possible deal?), and situational characteristics (as previously discussed).

Two interesting issues in decisions are:

- Variety seeking (where consumers seek to try new brands not because these brands are expected to be "better" in any way, but rather because the consumer wants a "change of pace," and
- "Impulse" purchases-unplanned buys. This represents a somewhat "fuzzy" group. For example, a shopper may plan to buy vegetables but only decide in the store to actually buy broccoli and corn. Alternatively, a person may buy an item which is currently on sale, or one that he or she remembers that is needed only once inside the store.

A number of factors involve consumer choices. In some cases, consumers will be more motivated.

For example, one may be more careful choosing a gift for an in-law than when buying the same thing for one self. Some consumers are also more motivated to comparison shop for the best prices, while others are more convenience oriented. Personality impacts decisions. Some like variety more than others, and some are more receptive to stimulation and excitement in trying new stores. Perception influences decisions. Some people, for example, can taste the difference between generic and name brand foods while many cannot. Selective perception occurs when a person is paying attention only to information of interest.

For example, when looking for a new car, the consumer may pay more attention to car ads than when this is not in the horizon. Some consumers are put off by perceived risk. Thus, many marketers offer a money back guarantee. Consumers will tend to change their behavior through learning-e.g., they will avoid restaurants they have found to be crowded and will settle on brands that best meet their tastes. Consumers differ in the values they hold (e.g., some people are more committed to recycling than others who will not want to go through the hassle). We will consider the issue of lifestyle under segmentation.

Attitudes. Consumer attitudes are a composite of a consumer's (1) beliefs about, (2) feelings about, (3) and behavioral intentions toward some "object"-within the context of marketing, usually a brand, product category, or retail store. These components are viewed together since they are highly interdependent and together represent forces that influence how the consumer will react to the object.

Beliefs. The first component is beliefs. A consumer may hold both positive beliefs toward an object (e.g., coffee tastes good) as well as negative beliefs (e.g., coffee is easily spilled and stains papers). In addition, some beliefs may be neutral (coffee is black), and some may be differ in valance depending on the person or the situation (e.g., coffee is hot and stimulates--good on a cold morning, but not good on a hot summer evening when one wants to sleep). Note also that the beliefs that consumers hold need not be accurate (e.g., that pork contains little fat), and some beliefs may, upon closer examination, be contradictory.

Affect. Consumers also hold certain feelings toward brands or other objects. Sometimes these feelings are based on the beliefs (e.g., a person feels nauseated when thinking about a hamburger because of the tremendous amount of fat it contains), but there may also be feelings which are relatively independent of beliefs. For example, an extreme environmentalist may believe that cutting down trees is morally wrong, but may have positive affect toward Christmas trees because he or she unconsciously associates these trees with the experience that he or she had at Christmas as a child. Behavioral intention. The behavioral intention is what the consumer plans to do with respect to the object (e.g., buy or not buy the brand). As with affect, this is sometimes a logical consequence of beliefs (or affect), but may sometimes reflect other circumstances--e.g., although a consumer does not really like a restaurant, he or she will go there because it is a hangout for his or her friends.

Changing attitudes is generally very difficult, particularly when consumers suspect that the marketer has a self-serving "agenda" in bringing about this change (e.g., to get the consumer to buy more or to switch brands). Here are some possible methods:

- *Changing Affect:* One approach is to try to change affect, which may or may not involve getting consumers to change their beliefs. One strategy uses the approach of classical conditioning try to "pair" the product with a liked stimulus. For example, we "pair" a car with a beautiful woman. Alternatively, we can try to get people to like the advertisement and hope that this liking will "spill over" into the purchase of a product. For example, the Pillsbury Doughboy does not really emphasize the conveyance of much information to the consumer; instead, it attempts to create a warm, "fuzzy" image. Although Energizer Bunny ads try to get people to believe that their batteries last longer, the main emphasis is on the likeable bunny. Finally, products which are better known, through the mere exposure effect, tend to be better liked-that is, the more a product is advertised and seen in stores, the more it will generally be liked, even if consumers to do not develop any specific beliefs about the product.
- *Changing Behavior:* People like to believe that their behavior is rational; thus, once they use our products, chances are that they will continue unless someone is able to get them to switch. One way to get people to

switch to our brand is to use temporary price discounts and coupons; however, when consumers buy a product on deal, they may justify the purchase based on that deal (i.e., the low price) and may then switch to other brands on deal later. A better way to get people to switch to our brand is to at least temporarily obtain better shelf space so that the product is more convenient. Consumers are less likely to use this availability as a rationale for their purchase and may continue to buy the product even when the product is less conveniently located.

- *Changing Beliefs:* Although attempting to change beliefs is the obvious way to attempt attitude change, particularly when consumers hold unfavorable or inaccurate ones, this is often difficult to achieve because consumers tend to resist. Several approaches to belief change exist:
  - *Change Currently held Beliefs:* It is generally very difficult to attempt to change beliefs that people hold, particularly those that are strongly held, even if they are inaccurate. For example, the petroleum industry advertised for a long time that its profits were lower than were commonly believed, and provided extensive factual evidence in its advertising to support this reality. Consumers were suspicious and rejected this information, however.
  - *Change the Importance of Beliefs:* Although the sugar manufacturers would undoubtedly like to decrease the importance of healthy teeth, it is usually not feasible to make beliefs less important--consumers are likely to reason, why, then, would you bother bringing them up in the first place? However, it may be possible to strengthen beliefs that favor us--e.g., a vitamin supplement manufacturer may advertise that it is extremely important for women to replace iron lost through menstruation. Most Add consumers already agree with this, but the belief can be made stronger. beliefs. Consumers are less likely to resist the addition of beliefs so long as they do not conflict

with existing beliefs. Thus, the beef industry has added beliefs that beef (1) is convenient and (2) can be used to make a number of creative dishes. Vitamin manufacturers attempt to add the belief that stress causes vitamin depletion, which sounds quite plausible to most people.

- *Change the Ideal:* It usually difficult, and very risky, to attempt to change ideals, and only few firms succeed. For example, Hard Candy may have attempted to change the ideal away from traditional beauty toward more unique self expression.

One-sided vs. two-sided appeals. Attitude research has shown that consumers often tend to react more favorably to advertisements which either (1) admit something negative about the sponsoring brand (e.g., the Volvo is a clumsy car, but very safe) or (2) admits something positive about a competing brand (e.g., a competing supermarket has slightly lower prices, but offers less service and selection). Two-sided appeals must, contain overriding arguments why the sponsoring brand is ultimately superior-that is, in the above examples, the "but" part must be emphasized.

Reference Groups: A useful framework of analysis of group influence on the individual is the so called reference group-the term comes about because an individual uses a relevant group as a standard of "reference" against which oneself is compared. Reference groups come in several different forms. The aspirational reference group refers to those others against whom one would like to compare oneself. For example, many firms use athletes as spokespeople, and these represent what many people would ideally like to be. Associative reference groups include people who more realistically represent the individuals' current equals or near-equals-e.g., coworkers, neighbors, or members of churches, clubs, and organizations. Finally, the dissociative reference group includes people that the individual would not like to be like.

For example, the store literally named The Gap came about because many younger people wanted to actively dissociate from parents and other older and "uncool" people. The Quality Paperback Book specifically suggests in its advertising that its members are "a breed apart" from conventional readers of popular books.

The Family Life Cycle. Individuals and families tend to go through a "life cycle." The simple life cycle goes from:

child/teenager — young single — young couple — full nest — empty nest — widow(er).

In real life, this situation is, of course, a bit more complicated. For example, many couples undergo divorce. Then we have the scenario:

full nest — single parent

This situation can result either from divorce or from the death of one parent. Divorce usually entails a significant change in the relative wealth of spouses. In some cases, the non-custodial parent (usually the father) will not pay the required child support, and even if he or she does, that still may not leave the custodial parent and children as well off as they were during the marriage. On the other hand, in some cases, some non-custodial parents will be called on to pay a large part of their income in child support. This is particularly a problem when the non-custodial parent remarries and has additional children in the second (or subsequent marriages). In any event, divorce often results in a large demand for:

- low cost furniture and household items
- time-saving goods and services.

Divorced parents frequently remarry, or become involved in other non-marital relationships; thus, we may see

full nest — single parent — blended family

Another variation involves

young single — single parent

Here, the single parent who assumes responsibility for one or more children may not form a relationship with the other parent of the child.

Generally, there are two main themes in the Family Life Cycle, subject to significant exceptions:

- As a person gets older, he or she tends to advance in his or her career and tends to get greater income (exceptions: maternity leave, divorce, retirement).

- Unfortunately, obligations also tend to increase with time (at least until one's mortgage has been paid off). Children and paying for one's house are two of the greatest expenses.

Note that although a single person may have a lower income than a married couple, the single may be able to buy more discretionary items since he or she has fewer current obligations. This will change when a house is bought or children come along.

Family Decision Making: Individual members of families often serve different roles in decisions that ultimately draw on shared family resources. Some individuals are information gatherers/holders, who seek out information about products of relevance. These individuals often have a great deal of power because they may selectively pass on information that favors their chosen alternatives. Influencers do not ultimately have the power decide between alternatives, but they may make their wishes known by asking for specific products or causing embarrassing situations if their demands are not met. The decision maker(s) have the power to determine issues such as:

- Whether to buy;
- Which product to buy (pick-up or passenger car?);
- Which brand to buy;
- Where to buy it; and
- When to buy.

Note, however, that the role of the decision maker is separate from that of the purchaser. From the point of view of the marketer, this introduces some problems since the purchaser can be targeted by point-of-purchase (POP) marketing efforts that cannot be aimed at the decision maker. Also note that the distinction between the purchaser and decision maker may be somewhat blurred:

- The decision maker may specify what kind of product to buy, but not which brand;
- The purchaser may have to make a substitution if the desired brand is not in stock;
- The purchaser may disregard instructions (by error or deliberately).

It should be noted that family decisions are often subject to a great deal of conflict. The reality is that few families are wealthy enough to avoid a strong tension between demands on the family's resources. Conflicting pressures are especially likely in families with children and/or when only one spouse works outside the home. Note that many decisions inherently come down to values, and that there is frequently no "objective" way to arbitrate differences. One spouse may believe that it is important to save for the children's future; the other may value spending now (on private schools and computer equipment) to help prepare the children for the future. Who is right? There is no clear answer here. The situation becomes even more complex when more parties-such as children or other relatives-are involved. Culture is part of the external influences that impact the consumer. That is, culture represents influences that are imposed on the consumer by other individuals. The United States has undergone some changes in its predominant culture over the last several decades. Again, however, it should be kept in mind that there are great variations within the culture. For example, on the average, Americans have become less materialistic and have sought more leisure; on the other hand, the percentage of people working extremely long hours has also increased.

Significant changes have occurred in gender roles in American society. One of the reasons for this is that more women work outside the home than before. However, women still perform a disproportionate amount of housework, and men who participate in this activity tend to do so reluctantly. In general, commercials tend to lag somewhat behind reality-e.g., few men are seen doing housework, and few women are seen as buyers and decision makers on automobile purchases.

Regional influence, both in the United States and other areas, is significant. Many food manufacturers offer different product variations for different regions. Joel Girardeau, in his book The Nine Nations of North America, proposed nine distinct regional subcultures that cut across state lines. Although significant regional differences undoubtedly exist, research has failed to support Garreau's specific characterizations/

Consumer behavior is frequently affected by the situation. For example, people may buy different products when shopping for others than they would for themselves. We tend to make quicker but less elaborate decisions when facing time pressure. There are also influences of mood. For example, people who are unhappy tend to make more rational and more critical decisions.

The Means-End Chain: Consumers often buy products not because of their attributes per se but rather because of the ultimate benefits that these attributes provide, in turn leading to the satisfaction of ultimate values. For example, a consumer may not be particularly interested in the chemistry of plastic roses, but might reason as follows:

Highly reliable synthetic content of roses — Roses will stay in original condition for a long time — Significant other will appreciate the roses longer — Significant other will continue to love one — Self esteem.

The important thing in a means-end chain is to start with an attribute, a concrete characteristic of the product, and then logically progress to a series of consequences (which tend to become progressively more abstract) that end with a value being satisfied. Thus, each chain must start with an attribute and end with a value. An important implication of means-end chains is that it is usually most effective in advertising to focus on higher level items. For example, in the flower example above, an individual giving the flowers to the significant other might better be portrayed than the flowers alone.

Organizational Buyers Come in Several Forms: Resellers involve either wholesalers or retailers that buy from one organization and resell to some other entity. For example, large grocery chains sometimes buy products directly from the manufacturer and resell them to end-consumers. Wholesalers may sell to retailers who in turn sell to consumers. Producers also buy products from sub-manufacturers to create a finished product. For example, rather than manufacturing the parts themselves, computer manufacturers often buy hard drives, motherboards, cases, monitors, keyboards, and other components from manufacturers and put them together to create a finished product. Governments buy a great deal of things. For example, the military needs an incredible amount of supplies to feed and equip troops. Finally, large institutions buy products in huge quantities. For example, UCR probably buys thousands of reams of paper every month. Organizational buying usually involves more people than individual buying. Often, many people are involved in making decisions as to (a) whether to buy, (b) what to buy, (c) at what quantity, and (d) from whom. An engineer may make a specification as to what is needed, which may be approved by a manager, with the final purchase being made by a purchase specialist who spends all his or her time finding the best deal on the goods that the organization needs.

Often, such long purchase processes can cause long delays. In the government, rules are often especially stringent-e.g., vendors of fruit cake have to meet fourteen pages of specifications put out by the General Services Administration. In many cases, government buyers are also heavily bound to go with the lowest price. Even if it is obvious that a higher priced vendor will offer a superior product, it may be difficult to accept that bid.

Organizational Buyers: A large portion of the market for goods and services is attributable to organizational, as opposed to individual, buyers. In general, organizational buyers, who make buying decisions for their companies for a living, tend to be somewhat more sophisticated than ordinary consumers. However, these organizational buyers are also often more risk averse. There is a risk in going with a new, possibly better (lower price or higher quality) supplier whose product is unproven and may turn out to be problematic. Often the fear of running this risk is greater than the potential rewards for getting a better deal. In the old days, it used to be said that "You can't get fired for buying IBM." This attitude is beginning to soften a bit today as firms face increasing pressures to cut costs.

TOURISM DEVELOPMENT

Tourism development has its greatest impacts at the community level. These impacts reach far beyond jobs, wages, and revenues. Social and environmental consequences such as crime, congestion, and water pollution also can have serious impacts on the quality of life of residents as well as on the quality of vacations for tourists. Community leaders and planners have indicated a need for information about these impacts. Since 1980, researchers at a number of universities in the Northeast and elsewhere have worked toward developing a framework and a database with which any locality could make "ball-park" estimates of the impacts of typical types of tourism development. A major research finding has been that it is not easy to define typical communities, typical developments, or average impacts.

Another finding has been that the complex interactions between residents, tourists, industry, and government make it difficult to justify a simple framework for analysis. On the other hand it is difficult to present the correct framework (assuming one exists) in a simple manner. In order to test our preliminary research hypotheses, a tourism-planning computer game has been developed which pits the player against the development pressures of a hypothetical small New England community.

In addition to meeting our objective of illustrating our long-term research goals in a palatable format the game has been used successfully in the classroom and, in fact, has taken on a project status of its own.

Project Background: A Game?

The Tourism Development Simulation Model (TDSM) is a computer program developed in conjunction with a series of projects on the impacts of tourism development. The emphasis in the earliest project was on the development of a methodology that could be used by individual municipalities and state agencies to estimate and project impacts caused by alternative tourism product mixes at the local level. A follow-up project focused on the fiscal impact portion of the model.

In the early stages of design and development of this model, it became readily apparent that the scope of the work was very broad-too broad to produce the quick and comprehensive results users wanted.

It was, in fact, difficult to describe the goals of the project or its potential value to targeted users. It was decided, therefore, that a simplified version of the model could provide the basis of a computer game, and that this game concerning tourism development in a hypothetical community could provide an alternative means of describing the usefulness of the major project objectives.

The production and distribution of the game has been so successful that it has taken on a project status of its own. Priced at cost, it was initially distributed as an amusing "think piece" for researchers and planners, and as an palatable introduction to related research projects.

The game is loosely based on the impact assessment framework developed in a study of the impacts of tourism on thirteen coastal communities in the Northeast (Tyrrell et al. 1985). A typical small New England community was characterized using some empirical results and some "best guess" approximations to relationships between major variables. The relationships were then refined to reflect the "reality" exhibited in recent community case studies (NE-137 Block 1985). In addition to providing the intended introduction to long-term project goals, the processes of designing and constructing the game and using it as a community behavior simulator have taught us much about the implications of "reality" and "reasonableness" on mathematical representations of community behavior. These lessons have had a considerable impact on our primary goal of developing a tourism development simulation model.

Designed to illustrate the principles of community budgeting and planning in the context of tourism industry development, the game has been used as an educational tool for students of tourism planning at the graduate and undergraduate level, and non-degree participants in leadership development programs in both the U.S. and Canada. For all audience types, the educational vehicle provided by the computer game is accepted enthusiastically. As with others (Loukissas 1983), we have found this approach to have definite advantages over traditional seminar presentations.

This paper describes the details of the game's design and describes the importance of the "reasonableness" criterion used in the development of the underlying model. It also attempts to persuade the reader that a computer game, based on a "best-guess" model, can provide a useful research and educational tool.

The Game Player

The game player assumes the role of an unusually potent town administrator who must guide development using tourism promotion and three other types of expenditure programs: "other" industrial development programs, social programs, and environmental projects. These expenditure categories are assumed to include all major expenditure items in a town's budget except for administration, which is ignored by the model. In order to balance the town's budget the player must adjust tax rates for residential and business property and decide upon daily tourist fees. The player's objective is to achieve balanced economic, social, and environmental development as measured by their respective indexes. At the end of each year of office the player is presented with quantitative and qualitative assessments of performance, and given the opportunity to change any of the seven fiscal controls. The game ends after 10 years of service or when the player quits or is fired, which ever comes first.

THE TOURISM DEVELOPMENT MODEL

Model Structure

Some 40 equations containing more than fifty parameters characterize the components of community activity and development in the small hypothetical town. Most of these (19 equations) characterize the tourism industry and "other" industry behavior. These include basic supply and demand relationships for the tourism product and the "other" product produced in the town, as well as derived demands for labor and supplies and business relocation. The multi-market model framework is common to macro modeling efforts (Pindyck and Rubinfeld 1976). Supply and demand equations are logarithmic and contain a lagged dependent variable. This formulation characterizes behavior as "partially" adjusting toward some distant equilibrium value. The amount of the adjustment declines each year following the initial change in the independent variable. The rate of adjustment is determined by the size of the lag coefficient. Such models are frequent in econometric research studies since their coefficients are directly interpretable, and the implied dynamics is intuitively appealing.

3

Management of Hotels

INTRODUCTION

The Committee may be comprised of the department heads for housekeeping, front office, food and beverage, security, sales and public relations, meetings and conventions, engineering and building maintenance, and human resources. Executive committee members bring a different perspective of guest service to the total management objective reflecting the unique expertise and training of their positions. A comfortable room, good food, and a helpful staff can make being away from home an enjoyable experience for both vacationing families and business travellers. While most lodging managers work in traditional hotels and motels, some work in other lodging establishments, such as camps, inns, boardinghouses, dude ranches, and recreational resorts.

In full-service hotels, lodging managers help their guests have a pleasant stay by providing many of the comforts of home, including cable television, fitness equipment, and voice mail, as well as specialized services such as health spas. For business travellers, lodging managers often schedule available meeting rooms and electronic equipment, including slide projectors and fax machines. Lodging managers are responsible for keeping their establishments efficient and profitable. In a small establishment with a limited staff, the manager may oversee all aspects of operations. However, large hotels may employ hundreds of workers, and the general manager usually is aided by a number of assistant managers assigned to the various departments of the operation. In hotels of every size, managerial duties vary significantly by job title. General managers have overall responsibility for the operation of the hotel. Within guidelines established by the owners of the hotel or executives of the hotel chain, the general manager sets room rates, allocates funds to departments, approves expenditures, and ensures expected standards for guest service, decor, housekeeping, food quality, and banquet operations.

Managers who work for chains also may organize and staff a newly built hotel, refurbish an older hotel, or reorganize a hotel or motel that is not operating successfully. In order to fill entry-level service and clerical jobs in hotels, some managers attend career fairs. Resident or hotel managers are responsible for the day-to-day operations of the property. In larger properties, more than one of these managers may assist the general manager, frequently dividing responsibilities between the food and beverage operations and the rooms or lodging services. At least one manager, either the general manager or a hotel manager, is on call 24 hours a day to resolve problems or emergencies. Assistant managers help run the day-to-day operations of the hotel. In large hotels, they may be responsible for activities such as personnel, accounting, office administration, marketing and sales, purchasing, security, maintenance, and pool, spa, or recreational facilities.

In smaller hotels, these duties may be combined into one position. Assistant managers may adjust charges on a hotel guest's bill when a manager is unavailable. An Executive Committee made up of a hotel's senior managers advises the general manager, assists in setting hotel policy, coordinates services that cross departmental boundaries, and collaborates on efforts to ensure consistent and efficient guest services throughout the hotel. Executive housekeepers ensure that guest rooms, meeting and banquet rooms, and public areas are clean, orderly, and well maintained. They also train, schedule, and supervise the work of housekeepers, inspect rooms, and order cleaning supplies.

Front office managers coordinate reservations and room assignments, as well as train and direct the hotel's front desk staff. They ensure that guests are treated courteously, complaints and problems are resolved, and requests for special services are carried out. Front office managers may adjust charges posted on a customer's bill.

Convention services managers coordinate the activities of various departments in larger hotels to accommodate meetings, conventions, and special events. They meet with representatives of groups or organizations to plan the number of rooms to reserve, the desired configuration of the meeting space, and banquet services. During the meeting or event, they resolve unexpected problems and monitor activities to ensure that hotel operations conform to the expectations of the group.

Food and beverage managers oversee all food service operations maintained by the hotel. They coordinate menus with the Executive Chef for the hotel's restaurants, lounges, and room service operations. They supervise the ordering of food and supplies, direct service and maintenance contracts within the kitchens and dining areas, and manage food service budgets. Catering managers arrange for food service in a hotel's meeting and convention rooms. They coordinate menus and costs for banquets, parties, and events with meeting and convention planners or individual clients. They coordinate staffing needs and arrange schedules with kitchen personnel to ensure appropriate food service.

Sales or marketing directors and public relations directors oversee the advertising and promotion of hotel operations and functions, including lodging and dining specials and special events, such as holiday or seasonal specials. They direct the efforts of their staff to purchase advertising and market their property to organizations or groups seeking a venue for conferences, conventions, business meetings, trade shows, and special events. They also coordinate media relations and answer questions from the press. Human resources directors manage the personnel functions of a hotel, ensuring that all accounting, payroll, and employee relations matters are handled in compliance with hotel policy and applicable laws. They also oversee hiring practices and standards and ensure that training and promotion programs reflect appropriate employee development guidelines.

Finance (or revenue) directors monitor room sales and reservations. In addition to overseeing accounting and cash-flow matters at the hotel, they also project occupancy levels, decide which rooms to discount and when to offer rate specials.

Computers are used extensively by lodging managers and their assistants to keep track of guests' bills, reservations, room assignments, meetings, and special events. In addition, computers are used to order food, beverages, and supplies, as well as to prepare reports for hotel owners and top-level managers. Managers work with computer specialists to ensure that the hotel's computer system functions properly. Should the hotel's computer system fail, managers must continue to meet the needs of hotel guests and staff.

Working Conditions

Because hotels are open around the clock, night and weekend work is common. Many lodging managers work more than 40 hours per week, and may be called back to work at any time. Some managers of resort properties or other hotels where much of the business is seasonal have other duties on the property during the off-season or find work at other hotels or in other areas.

Lodging managers experience the pressures of coordinating a wide range of activities. At larger hotels, they also carry the burden of managing a large staff and finding a way to satisfy guest needs while maintaining positive attitudes and employee morale. Conventions and large groups of tourists may present unusual problems or require extended work hours. Moreover, dealing with irate guests can be stressful. The job can be particularly hectic for front office managers during check-in and check-out times. Computer failures can further complicate processing and add to frustration levels.

TRAINING, QUALIFICATIONS AND ADVANCEMENT

Hotels increasingly emphasize specialized training. Postsecondary training in hotel, restaurant, or hospitality management is preferred for most hotel management positions; however, a college liberal arts degree may be sufficient when coupled with related hotel experience or business education. Internships or part-time or summer work experience in a hotel are an asset to students seeking a career in hotel management. The experience gained and the contacts made with employers can greatly benefit students after graduation. Most degree programs include work-study opportunities.

Community colleges, junior colleges, and many universities offer certificate or degree programs in hotel, restaurant, or hospitality management leading to an associate, bachelor, or graduate degree. Technical institutes, vocational and trade schools, and other academic institutions also offer courses leading to formal recognition in hospitality management. In total, more than 800 educational facilities provide academic training for would-be lodging managers. Hotel management programs include instruction in hotel administration, accounting, economics, marketing, housekeeping, food service management and catering, and hotel maintenance engineering. Computer training also is an integral part of hotel management training, due to the widespread use of computers in reservations, billing, and housekeeping management.

More than 450 high schools in 45 States offer the Lodging Management Program created by the Educational Institute of the American Hotel and Lodging Association. This two-year program offered to high school juniors and seniors teaches management principles and leads to a professional certification called the "Certified Rooms Division Specialist." Many colleges and universities grant participants credit towards a post-secondary degree in hotel management. Lodging managers must be able to get along with many different types of people, even in stressful situations. They must be able to solve problems and concentrate on details. Initiative, self-discipline, effective communication skills, and the ability to organize and direct the work of others also are essential for managers at all levels.

Persons wishing to make a career in the hospitality industry may be promoted into a management trainee position sponsored by the hotel or a hotel chain's corporate parent. Typically, trainees work as assistant managers and may rotate assignments among the hotel's departments—front office, housekeeping, or food and beverage—to gain a wide range of experiences. Relocation to another property may be required to help round out the experience and to help grow a trainee into the position.

Work experience in the hospitality industry at any level or in any segment, including summer jobs or part-time work in a hotel or restaurant, is good background for entering hotel management. Most employers require a bachelor's degree with some education in business and computer literacy, while some prefer a master's degree for hotel management positions. However, employees who demonstrate leadership potential and possess sufficient length or breadth of experience may be invited to participate in a management training program and advance to hotel management positions without the education beyond high school. Large hotel and motel chains may offer better opportunities for advancement than small, independently owned establishments, but relocation every several years often is necessary for advancement. The large chains have more extensive career ladder programs and offer managers the opportunity to transfer to another hotel or motel in the chain or to the central office. Career advancement can be accelerated by the completion of certification programs offered by various associations. These programs usually require a combination of course work, examinations, and experience. For example, outstanding lodging managers may advance to higher level manager positions.

Employment

Lodging managers held about 58,000 jobs in 2004. Self-employed managers—primarily owners of small hotels, motels, and inns—held about 45 percent of these jobs. Companies that manage hotels and motels under contract employed many managers.

Job Outlook

Employment of lodging managers is expected to grow about as fast as the average for all occupations through 2014. Additional job openings are expected to occur as experienced managers transfer to other occupations or leave the labour force, in part because of the long hours and stressful working conditions. Job opportunities are expected to be best for persons with college degrees in hotel or hospitality management.

Renewed business travel and domestic and foreign tourism will drive employment growth of lodging managers in full-service hotels. The numbers of economy-class rooms and extended-stay hotels also are expected to increase to accommodate leisure travellers and bargain-conscious guests. An increasing range of lodging accommodations is available to travellers, from economy hotels which offer clean, comfortable rooms and front desk services without costly extras such as restaurants and room service, to luxury and boutique inns that offer sumptuous furnishings and personal services.

The accommodation industry is expected to continue to consolidate as lodging chains acquire independently owned establishments or undertake their operation on a contract basis. The increasing number of extended-stay hotels will moderate growth of manager jobs because these properties usually have fewer departments and require fewer managers. Also, these establishments often do not require a manager to be available 24 hours a day, instead assigning front desk clerks on duty at night some of the responsibilities previously reserved for managers. Additional demand for managers is expected in suite hotels, because some guests—especially business customers—

are willing to pay higher prices for rooms with kitchens and suites that provide the space needed to conduct small meetings. In addition, large full-service hotels—offering restaurants, fitness centers, large meeting rooms, and play areas for children, among other amenities—will continue to provide many trainee and managerial opportunities.

Earnings

Median annual earnings of lodging managers were $37,660 in May 2004. The middle 50 percent earned between $28,640 and $51,030. The lowest 10 percent earned less than $22,680, while the highest 10 percent earned more than $72,160. Median annual earnings for lodging managers in traveler accommodations were $37,420.

Salaries of lodging managers vary greatly according to their responsibilities and the segment of the hotel industry in which they are employed, as well as the location and region where the hotel is located. Managers may earn bonuses of up to 25 percent of their basic salary in some hotels and also may be furnished with meals, parking, laundry, and other services. In addition to providing typical benefits, some hotels offer profit-sharing plans and educational assistance to their employees.

HOTEL AND RESORT DESK CLERK

Desk clerks, also known as front office clerks or room clerks, are part of the front office staff of hotels, motels, and resorts. They are responsible for checking guests in and out, giving information about rates and the kinds of services their establishment provides, and assigning guests to rooms. Of all lodging employees, desk clerks have the most contact with the public; therefore, it is especially important that they make a good impression and ensure that guests' needs are being met.

There are many kinds of desk clerks in the hospitality industry. Key clerks issue and receive room keys. Reservations clerks handle reservations that guests make by mail, by telephone, or via the Internet and inform the room clerks when the guests plan to arrive. Rack clerks keep track of which rooms are occupied and unoccupied and oversee the work of the housekeepers and maintenance crew. Mail clerks are in charge of the guests' mail and messages. Information clerks tell guests about local places of interest and provide directions. However, only in the very largest hotels are the clerks so specialized. Usually one hotel desk clerk performs several duties such as handling reservations, checking guests in or out, and giving them directions to local sites.

Desk clerks work throughout the country in all kinds of hotels, motels, and resorts. The differences in these types of lodgings lie in their location and needs of their clientele. Hotels are typically found in cities; residential hotels serve people who desire hotel service on a long-term basis.

Most motels are located along highways rather than in large urban areas. Because they are designed to serve motorists who are driving a long way, motels are sometimes referred to as motor lodges. Resort hotels are usually located in vacation areas. In addition to providing rooms, many resort hotels provide recreational activities such as horseback riding and swimming. Most hotels, motels, and resorts are open twenty-four hours every day of the year. There is almost always a desk clerk on duty to take care of the guests' needs. The desk clerk has the most contact with hotel guests. It is important for the desk clerk to be friendly, helpful, and well groomed.

Education and Training Requirements

Managers of lodging establishments like to hire people who have at least a high school education. Some large hotels prefer hiring individuals with some college experience. On-the-job training is provided.

It is helpful to be good at typing, bookkeeping, and office machine and computer operation. Clerks should also have strong interpersonal and problem-solving skills. Many desk clerks begin as bellhops, switchboard operators, or key clerks. After they gain some experience these workers may be promoted to desk clerk. Desk clerks must have a neat appearance and be able to get along well with people.

Getting the Job

Prospective desk clerks can learn about job openings from state employment agencies, newspaper want ads, or job banks on the Internet. They can also apply directly to hotels, motels, and resorts in which they want to work. Students attending training schools that specialize in hotel work should check for job listings with the school's placement office.

Advancement Possibilities and Employment Outlook

Lodging managers generally prefer to promote their employees rather than hire people from outside the staff. Desk clerks who do their jobs well can move up to the position of assistant manager or front office manager. Education beyond high school is useful in getting a promotion. Many colleges and junior colleges now offer courses and programs in hotel management. The hotel, motel, and resort industry is expected to grow faster than the average through the year 2014. An increase in business travel as well as in domestic and foreign tourism will create a demand for all lodging workers. Also, the turnover rate for desk clerks is high so jobs open up regularly.

Working Conditions

Hotels, motels, and resorts are pleasant places to work. They are usually open seven days a week, twenty-four hours a day. Desk clerks may be asked to work nights, weekends, and holidays. They often put in a five-or six-day forty-to forty-eight-hour week. Employees are usually given extra pay for working irregular hours. Most room clerks rotate their shifts with other workers. Front desks are generally clean and well lighted and the work is not strenuous. However, clerks may be on their feet much of the time, and their work can become quite hectic, especially in busy hotels and resorts; desk clerks in the hospitality industry need to be patient and tolerant even when guests are unreasonable.

Earnings and Benefits

According to the U.S. Bureau of Labour Statistics, hotel, motel, and resort desk clerks earned a median salary of $17,700 per year in 2004. Those working in large metropolitan areas usually earn more. Benefits for full-time workers include paid vacations and holidays, health insurance, life insurance, and retirement plans. Educational assistance is sometimes available as well.

MOTION PICTURE PROJECTIONIST

Motion picture projectionists operate all of the equipment in the projection booths of indoor cinemas and drive-ins. They use movie projectors, audio equipment, and machines that rewind film to provide film entertainment for the theater's customers. Projectionists must inspect films before they are shown. To do this they place each film reel on a hand rewinding machine and look for holes, worn places, or other defects. If necessary they repair any defects found in the film.

In most cases full-length motion pictures are recorded on several reels of film so projectionists must operate two projectors at a time. When one reel of film is ending, projectionists must have the other projector and film reel ready for showing. Projectionists know when to change projectors by watching for cue marks on the movie screen. When the cue marks appear, they close the shutter of the first projector, open the shutter of the second projector, and then rewind the first reel on a rewinding machine. The first projector is then ready for threading the next reel of film. An average reel runs about twenty minutes. This process is repeated until the entire film is shown. Some projectionists are assisted by a motion picture projectionist's apprentice. Projectionists also clean and oil the equipment, check for defective parts, and make repairs. For major repairs they are assisted by a service repair worker.

Education and Training Requirements

There are no specific education requirements for motion picture projectionists, although a few cities and states require that they be licensed. Projectionists must have good mechanical ability because the equipment they use and repair is complex. Excellent hearing, eyesight, and manual dexterity are also important. Many projectionist jobs are unionized. To qualify as a union projectionist a candidate must serve a one-to two-year apprenticeship and pass a union examination. Apprentices must be at least eighteen years old and have a high school diploma. They learn to operate projectors and other equipment by working on the job with experienced projectionists. Some do not get paid while they are learning; others do and they may also hold other jobs in the theater. Some projectionists learn their skills at vocational or technical schools or on the job at small, nonunion theatres; however, theatres with union contracts will not hire nonunion projectionists. In large cities projectionists who have served an apprenticeship usually find jobs through their union. Nonunion members can apply directly to local nonunion theatres. Projectionist positions are also listed in the want ads of local newspapers.

Advancement Possibilities and Employment Outlook

Motion picture projectionists who work in large multiscreen theatres may advance to the position of chief operator. Some projectionists become service repair workers who fix sound equipment and projectors. Occasionally an experienced projectionist becomes a theater manager. The job outlook for motion picture projectionists is poor. Although the number of theatres is expected to grow slightly through the year 2014, increasingly sophisticated projection equipment does much of the work automatically. Most openings will occur as workers retire or change jobs.

Working Conditions

Both indoor and drive-in theatres are usually nice places to work. Most projection rooms are comfortable, clean, well lighted, and well ventilated. Projectionists must be able to work independently and be willing to view movies over and over again. Many motion picture projectionists work part time. Full-time projectionists work forty hours a week, including days and evenings. Their hours may be split over six days of the week instead of five. Some work in more than one theater, especially in multiscreen complexes.

Earnings and Benefits

Generally theatres in cities pay better wages than suburban or drive-in theatres. According to data from the 2004 Occupational Employment Statistics survey, motion picture projectionists earn a median salary of $8.32 per hour. Benefits for full-time workers may include paid vacations and health insurance as well as retirement plans.

RESTAURANT HOST OR HOSTESS

Restaurant hosts and hostesses serve as personal representatives of the restaurant for which they work. They are in charge of making reservations and greeting guests when they arrive at the restaurant. They also seat the guests and make sure that they enjoy their meal. Hosts and hostesses try to give guests a good impression of the restaurant by greeting them in a warm, friendly manner. If guests have to wait to be seated, hosts and hostesses make them comfortable while they wait. The guests are given an idea of how long they will have to wait and are seated in a waiting area. Sometimes hosts and hostesses suggest that the diners wait at the bar and have a drink. Hosts and hostesses locate a table that is the right size for the guests, take the guests to the table, and give them menus. They may also assist guests in seating small children, or fill their water glasses. While greeting incoming guests, hosts and hostesses must take care of guests who are leaving. Some hosts and hostesses receive the money for the guests' food and make change. To do this they must know how to operate a cash register. Restaurants sometimes have a candy or cigarette counter. If guests want to buy these items, hosts and hostesses add their cost to the guests' checks. In some restaurants this work is done by a cashier.

At the end of their work shifts, hosts and hostesses record the transactions that have taken place and total all guest checks to determine how much money has been received. These records are used to balance the accounts at the end of the day. The records are then turned in to the restaurant manager for inspection. The host and hostess stand near the restaurant entrance so they can greet guests as they arrive and then seat them at tables.

Education and Training Requirements

Individuals interested in becoming a host or hostess should take courses in business, arithmetic, bookkeeping, family and consumer science, and public speaking. Hosts and hostesses should be friendly and outgoing people who can remain calm and courteous during rush periods.

They also must be neat and well groomed. Most restaurants prefer to hire people who have a high school education. Some vocational schools have programs in food service that can help prepare students for this kind of work; however, most restaurant hosts and hostesses are trained on the job.

Getting the Job

Prospective hosts and hostesses should apply directly to restaurants in which they would like to work. Newspaper want ads sometimes have listings for these positions, as do state employment offices. Previous restaurant experience is helpful in landing a hosting job.

Advancement Possibilities and Employment Outlook

Hosts and hostesses advance by transferring to more expensive restaurants that pay higher salaries. Experienced and responsible restaurant hosts and hostesses may become restaurant managers. One big trend in the twenty-first century was an increase in the number of Americans dining out. With the restaurant business growing, the job outlook for hosts and hostesses is good, with positions expected to grow about as fast as the average through the year 2014.

Working Conditions

Because restaurants serve the public, they are usually attractive places in which to work. Expensive restaurants often provide elegant work surroundings. Hosts and hostesses are usually stationed near the restaurant entrance and are on their feet throughout their shifts. They must maintain a neat appearance and always be courteous to guests. Full-time hosts and hostesses work forty hours a week and may rotate shifts, but there are many part-time workers in this field as well. Hosts and hostesses must work their share of weekends, evenings, and holidays. Many of these workers belong to labour unions.

Earnings and Benefits

Earnings depend on the restaurant, with expensive restaurants generally paying higher salaries. According to the U.S. Bureau of Labour Statistics, hosts and hostesses earned a median wage of $7.52 per hour in 2004. Their wages tend to be higher than that of waitpersons because they usually do not receive tips. (In some restaurants, however, they are included in a tip pool that gives them a small share of the day's tips.) Restaurants often offer full-time employees paid holidays and vacations, health insurance, and retirement plans. Most hosts and hostesses receive free meals when they are at work.

PROCESS OF HOTEL ORGANIZING

A key issue in accomplishing the goals identified in the planning process is structuring the work of the organization. Organizations are groups of people, with ideas and resources, working toward common goals. The purpose of the organizing function is to make the best use of the organization's resources to achieve organizational goals. Organizational structure is the formal decision-making framework by which job tasks are divided, grouped, and coordinated. Formalization is an important aspect of structure. It is the extent to which the units of the organization are explicitly defined and its policies, procedures, and goals are clearly stated. It is the official organizational structure conceived and built by top management. The formal organization can be seen and represented in chart form. An organization chart displays the organizational structure and shows job titles, lines of authority, and relationships between departments.

The informal organization is the network, unrelated to the firm's formal authority structure, of social interactions among its employees. It is the personal and social relationships that arise spontaneously as people associate with one another in the work environment. The supervisor must realize that the informal organization affects the formal organization. The informal organization can pressure group members to conform to the expectations of the informal group that conflict with those of the formal organization. This can result in the generation of false information or rumors and resistance to change desired by management. The supervisor should recognize the existence of information groups, identify the roles member play within these groups, and use knowledge of the groups to work effectively with them. The informal organization can make the formal organization more effective by providing support to management, stability to the environment, and useful communication channels.

ORGANIZATIONAL STRUCTURE AND FUNCTIONS IN HOTELS

Even though the differences among organizations are enormous, there are many similarities that enable them to be classified. One widely used classification is the twofold system (mechanistic versus organic forms of organizational structure) developed by Tom Burns and G. M. Stalker in their study of electronics, firms in the United Kingdom.

The mechanistic structure is the traditional or classical design, common in many medium-and large-size organizations. Mechanistic organizations are somewhat rigid in that they consist of very clearly delineated jobs, have a well-defined hierarchical structure, and rely heavily on the formal chain of command for control.

Bureaucratic organizations, with their emphasis on formalization, are the primary form of mechanistic structures. According to Max Weber, bureaucracy is a form of organization characterized by a rational, goal-directed hierarchy, impersonal decision making, formal controls, and subdivision into managerial positions and specialization of labour. Bureaucratic organizations are tall consisting of hierarchies with many levels of management.

In a tall structure, people become relatively confined to their own area of specialization. Bureaucracies are driven by a top-down or command and control approach in which managers provide considerable direction and have considerable control over others. Other features of the bureaucratic organization include functional division of labour and work specialization.

On the other hand, the organic structure is more flexible, more adaptable to a participative form of management, and less concerned with a clearly defined structure. The organic organization is open to the environment in order to capitalize upon new opportunities.

Organic organizations have a flat structure with only one or two levels of management. Flat organizations emphasize a decentralized approach to management that encourage high employee involvement in decisions. The purpose of this structure is to create independent small businesses or enterprises that can rapidly respond to customers' needs or changes in the business environment. The supervisor tends to have a more personal relationship with his or her employees.

Rensis Likert has conducted extensive research on a non-bureaucratic organization design referred to as System 4 (participative-democratic). Management and employees interact in a friendly environment characterized by mutual confidence and trust.

Contingency organization means that the most appropriate organization structure for each situation depends upon technology, organizational size, goals and strategy, environmental stability, and characteristics of the employees.

Mechanistic organizations are best suited to repetitive operations and stable environments, while organic organizations are best suited to an uncertain task and a changing environment.

ORGANIZATION DESIGN

Designing an organization involves choosing an organizational structure that will enable the company to most effectively achieve its goals. Organization design is the creation of an organization's structure, traditionally functional, divisional, and/or matrix.

Functions or divisions arrange traditional organizations. In a functional organization, authority is determined by the relationships between group functions and activities. Functional structures group similar or related occupational specialties or processes together under the familiar headings of finance, manufacturing, marketing, accounts receivable, research, surgery, and photo finishing. Economy is achieved through specialization. However, the organization risks losing sight of its overall interests as different departments pursue their own goals.

In a divisional organization, corporate divisions operate as relatively autonomous businesses under the larger corporate umbrella. In a conglomerate organization, divisions may be unrelated. Divisional structures are made up of self-contained strategic business units that each produces a single product. For example, General Motors' divisions include Chevrolet, Oldsmobile, Pontiac, and Cadillac. A central headquarters, focusing or results, coordinates and controls the activities, and provides support services between divisions. Functional departments accomplish division goals. A weakness however, is the tendency to duplicate activities among divisions.

In a matrix organization, teams are formed and team members report to two or more managers. Matrix structures utilize functional and divisional chains of command simultaneously in the same part of the organization, commonly for one-of-a-kind projects. It is used to develop a new product, to ensure the continuing success of a product to which several departments directly contribute, and to solve a difficult problem. By superimposing a project structure upon the functional structure, a matrix organization is formed that allows the organization to take advantage of new opportunities. This structure assigns specialists from different functional departments to work on one or more projects being led by project managers. The matrix concept facilitates working on concurrent projects by creating a dual chain of command, the project (program, systems, or product) manager and the functional manager. Project managers have authority over activities geared toward achieving organizational goals while functional managers have authority over promotion decisions and performance reviews. An example is an aerospace firm with a contract from NASA.

Matrix organizations are particularly appealing to firms that want to speed up the decision-making process. However, the matrix organization may not allow long-term working relationships to develop. Furthermore, using multiple managers for one employee may result in confusion as to manager evaluation and accountability. Thus, the matrix system may elevate the conflict between product and functional interests.

Boundaryless organizations are not defined or limited by horizontal, vertical, or external boundaries imposed by a predetermined structure. They share many of the characteristics of flat organizations, with a strong emphasis on teams. Cross-functional teams dissolve horizontal barriers and enable the organization to respond quickly to environmental changes and to spearhead innovation. Boundaryless organizations can form relationships (joint ventures, intellectual property, distribution channels, or financial resources) with customers, suppliers, and/or competitors. Telecommuting, strategic alliances and customer-organization linkages break down external barriers, streamlining work activities. Jack Welch, former CEO of General Electric, to facilitate interactions with customers and suppliers, first used this un-structure.

A boundaryless environment is required by learning organizations to facilitate team collaboration and the sharing of information. When an organization develops the continuous capacity to adapt and survive in an increasingly competitive environment because all members take an active role in identifying and resolving work-related issues, it has developed a learning culture. A learning organization is one that is able to adapt and respond to change. This design empowers employees because they acquire and share knowledge and apply this learning to decision-making. They are pooling collective intelligence and stimulating creative thought to improve performance. Supervisors facilitate learning by sharing and aligning the organization's vision for the future and sustaining a sense of community and strong culture.

ORGANIZING FUNCTION

The organizing function deals with all those activities that result in the formal assignment of tasks and authority and a coordination of effort. The supervisor staffs the work unit, trains employees, secures resources, and empowers the work group into a productive team. The steps in the organizing process include (1) review plans, (2) list all tasks to be accomplished, (3) divide tasks into groups one person can accomplish-a job, (4) group related jobs together in a logical and efficient manner, (5) assign work to individuals, (6) delegate authority to establish relationships between jobs and groups of jobs.

The nature and scope of the work needed to accomplish the organization's objectives is needed to determine work classification and work unit design. Division of labour, or work specialization, is the degree to which tasks in an organization are divided into separate jobs. Work process requirements and employee skill level determine the degree of specialization. Placing capable people in each job ties directly with productivity improvement. In order to maximize productivity, supervisors match employee skill level with task requirements.

Supervisors should perform workflow analysis to examine how work creates or adds value to the ongoing processes in an organization. Workflow analysis looks at how work moves from the customer or the demand source through the organization to the point at which the work leaves the organization as a product or service to meet customer demand.

Thus, workflow analysis can be used to tighten the connection between employees' work and customers' needs. Also, it can help to make major performance breakthroughs throughout business process reengineering (BPR), a fundamental rethinking and radical redesign of business processes to achieve dramatic improvements in costs, quality, service, and speed. BPR uses workflow analysis to identify jobs that can be eliminated or recombined to improve company performance.

DEPARTMENTALIZATION

After reviewing the plans, usually the first step in the organizing process is departmentalization. Once jobs have been classified through work specialization, they are grouped so those common tasks can be coordinated. Departmentalization is the basis on which work or individuals are grouped into manageable units. There are five traditional methods for grouping work activities.

— Departmentalization by function organizes by the functions to be performed. The functions reflect the nature of the business. The advantage of this type of grouping is obtaining efficiencies from consolidating similar specialties and people with common skills, knowledge and orientations together in common units.

— Departmentalization by product assembles all functions needed to make and market a particular product are placed under one executive. For instance, major department stores are structured around product groups such as home accessories, appliances, women's clothing, men's clothing, and children's clothing.

— Departmentalization by geographical regions groups jobs on the basis of territory or geography. For example, Merck, a major pharmaceutical company, has its domestic sales departmentalized by regions such as Northeast, Southeast, Midwest, Southwest, and Northwest.

— Departmentalization by process groups jobs on the basis of product or customer flow. Each process requires particular skills and offers a basis for homogeneous categorizing of work activities. A patient preparing for an operation would first engage in preliminary diagnostic tests, then go through the admitting process, undergo a procedure in surgery, receive post operative care, be discharged and perhaps receive out-patient attention. These services are each administered by different departments.

— Departmentalization by customer groups jobs on the basis of a common set of needs or problems of specific customers. For instance, a plumbing firm may group its work according to whether it is serving private sector, public sector, government, or not-for-profit organizations. A current departmentalization trend is to structure work according to customer, using cross-functional teams. This group is chosen from different functions to work together across various departments to interdependently create new products or services. For example, a cross-functional team consisting of managers from accounting, finance, and marketing is created to prepare a technology plan.

POWER AND AUTHORITY

Organizational structure is a means of facilitating the achievement of organizational objectives. Such structures are not static, but dynamic. They reorganize in response to changing conditions that occur in the environment, new technology, or organizational growth. Organization structures are dependent upon the employees whose activities they guide. Supervisors rely upon power and authority to ensure that employees get things done.

Authority

The organizational structure provides the framework for the formal distribution of authority. Formalization is the degree to which tasks are standardized and rules and regulations govern employee behaviour.

It influences the amount of discretion an employee has over his or her job. In an organization with high degrees of formalization, job descriptions and policies provide clear direction. Where formalization is low, employees have a great deal of freedom in deciding how thy conduct their work. Within the same organization, different departments may have different degrees of formalization.

For example, in a hospital, doctors have freedom in selecting treatments, drugs, and methods for treating patients. However, the hospital physical plant staff has a strict schedule for cleaning buildings, mowing lawns, and maintaining the facilities. Authority is the legitimate power of a supervisor to direct subordinates to take action within the scope of the supervisor's position. Formal authority in the organization can be traced all the way back to the U.S. constitutional right to own property. The owner of the organization has the authority to make decisions. For example, entrepreneurial firms have an informal arrangement of employees and centralization of decision-making authority, the owner.

Forms of Authority

Three forms of authority are line authority, staff authority, and team authority. Line authority is direct supervisory authority from superior to subordinate. Authority flows in a direct chain of command from the top of the company to the bottom. Chain of command is an unbroken line of reporting relationships that extends through the entire organization that defines the formal decision-making structure. It helps employees know to whom they are accountable, and whom to go to with a problem. Line departments are directly linked to the production and sales of specific products.

Supervisors--in line departments, such as marketing and production--give direct orders, evaluate performance, and reward or punish those employees who work for them. Unity of command within the chain states that each person in an organization should take orders from and reports to only one person. This helps prevent conflicting demands being placed on employees by more than one boss. However, the trend toward employee empowerment, fuelled by advances in technology and changes in design from downsizing and reengineering have tempered the importance of being accountable to only one superior. Span of control refers to the number of employees that should be placed under the direction of one manager. Spans within effective organizations vary greatly. The actual number depends on the amount of complexity and the level of specialization. In general, a wide span of control is possible with better-trained, more experienced, and committed employees.

Staff authority is more limited authority to advise. It is authority that is based on expertise and which usually involves advising line managers. Staff members are advisers and counsellors who aid line departments in making decisions but do not have the authority to make final decisions. Staff supervisors help line departments decide what to do and how to do it. They coordinate and provide technical assistance or advice to all advisors, such as accounting, human resources, information technology, research, advertising, public relations, and legal services.

Team authority is granted to committees or work teams involved in an organization's daily operations. Work teams are groups of operating employees empowered to plan and organize their own work and to perform that work with a minimum of supervision. Team-Based structures organize separate functions into a group based on one overall objective. Empowered employees create their own schedules, design their own processes, and are held responsible for outcomes. This facilitates efficiencies in work process, and the ability to detect and react to changes in the environment. Employees with the skills and knowledge to manage more than one specialized task are able to promptly provide customers with quality products and services. Cross-functionally training team members allows any member to perform a variety of problem-solving tasks. Teamwork is an imperative in a flat, boundaryless organizational structure. A team is a small number of people with complementary skills who work toward common goals for which they hold themselves mutually accountable. Self-managed teams are responsible for producing an entire product, a component, or an ongoing service. In most cases, members are cross-trained on the different tasks assigned to the team. Often, these teams are trained in technical, administrative, and interpersonal skills. Problem-solving teams do not affect an organization's structure because they exist for only a limited period. They are often used when organizations decide to make improvements in the quality of a product or service. Special-purpose teams consist of members who span functional or organizational boundaries and whose purpose is to examine complex issues such as introducing new technology, improving the quality of work process, or encouraging cooperation between labour and management in a unionized setting.

Power

In addition to authority, supervisors have more personal sources of power to draw upon for getting things done. Everyone has power in one form or another and it is by exercising this power that organizations get things accomplished. Supervisors who are capable of achieving their objectives independently of others are said to possess strength. When these "strong" supervisors involve and incorporate others into their plans and activities they are making use of power, and in fact increasing the total amount of power available to incorporate into a particular situation or problem. Involving employees in setting objectives and making decisions as it relates to their jobs empowers everyone, and results in greater job satisfaction and commitment, as well as increased productivity. Empowering employees provides them with greater autonomy.

Power is the ability to exert influence in the organization beyond authority, which is derived from position. The supervisor's personal power could include job knowledge, personal influence, interpersonal skills, and ability to get results, empathetic ability, persuasive ability, and physical strength. J.P. French and B. Raven identify six sources of power: legitimate, coercive, reward, expert, referent, and information. Legitimate power is a result of the position a person holds in the organization hierarchy. This position power is broader than the ability to reward and punish, as members need to accept the authority of the position. Coercive power is the threat of sanctions. It is dependent on fear and includes, but is not limited to the ability to dismiss, assign undesirable work, or restriction of movement. Reward power results in people doing what is asked because they desire positive benefits or rewards. Rewards can be anything a person values (praise, raises, and promotions). Expert power comes from expertise, skill, or knowledge. Referent power refers to a person who has desirable resources or personal traits. It results in admiration and the desire to emulate. Information power is based upon the persuasiveness or content of a communication and is independent of the influencing individual. In most instances, supervisors do not need to offer incentives or threaten retribution to get employees to do what they request. They influence employees because the employees want to follow. This power to influence comes from the employee granting authority to the supervisor.

Centralization versus Decentralization

Centralization is the degree to which decision-making is concentrated in top management's hands. Decentralization is the extent to which decision-making authority is pushed down the organization structure and shared with many lower-level employees. Centralized organizations have more levels of management with narrow spans of control. Employees are not free to make decisions. Decentralized organizations have fewer levels of management with wide spans of control giving employees more freedom of action. All other things being equal, a wide span of control is more efficient because it requires fewer managers. However, it is important to recognize that, at some point, effectiveness will decline.

The current trend is toward broadening decentralization. As competition intensifies, the need for organizations to be responsive increases. This has made employees, usually those at the lower levels, who are closest to customers extremely important. They are an excellent source of knowledge and implement changes that directly impact performance. Giving this group more input into certain decision-making activities can result in increased firm performance. Teamwork is an imperative in a flat, boundaryless organizational structure. A team is a small number of people with complementary skills who work toward common goals for which they hold themselves mutually accountable. Self-managed teams are responsible for producing an entire product, a component, or an ongoing service. In most cases, members are cross-trained on the different tasks assigned to the team. Often, these teams are trained in technical, administrative, and interpersonal skills. Problem-solving teams do not affect an organization's structure because they exist for only a limited period.

They are often used when organizations decide to make improvements in the quality of a product or service. Special-purpose teams consist of members who span functional or organizational boundaries and whose purpose is to examine complex issues such as introducing new technology, improving the quality of work process, or encouraging cooperation between labour and management in a unionized setting.

Power

In addition to authority, supervisors have more personal sources of power to draw upon for getting things done. Everyone has power in one form or another and it is by exercising this power that organizations get things accomplished. Supervisors who are capable of achieving their objectives independently of others are said to possess strength. When these "strong" supervisors involve and incorporate others into their plans and activities they are making use of power, and in fact increasing the total amount of power available to incorporate into a particular situation or problem. Involving employees in setting objectives and making decisions as it relates to their jobs empowers everyone, and results in greater job satisfaction and commitment, as well as increased productivity. Empowering employees provides them with greater autonomy.

Power is the ability to exert influence in the organization beyond authority, which is derived from position. The supervisor's personal power could include job knowledge, personal influence, interpersonal skills, and ability to get results, empathetic ability, persuasive ability, and physical strength. J.P. French and B. Raven ("The Bases of Social Power" in Studies in Social Power, edited by D. Cartwright, Institute for Social Research, 1959, pp. 150-167) identify six sources of power: legitimate, coercive, reward, expert, referent, and information.

Legitimate power is a result of the position a person holds in the organization hierarchy. This position power is broader than the ability to reward and punish, as members need to accept the authority of the position. Coercive power is the threat of sanctions.

It is dependent on fear and includes, but is not limited to the ability to dismiss, assign undesirable work, or restriction of movement. Reward power results in people doing what is asked because they desire positive benefits or rewards. Rewards can be anything a person values (praise, raises, and promotions). Expert power comes from expertise, skill, or knowledge. Referent power refers to a person who has desirable resources or personal traits.

It results in admiration and the desire to emulate. Information power is based upon the persuasiveness or content of a communication and is independent of the influencing individual. In most instances, supervisors do not need to offer incentives or threaten retribution to get employees to do what they request. They influence employees because the employees want to follow. This power to influence comes from the employee granting authority to the supervisor.

Centralization versus Decentralization

Centralization is the degree to which decision-making is concentrated in top management's hands. Decentralization is the extent to which decision-making authority is pushed down the organization structure and shared with many lower-level employees.

Centralized organizations have more levels of management with narrow spans of control. Employees are not free to make decisions. Decentralized organizations have fewer levels of management with wide spans of control giving employees more freedom of action. All other things being equal, a wide span of control is more efficient because it requires fewer managers. However, it is important to recognize that, at some point, effectiveness will decline.

The current trend is toward broadening decentralization. As competition intensifies, the need for organizations to be responsive increases.

This has made employees, usually those at the lower levels, who are closest to customers extremely important. They are an excellent source of knowledge and implement changes that directly impact performance. Giving this group more input into certain decision-making activities can result in increased firm performance.

It is impractical for the supervisor to handle all of the work of the department directly. In order to meet the organization's goals, focus on objectives, and ensure that all work is accomplished, supervisors must delegate authority. Authority is the legitimate power of a supervisor to direct subordinates to take action within the scope of the supervisor's position.

By extension, this power, or a part thereof, is delegated and used in the name of a supervisor. Delegation is the downward transfer of formal authority from superior to subordinate. The employee is empowered to act for the supervisor, while the supervisor remains accountable for the outcome. Delegation of authority is a person-to-person relationship requiring trust, commitment, and contracting between the supervisor and the employee.

The supervisor assists in developing employees in order to strengthen the organization. He or she gives up the authority to make decisions that are best made by subordinates. This means that the supervisor allows subordinates the freedom to make mistakes and learn from them. He or she does not supervise subordinates' decision-making, but allows them the opportunity to develop their own skills. The supervisor lets subordinates know that he or she is willing to help, but not willing to do their jobs for them. The supervisor is not convinced that the best way for employees to learn is by telling them how to solve a problem. This results in those subordinates becoming dependent on the supervisor. The supervisor allows employees the opportunity to achieve and be credited for it.

An organization's most valuable resource is its people. By empowering employees who perform delegated jobs with the authority to manage those jobs, supervisors free themselves to manage more effectively. Successfully training future supervisors means delegating authority. This gives employees the concrete skills, experience, and the resulting confidence to develop themselves for higher positions. Delegation provides better managers and a higher degree of efficiency. Thus, collective effort, resulting in the organization's growth, is dependent on delegation of authority.

Responsibility and Accountability

Equally important to authority is the idea that when an employee is given responsibility for a job, he or she must also be given the degree of authority necessary to carry it out. Thus, for effective delegation, the authority granted to an employee must equal the assigned responsibility. Upon accepting the delegated task, the employee has incurred an obligation to perform the assigned work and to properly utilize the granted authority. Responsibility is the obligation to do assigned tasks. The individual employee is responsible for being proficient at his or her job. The supervisor is responsible for what employees do or fail to do, as well as for the resources under their control. Thus, responsibility is an integral part of a supervisor's authority. Responsibilities fall into two categories: individual and organizational. Employees have individual responsibilities to be proficient in their job. They are responsible for their actions. Nobody gives or delegates individual responsibilities. Employees assume them when they accept a position in the organization.

Organizational responsibilities refer to collective organizational accountability and include how well departments perform their work. For example, the supervisor is responsible for all the tasks assigned to his or her department, as directed by the manager. When someone is responsible for something, he or she is liable, or accountable to a superior, for the outcome. Thus, accountability flows upward in the organization. All are held accountable for their personal, individual conduct. Accountability is answering for the result of one's actions or omissions. It is the reckoning, wherein one answers for his or her actions and accepts the consequences, good or bad. Accountability establishes reasons, motives and importance for actions in the eyes of managers and employees alike. Accountability is the final act in the establishment of one's credibility. It is important to remember that accountability results in rewards for good performance, as well as discipline for poor performance.

The Delegation Process

The delegation process has five phases: (1) preparing, (2) planning, (3) discussing, (4) auditing, and (5) appreciating. The first step in delegating is to identify what should and should not be delegated.

The supervisor should delegate any task that a subordinate performs better. Tasks least critical to the performance of the supervisor's job can be delegated. Any task that provides valuable experience for subordinates should be delegated. Also, the supervisor can delegate the tasks that he or she dislikes the most. But, the supervisor should not delegate any task that would violate a confidence.

— Preparing includes establishing the objectives of the delegation, specifying the task that needs to be accomplished, and deciding who should accomplish it.

— Planning is meeting with the chosen subordinate to describe the task and to ask the subordinate to devise a plan of action. As Andrew Carnegie once said, "The secret of success is not in doing your own work but in recognizing the right man to do it." Trust between the supervisor and employee-that both will fulfill the commitment-is most important.

— Discussing includes reviewing the objectives of the task as well as the subordinate's plan of action, any potential obstacles, and ways to avoid or deal with these obstacles. The supervisor should clarify and solicit feedback as to the employee's understanding. Clarifications needed for delegation include the desired results (what not how), guidelines, resources available, and consequences (good and bad). Delegation is similar to contracting between the supervisor and employee regarding how and when the work will be completed. The standards and time frames are discussed and agreed upon. The employee should know exactly what is expected and how the task will be evaluated.

— Auditing is monitoring the progress of the delegation and making adjustments in response to unforeseen problems.

— Appreciating is accepting the completed task and acknowledging the subordinate's efforts.

Since motivation influences productivity, supervisors need to understand what motivates employees to reach peak performance. It is not an easy task to increase employee motivation because employees respond in different ways to their jobs and their organization's practices. Motivation is the set of processes that moves a person toward a goal. Thus, motivated behaviours are voluntary choices controlled by the individual employee.

The supervisor (motivator) wants to influence the factors that motivate employees to higher levels of productivity. Factors that affect work motivation include individual differences, job characteristics, and organizational practices. Individual differences are the personal needs, values, and attitudes, interests and abilities that people bring to their jobs. Job characteristics are the aspects of the position that determine its limitations and challenges.

Organizational practices are the rules, human resources policies, managerial practices, and rewards systems of an organization. Supervisors must consider how these factors interact to affect employee job performance.

Simple Model of Motivation

The purpose of behaviour is to satisfy needs. A need is anything that is required, desired, or useful. A want is a conscious recognition of a need. A need arises when there is a difference in self-concept (the way I see myself) and perception (the way I see the world around me). The presence of an active need is expressed as an inner state of tension from which the individual seeks relief.

Theories of Motivation

Many methods of employee motivation have been developed. The study of work motivation has focused on the motivator (supervisor) as well as the motivatee (employee). Motivation theories are important to supervisors attempting to be effective leaders. Two primary approaches to motivation are content and process.

The content approach to motivation focuses on the assumption that individuals are motivated by the desire to fulfill inner needs. Content theories focus on the needs that motivate people.

Maslow's Hierarchy of Needs identifies five levels of needs, which are best seen as a hierarchy with the most basic need emerging first and the most sophisticated need last. People move up the hierarchy one level at a time. Gratified needs lose their strength and the next level of needs is activated. As basic or lower-level needs are satisfied, higher-level needs become operative. A satisfied need is not a motivator. The most powerful employee need is the one that has not been satisfied. Abraham Maslow first presented the five-tier hierarchy in 1942 to a psychoanalytic society and published it in 1954 in Motivation and Personality (New York: Harper and Row).

Level I-Physiological needs are the most basic human needs. They include food, water, and comfort. The organization helps to satisfy employees' physiological needs by a paycheck.

Level II-Safety needs are the desires for security and stability, to feel safe from harm. The organization helps to satisfy employees' safety needs by benefits.

Level III-Social needs are the desires for affiliation. They include friendship and belonging. The organization helps to satisfy employees' social needs through sports teams, parties, and celebrations. The supervisor can help fulfill social needs by showing direct care and concern for employees.

Level IV-Esteem needs are the desires for self-respect and respect or recognition from others. The organization helps to satisfy employees' esteem needs by matching the skills and abilities of the employee to the job. The supervisor can help fulfill esteem needs by showing workers that their work is appreciated.

Level V-Self-actualization needs are the desires for self-fulfilment and the realization of the individual's full potential. The supervisor can help fulfill self-actualization needs by assigning tasks that challenge employees' minds while drawing on their aptitude and training. Alderfer's ERG identified three categories of needs. The most important contribution of the ERG model is the addition of the frustration-regression hypothesis, which holds that when individuals are frustrated in meeting higher level needs, the next lower level needs reemerge. Existence needs are the desires for material and physical well being. These needs are satisfied with food, water, air, shelter, working conditions, pay, and fringe benefits.

Relatedness needs are the desires to establish and maintain interpersonal relationships. These needs are satisfied with relationships with family, friends, supervisors, subordinates, and co-workers. Growth needs are the desires to be creative, to make useful and productive contributions and to have opportunities for personal development.

McClelland's Learned Needs divides motivation into needs for power, affiliation, and achievement.

Achievement motivated people thrive on pursuing and attaining goals. They like to be able to control the situations in which they are involved. They take moderate risks. They like to get immediate feedback on how they have done. They tend to be preoccupied with a task-orientation towards the job to be done.

Power motivated individuals see almost every situation as an opportunity to seize control or dominate others. They love to influence others. They like to change situations whether or not it is needed. They are willing to assert themselves when a decision needs to be made.

Affiliation motivated people are usually friendly and like to socialize with others. This may distract them from their performance requirements. They will usually respond to an appeal for cooperation.

Herzberg's Two-Factor Theory describes needs in terms of satisfaction and dissatisfaction. Frederick Herzberg examined motivation in the light of job content and contest. Motivating employees is a two-step process. First provide hygienes and then motivators. One continuum ranges from no satisfaction to satisfaction. The other continuum ranges from dissatisfaction to no dissatisfaction. Satisfaction comes from motivators that are intrinsic or job content, such as achievement, recognition, advancement, responsibility, the work itself, and growth possibilities. Herzberg uses the term motivators for job satisfiers since they involve job content and the satisfaction that results from them. Motivators are considered job turn-ons. They are necessary for substantial improvements in work performance and move the employee beyond satisfaction to superior performance. Motivators correspond to Maslow's higher-level needs of esteem and self-actualization.

Dissatisfaction occurs when the following hygiene factors, extrinsic or job context, are not present on the job: pay, status, job security, working conditions, company policy, peer relations, and supervision. Herzberg uses the term hygiene for these factors because they are preventive in nature.

They will not produce motivation, but they can prevent motivation from occurring. Hygiene factors can be considered job stay-ons because they encourage an employee to stay on a job. Once these factors are provided, they do not necessarily promote motivation; but their absence can create employee dissatisfaction. Hygiene factors correspond to Maslow's physiological, safety, and social needs in that they are extrinsic, or peripheral, to the job. They are present in the work environment of job context.

Motivation comes from the employee's feelings of accomplishment or job content rather than from the environmental factors or job context. Motivators encourage an employee to strive to do his or her best. Job enrichment can be used to meet higher-level needs. To enrich a job, a supervisor can introduce new or more difficult tasks, assign individuals specialized tasks that enable them to become experts, or grant additional authority to employees.

The process approach emphasizes how and why people choose certain behaviours in order to meet their personal goals. Process theories focus on external influences or behaviours that people choose to meet their needs. External influences are often readily accessible to supervisors.

Vroom's Expectancy Model suggests that people choose among alternative behaviours because they anticipate that particular behaviours will lead to one or more desired outcomes and that other behaviours will lead to undesirable outcomes. Expectancy is the belief that effort will lead to first-order outcomes, any work-related behaviour that is the direct result of the effort an employee expends on a job.

Equity is the perception of fairness involved in rewards given. A fair or equitable situation is one in which people with similar inputs experience similar outcomes. Employees will compare their rewards with the rewards received by others for their efforts. If employees perceive that an inequity exists, they are likely to withhold some of their contributions, either consciously or unconsciously, to bring a situation into better balance.

For example, if someone thinks he or she is not getting enough pay (output) for his or her work (input), he or she will try to get that pay increased or reduce the amount of work he or she is doing. On the other hand, when a worker thinks he or she is being paid too much for the work he or she is doing, he or she tends to increase the amount of work. Not only do workers compare their own inputs and outputs; they compare their input/output ratio with the input/output ratio of other workers. If one work team believes they are doing more work than a similar team for the same pay, their sense of fairness will be violated and they will tend to reduce the amount of work they are doing. It is a normal human inclination to want things to be fair.

Bowditch and Buono note (see Bowditch, James L. and Anthony F. Buono, A Primer on Organizational Behaviour, 4th, John Wiley & Sons, 1997) that while equity theory was originally concerned with differences in pay, it may be applied to other forms of tangible and intangible rewards in the workplace. That is, if any input is not balanced with some fair output, the motivation process will be difficult. Supervisors must manage the perception of fairness in the mind of each employee. If subordinates think they are not being treated fairly, it is difficult to motivate them.

Reinforcement involves four types of consequence. Positive reinforcement creates a pleasant consequence by using rewards to increase the likelihood that a behaviour will be repeated. Negative reinforcement occurs when a person engages in behaviour to avoid unpleasant consequences or to escape from existing unpleasant consequences.

Punishment is an attempt to discourage a target behaviour by the application of negative outcomes whenever it is possible. Extinction is the absence of any reinforcement, either positive or negative, following the occurrence of a target behaviour. Employees have questions about their jobs. Can I do what management is asking me to do? If I do the job, will I be rewarded? Will the reward I receive be satisfactory to me?

Reinforcement is based primarily on the work of B.F. Skinner, a psychologist, who experimented with the theories of operant conditioning. Skinner's work shows that many behaviours can be controlled through the use of rewards. In fact, a person might be influenced to change his or her behaviour by giving him or her rewards.

Employees who do an exceptionally good job on a particular project should be rewarded for that performance. It will motivate them to try to do an exceptional job on their next project. Employees must associate the reward with the behaviour. In other words, the employee must know for what specifically he or she is being rewarded!

The reward should come as quickly as possible after the behaviour. The reward can be almost anything, but it must be something desired by the employee. Some of the most powerful rewards are symbolic; things that cost very little but mean a lot to the people who get them. Examples of symbolic rewards are things like plaques or certificates.

4

Techniques of Management

INTRODUCTION

To meet the many demands of performing their functions, managers assume multiple roles. A role is an organized set of behaviours. Henry Mintzberg has identified ten roles common to the work of all managers. The ten roles are divided into three groups: interpersonal, informational, and decisional. The informational roles link all managerial work together. The interpersonal roles ensure that information is provided. The decisional roles make significant use of the information. The performance of managerial roles and the requirements of these roles can be played at different times by the same manager and to different degrees depending on the level and function of management. The ten roles are described individually, but they form an integrated whole.

The three interpersonal roles are primarily concerned with interpersonal relationships. In the figurehead role, the manager represents the organization in all matters of formality. The top level manager represents the company legally and socially to those outside of the organization. The supervisor represents the work group to higher management and higher management to the work group. In the liaison role, the manger interacts with peers and people outside the organization. The top level manager uses the liaison role to gain favours and information, while the supervisor uses it to maintain the routine flow of work. The leader role defines the relationships between the manger and employees. The direct relationships with people in the interpersonal roles place the manager in a unique position to get information. Thus, the three informational roles are primarily concerned with the information aspects of managerial work. In the monitor role, the manager receives and collects information. In the role of disseminator, the manager transmits special information into the organization. The top level manager receives and transmits more information from people outside the organization than the supervisor. In the role of spokesperson, the manager disseminates the organization's information into its environment. Thus, the top level manager is seen as an industry expert, while the supervisor is seen as a unit or departmental expert.

The unique access to information places the manager at the center of organizational decision making. There are four decisional roles. In the entrepreneur role, the manager initiates change. In the disturbance handler role, the manger deals with threats to the organization. In the resource allocator role, the manager chooses where the organization will expend its efforts. In the negotiator role, the manager negotiates on behalf of the organization.

The top level manager makes the decisions about the organization as a whole, while the supervisor makes decisions about his or her particular work unit. The supervisor performs these managerial roles but with different emphasis than higher managers. Supervisory management is more focused and short-term in outlook.

Thus, the figurehead role becomes less significant and the disturbance handler and negotiator roles increase in importance for the supervisor. Since leadership permeates all activities, the leader role is among the most important of all roles at all levels of management. In order to perform the functions of management and to assume multiple roles, managers must be skilled. Robert Katz identified three managerial skills that are essential to successful management: technical, human, and conceptual.

Technical skill involves process or technique knowledge and proficiency. Managers use the processes, techniques and tools of a specific area. Human skill involves the ability to interact effectively with people. Managers interact and cooperate with employees. Conceptual skill involves the formulation of ideas. Managers understand abstract relationships, develop ideas, and solve problems creatively. Thus, technical skill deals with things, human skill concerns people, and conceptual skill has to do with ideas.

A manager's level in the organization determines the relative importance of possessing technical, human, and conceptual skills. Top level managers need conceptual skills in order to view the organization as a whole. Conceptual skills are used in planning and dealing with ideas and abstractions. Supervisors need technical skills to manage their area of specialty. All levels of management need human skills in order to interact and communicate with other people successfully.

As the pace of change accelerates and diverse technologies converge, new global industries are being created (for example, telecommunications). Technological change alters the fundamental structure of firms and calls for new organizational approaches and management skills. Successful organizations continually innovate and change based upon customer needs and feedback. Values, mission, and vision form the foundation for the execution of the functions of management. They are an organization's guidelines that affect how it will operate. They work only if visible and used in everyday activities and decisions. An organization's values are its beliefs or those qualities that have intrinsic worth and will not be compromised. Its mission is its purpose for existing. The vision is the image of itself in the future.

Values

Each supervisor's approach to management will reflect his or her values, as well as those of the organization. Building trust starts with creating culture based on shared values. Values are traits or qualities having intrinsic worth, such as courage, respect, responsibility, caring, truthfulness, self-discipline, and fairness. Values serve as a baseline for actions and decision-making and guide employees in the organization's intentions and interests. The values driving behaviour define the organizational culture. A strong value system or clearly defined culture turns beliefs into standards such as best quality, best performance, most reliable, most durable, safest, fastest, best value for the money, least expensive, most prestigious, best designed or styled, easiest to use. If asked, "What do we believe in?" or "List our organization's values" all employees in the organization should write down the same values. For example, McDonald's values were captured in its motto of "Q.S.C. & V." which stands for quality, service, cleanliness, and value.

Supervisors need to appreciate the significance of values and value systems. Values affect how a supervisor views other people and groups, thus influencing interpersonal relationships. Values affect how a supervisor perceives situations and solves problems. Values affect how a supervisor determines what is and is not ethical behaviour. Values affect how a supervisor leads and controls employees. Since employees often base behaviour on perceived values it is critical to ensure their perceptions reflect organizational values. Supervisors must communicate, encourage and reinforce the desired values and related behaviours to integrate them into the organizational culture.

Geert Hofstede identified a work-related value framework that has four dimensions: power distance, uncertainty avoidance, individualism, and polarization. Power distance is the attitude to human inequality and relationships to superiors and inferiors in any hierarchy. Uncertainty avoidance is the tolerance for uncertainty that determines choices and rituals to cope with it in social structures and belief systems. Individualism is the relationship between the individual and the collectivity, especially in the way individuals choose to live and work together. Polarization is the extent to which differences such as masculinity or femininity have implications for social organization and the organizations of beliefs. Every person has a different mental program, based on patterns of thinking, feeling, and acting, which are learned throughout a lifetime. The effects of these differences have many practical implications for those who work or are managers in multinational business and for those involved in international negotiations.

Mission

A mission is a broad definition of a business that differentiates it from all other organizations. It is the justification for the organization's existence. The mission statement is the "touchstone" by which all offerings are judged. In addition to the organization's purpose other key elements of the mission statement should include whom it serves, how, and why. The most effective mission statements are easily recalled and provide direction and motivation for the organization.

Since an organization exists to accomplish something in the larger environment, its specific mission or purpose provides employees with a shared sense of opportunity, direction, significance, and achievement. An explicit mission guides employees to work independently and yet collectively toward the realization of the organization's potential. Thus, a good mission statement gets the emotional bonding and commitment needed. It allows the individual employee to say; "I know how I should do my job differently."

For example, many people might think that The Walt Disney Company's mission is to run theme parks. But, Disney's mission is always moving toward an expanded view. Disney provides entertainment. "Disney's overriding objective is to create shareholder value by continuing to be the world's premier entertainment company from a creative, strategic, and financial standpoint."

Also, many people might think that Revlon's mission is to make cosmetics. Yet, Revlon provides glamour, excitement and innovation. Charles Revson, Revlon's founder understood the importance of mission. He said "In the factory, we make cosmetics; in the store, we sell hope."

Vision

Erich Fromm pointed out; "The best way to predict your future is to create it." A vision might be a picture, image, or description of the preferred future. A visionary has the ability to foresee something and sees the need for change first. He or she challenges the status quo and forces honest assessments of where the industry is headed and how the company can best get there. A visionary is ready with solutions before the problems arise.

A study over the period from 1926 to 1990 found visionary companies that set a purpose beyond making money outperformed other companies in the stock market by more than six to one. (See Gilbert Fuchsberg, "Visioning' Mission Becomes Its Own Mission," The Wall Street Journal, January 7, 1994, B1, 3.) Managers require more vision than ever because change is coming faster than ever. Leaders have the ability to make their vision real by engaging the minds, as well as the hearts of others.

Microsoft's early vision statement was "A Computer on Every Desk and In Every Home." (At approximately the same time, President John Akers said IBM's goal was to become a $100 billion company by then end of the century. At that time IBM sales were $50 billion.) Microsoft's vision has evolved [1998 the "Connected PC and the Connected TV"-the idea of integrating the intelligence and interactivity of PCs with the video and sound of TV] to 2002 "to enable people and businesses throughout the world to realize their full potential."

Life consists in what a man is thinking of all day.--Ralph Waldo Emerson.

A goal is an end that the organization strives to attain. However, the supervisor cannot "do" a goal. Supervisors break down processes, analyze them, set objectives and then drive hard to achieve them. Doing the same thing and expecting different results doesn't work. The supervisor must write an objective for what he or she is trying to accomplish. Thus, an objective is the object or aim of an action. It implies an explicit direction for the action to take and a specific quality of work to be accomplished within a given period of time. Objectives reflect the desired outcomes for individuals, groups and organizations. They provide direction for decision-making and a criterion against which outcomes are measured. Thus, objectives are the foundation of planning.

MANAGEMENT BY OBJECTIVES

An effective planning tool to help the supervisor set objectives is Management by Objectives (MBO). MBO gained recognition in 1954 with the publication of Peter Drucker's book The Practice of Management. MBO is a collaborative process whereby the manager and each subordinate jointly determine objectives for that subordinate. To be successful MBO programs should include commitment and participation in the MBO process at all levels, from top management to the lowest position in the organization. MBO begins when the supervisor explains the goals for the department in a meeting. The subordinate takes the goals and proposes objectives for his or her particular job. The supervisor meets with the subordinate to approve and, if necessary, modify the individual objectives.

Modification of the individual's objectives is accomplished through negotiation since the supervisor has resources to help the subordinate commit to the achievement of the objective. Thus, a set of verifiable objectives for each individual are jointly determined, prioritized, and formalized. The supervisor and the subordinate meet periodically to review the latter's progress. Communication is the key factor in determining MBO's success or failure. The supervisor gives feedback and may authorize modifications to the objectives or their timetables as circumstances dictate. Finally, the employee's performance is measured against his or her objectives, and he or she is rewarded . accordingly.

Steps in MBO Process

Research has demonstrated that when top management is committed and personally involved in implementing MBO programs, they significantly improve performance. This finding is not surprising when one considers that during the MBO process employees determine what they will accomplish. After all, who knows what a person is capable of doing better than the person does him or herself? Objectives are the driver of planning processes. It is imperative that top managers safeguard the intention of their goals to facilitate middle and lower management's effective translation and implementation of them. Objectives guide managerial activities such as budgeting, the development of action plans, staffing, and the purchasing of equipment. The organization's success ultimately depends on the combined outcomes of its objectives.

Objectives

Most supervisors set objectives, but not with equal skill. Few, who do not correctly write objectives, will reap MBO's full benefits. An objective is simply a statement of what is to done and should be stated in terms of results. A mnemonic aid to write objectives is SMART (Specific, Measurable, Attainable, Result-oriented, Time-limited).

Specific

An objective must be specific with a single key result. If more than one result is to be accomplished, more than one objective should be written. Just knowing what is to be accomplished is a big step toward achieving it. What is important to you? Once you clarify what you want to achieve, your attention will be focused on the objective that you deliberately set. You will be doing something important to you.

Measurable

An objective must be measurable. Only an objective that affects behaviour in a measurable way can be optimally effective. If possible, state the objective as a quantity. Some objectives are more difficult to measure than others are. However, difficulty does not mean that they cannot be measured. Treatment of salespeople might be measured by looking at the absenteeism and turnover rates among the sales force. Also, salespeople could be asked to fill out a behavioural questionnaire anonymously giving their observations of the supervision they receive. Customer service could be measured by such indices as the number of complaints received, by the number of customers lost, and by customer interviews or responses to questionnaires. Development of subordinates could be measured by determining the number of tasks the subordinate has mastered. Cooperation with other functions could be measured by length of delay in providing requested information, or by peer ratings of degree of cooperation. Avoid statements of objectives in generalities. Infinitives to avoid include to know, to understand, to enjoy, and to believe. Action verbs are observable and better communicate the intent of what is to be attempted. They include to write, to apply, to recite, to revise, to contrast, to install, to select, to assemble, to compare, to investigate, and to develop.

Scaling the Progress

Attainable

An objective must be attainable with the resources that are available. It must be realistic. Many objectives are realistic. Yet, the time it takes to achieve them may be unrealistic. For example, it is realistic to want to lose ten pounds. However, it is unrealistic to want to lose ten pounds in one week. What barriers stand between you and your objective? How will each barrier be overcome and within what time frame?

Result-oriented

The objective should be central to the goals of the organization. The successful completion of the objective should make a difference.How will this objective help the organization move ahead? Is the objective aligned with the mission of the organization?

Time-limited

The objective should be traceable. Specific objectives enable time priorities to be set and time to be used on objectives that really matter. Are the time lines you have established realistic? Will other competing demands cause delay? Will you be able to overcome those demands to accomplish the objective you've set in the time frame you've established?

Write Meaningful Objectives

Although the rules are difficult to establish, the following may be useful when writing an objective.

1. Start with an action or accomplishment verb. (Use the infinitive form of the verb. This means to start the with "to.")
2. Identify a single key result for each objective.
3. Give the date of the estimated completion.
4. Be sure the objective is one you can control.
5. To test for validity of SMART objectives, ask yourself the following questions.
   * S = Exactly what is my objective?
   * M = What would a good job look like?
   * A = Is my objective feasible?
   * R = Is my objective meaningful?
   * T = Is my objective traceable?

The following fill-in-the-blank equation may be useful when writing an objective.

Objective: To (+ action verb + single key result + target date).

A RACE TOWARDS A PROCESS-ORIENTED MANAGEMENT

Approaches to management of operational goals may be divided in two types-function-oriented and project-oriented. The function-oriented management (Fn-management) is usually used in the environments where a lot of relatively simple operational goals pop up very frequently. The Fn-management implies that operational goals are handled in a routine manner by the staff where each member has his own function in achieving operational goals. A manager does not coordinate the execution of activities for each goal, workers just react on the incoming documents, phone calls, etc., by completing activities they are assigned, and forwarding the received or newly composed documents further to their colleagues.

The project-oriented management (Pj-management) is usually used with more sophisticated goals such as construction or software projects. The Pj-management implies that a process for a new goal is planned in detail before the work on it starts, and there is someone (e.g., a project manager) who supervises all the work being done.

Fn-management is most cost-effective, but it works poorly when a process of achieving an operational goal deviates from a standard pattern, as it lacks control over individual processes. Pj-management gives full control over an individual process, but it's inefficient when a lot of coexisting processes are involved. There are working environments where one or the other type of management fits well. But in most environments a combination of these two approaches would be the way to obtain both full control over all processes and efficiency.

Below, we discuss our proposals for integration of the Fn- and Pj-managements. The result is a new type of management which we call the process-oriented management, or Pc-management, for short. This name highlights the main objective of the Pc-management-to control the processes, in contrast to Fn-management that places the emphasis on the execution of activities, and the Pj-management that emphasizes plans. We describe the Pc-management here in the following way. We consider an environment typical for the function-oriented management-a trading company, and try to introduce the project-oriented management in it.

The process-oriented management is presented thus as a result of tailoring the project-oriented approach to fit a different kind of environment. We find this way most convenient for discussing our ideas, but it's not, naturally, the only possible one. The Pc-management is based on the notions of "orgobject", "history" and "dynamic and distributed planning", which we can now turn our attention to. The Pj-management involves developing a detailed plan for achieving a project's goal before the work on the project can start. This plan is premised on certain assumptions that may turn out wrong after the project is under way. The plan should then be adapted to the changed conditions. For this purpose, a clear picture of the current state of the project is required to figure out what should be done to complete the project.

A project often involves developing some product that is a physical object, e.g. a software system, a building, etc. This product comes into existence in some form already at the earlier stages of the project, e.g. a half-ready software system or a building under construction. This half-ready product serves as a good representation of the current state of the project. As the half-ready product can be studied without regards to how it has been produced, the plan can be revised without going into details of the project's history.

In cases where the Fn-management is involved, there is no half-ready product to represent the current state of achieving an operational goal. A kind of an abstract object that contains all information on the current state of the process would be helpful here. As it would serve as an organizing device for achieving the goal, we call it an "orgobject".

For example, an orgobject representing a process of "Get payment for an incoming order" may be a record that contains information on: the name and address of the buyer, a description of each kind of goods ordered, the quantity and price per unit of each kind, the quantities of goods already delivered; the amount of money invoiced; the amount of money received. Having this orgobject, the conditions for the successful achievement of the "get payment" goal could be formulated as follows:

- have the numbers representing the quantities of 'goods ordered' and 'goods delivered' equal for each goods kind

- have 'money invoiced' equal to the sum of 'ordered' multiplied by 'price per unit' for all goods kinds, and
- have 'money received' equal to 'money invoiced'.

As the process develops, the corresponding orgobject should change so that it reflects all the time the current state of the process. As soon as some activity is completed, the orgobject representing the process is to be modified.

Thus, in the above example, after the delivery (full or partial), the quantities of the goods delivered are modified; if the customer has changed the order, the types and quantities of the goods ordered are modified, etc. To ensure that the orgobjects are always up-to-date, the routines for every type of activity should list not only the operations required for completing the activity (e.g., packing and shipping for delivery), but also instructions for the appropriate modifications of the relevant orgobjects.

Thus, the current state of an orgobject reflects the overall result of all activities completed earlier, and shows what actions should be taken to achieve the goal. To return to our example, if the quantity of the goods ordered is greater than the quantity of the goods delivered, the missing goods are to be delivered. If, on the other hand, the quantity of the goods ordered is less than the quantity of the goods delivered, then the customer should be asked to return some of the goods. Other examples: if the amount of money invoiced exceeds the payment received, then the customer should pay the difference. If the amount of the money received exceeds that of invoiced, then a credit note should be issued.

History

The current state of an orgobject contains only the result of the completed activities, but not a list of them, e.g.: the quantity of the goods delivered, but not the number of separate deliveries; the amount of money invoiced, but not the number of separate invoices, etc. This is OK if all goes as it should. But if something goes wrong, e.g., some goods sent off did not arrive, then the information on all activities performed is vital when figuring out what actions should be taken. This information can be collected through logging all the activities completed in the frame of the given process. Let's consider the following logging scheme. Every time a worker executes an activity, he/she doesn't physically change the previous state of the relevant orgobject. He/she makes a new record instead which contain the new state of the orgobject and leaves the former one unchanged. For example, after a delivery, a new record is made containing the same information as the previous one except the information on the quantities of the goods delivered. The latter is updated according to the packing list.

The record on the previous state of an orgobject is placed in a special file containing the history of the given orgobject. The worker who completes an activity composes also a report where he/she records: the kind of activity completed, the name of a person who completed it, the date, time, comments, etc. This report is saved together with the previous state of the orgobject in the history file. Given two consequent states of an orgobject and an activity report, we can reconstruct exactly what happened during the activity execution. For example, in case of delivery, we know exactly by whom and when the goods were delivered, and in what quantities. Thus, our log provides an easy access to the information on both the activity performed, and the state of events before and after it was performed.

Dynamic and Distributed Planning

As it was mentioned above, the Pj-management involves designing a detailed plan for each new process. If we try to apply the same to a Fn-management environment, two problems would arise:

- as Fn-processes are often trivial, their plans would be trivial too, e.g.: 'delivering goods'-'invoicing the buyer'-'getting payment'. It would be meaningless to record such plan for every process (and there are many in this kind of environments),

- unpredictable external events that often occur in Fn-management environments would demand revising the whole plan, e.g.: a customer has changed his order-additional delivery can be required, an invoice is to be sent later than it was initially planned, etc.

Dynamic planning is our answer to these problems. Dynamic planning involves planning only the first few activities at the first stage. As soon as one or several of these are completed, new activities are planned with regard to the emerging state of the relevant orgobject (and standard routines adopted in the company). For example, after a delivery, another delivery is planned if not all ordered goods have been delivered, or invoicing is planned if all goods have been delivered. The use of dynamic planning is fully beneficial in case of processes that follow a standard pattern. Otherwise, the usual planning is preferable. In case the character of the process (standard/deviating) is difficult to foresee, dynamic planning can be used at first, followed by conventional planning if necessary.

Another poser when trying to introduce the Pj-management in an Fn-environment is how to supervise a process. In cases where the Pj-management is involved, there is usually a project manager who supervises the execution of planned activities, and corrects the plan if needed. In an environment typical for the Fn-management, a project manager supervising each process would result in significant overheads.

A solution to this can be described as "distributed planning". Distributed planning implies that the worker who has completed a planned activity himself plans the subsequent activities. Moreover, he/she can assign these new activities not only to himself, but to other people too. For example, a worker who completes a delivery himself plans invoicing to be completed by another worker.

Distributed planning doesn't exclude the possibility of a centralized supervision of a process. In fact, a supervisor may intervene at any time and correct the plan if needed. Moreover, any member of staff can consult the supervisor in case he/she has some problems with his/her work on a particular process. He/she can do it by planning a special activity, e.g., "asking for help", and assigning his/her supervisor to complete it.

Let's have a look at the issue of implementing dynamic and distributed planning. Above, we considered orgobjects and plans as separate entities. Now, we put a plan inside the orgobject representing the corresponding process. As a result an orgobject besides the information on the current state of the process (e.g., on the customer, goods, delivery and payment) will also include a list of planned activities (e.g., delivery, invoicing, etc.), each of them containing information on what should be done, who's to do that and when.

Thus, a plan becomes part of an orgobject. Consequently, we can treat correction of the plan as one of the operations of changing the orgobject in the course of completing an activity. In section 3.1, we've already mentioned that instructions for modifying orgobjects should be included in the working procedures for each type of activities. To ensure proper dynamic planning, these instructions should embrace modification of the process's plan. In a simple case, a worker who has completed an activity modifies the relevant orgobject by removing this activity from the list of planned activities. In more complex cases, he/she adds new activities to the list, and/or removes some other activities from it.

Being an integral part of the orgobject representing a process, a plan is subjected to the logging we described above. As a result, all acts of replanning are registered in the same way as other modifications of orgobjects. Thus, for example, the name of a person who modified the plan is recorded, which may prove to be useful in case of conflicts.

Advantages

The main advantage of the Pc-management is its flexibility. The Pc-management permits to choose the optimum approach to coping with each process, and within the same management scheme. Thus, simple processes that follow a standard pattern are dealt with in a completely decentralized manner, whereas some more sophisticated case will be dealt with by centralized individual planning and supervising. Moreover, the same process may be treated differently at different stages. For example, it may be started as a standard one, but later it can be planned and supervised individually. As a result, full control over all kinds of processes is gained and efficiency is not sacrificed.

Another important thing is that the Pc-management is not bound to any particular type of organizational structure. It can be used both in case the same member of staff completes all the activities required for achieving an operational goal, and in case each activity type is assigned to a particular worker. This permits to preserve the same management scheme when the organizational structure is changed, e.g., in case of a company's expansion.

Some other advantages are as follows:

1. Orgobjects provide a perfect insight into the company's state of affairs. The information stored in the orgobjects is of great help to the management staff as it permit to quickly evaluate the state of a process (without going into its history). It also helps to give prompt answers to customers' questions. This kind of information is not easily obtainable when traditional managements schemes are used. Thus, when the Fn-management is used, only the information on the executed activities of a given type is easily accessible, and when the Pj-management is used, only the information on the state of the plans execution is easily accessible.
2. Histories of orgobjects permit to easily trace all the activities completed on a given process, which helps to devise plans for complicated cases. They are also a very important source of data for all kinds of statistical analysis, and other types of information processing required for decision-making.
3. The company's staff becomes goal-and process-conscious, as it is easy for any person to overview all the activities

(one's own and those of others) completed in a process he/she is involved in. The history of old orgobjects is useful for "learning by example", which may help a worker to find solutions in difficult cases. The goal-and process-consciousness isn't easy to acquire with a traditional management scheme. Under the Fn-management, a worker doesn't see how a process he/she's in is accomplished. His/her personal goal becomes to complete as efficient as possible the activities he/she is responsible for. That may result in, e.g., a seller concentrating on making telephone calls most of which don't get him to closing a deal.

4. The Pj-management emphasizes following the schedule, which becomes the main goal of the workers engaged in a project. There is a danger that the workers do not keep their eyes open for changes in the surrounding world, which is, e.g., the main reason why large software projects often produce out-of-day systems.
5. As all the information on the past is being stored, the management staff is in a better position concerning various kinds of conflicts, internal conflicts among workers engaged in the same process, and external ones, e.g., with customers or suppliers.
6. Distributed planning is a very powerful tool for coordinating the work which makes unnecessary the intensive communication (exchanges of documents, phone calls, etc.) among the workers engaged in the same processes. They get the required information from the current states of orgobjects and their histories.

An Orgsystem Wanted

Let's imagine you are fascinated by the Pc-management and decide to implement it in your company. A lot of orgobjects start circulating around, each accompanied by a huge history file. You don't find the one you need, you never know which of the orgobjects contains the planned activities assigned to you, and when these activities should be completed. You strove for a better order and got yourself into a mess. And, as if that were not enough, you have a lot of extra work to do. You should construct a new state of an orgobject for each completed activity, and remember to put the new activities on the list and assign them to yourself and others. You wanted to improve the efficiency, but it sinks instead.

There is no need to worry, there is a means to restore the order and efficiency, and that's, naturally a computer system. It's primary aim is to make you happy with the Pc-management doing away with the chaos, that's why we call it an "organizing system", or orgsystem for short.

Let's have another look at the Pc-management, this time supported by an orgsystem. Orgobjects do not circulate between various members of the staff who are to work with them, they stay in the same place together with their history and plans, and are easily accessible to all workers involved. All planned activities assigned to a given individual appear immediately in his/her personal calendar, so that each worker knows exactly what activities he/she has to complete and when. An orgsystem provides the means to increase the efficiency by:

- assisting workers in executing each activity,
- providing an extremely user-friendly interface.

These two features are a key to successful implementation of an orgsystem. Without them people would not be motivated to use the system, consequently the Pc-management wouldn't work. Let's look at these features in more detail.

Level of Help

All operations needed for executing an activity under the Pc-management belong to one of the two groups:

- external operations-operations that affect the "external world", and
- maintaining operations-operations aimed at maintaining orgobjects.

The character of external operation depends on the type of activity, e.g., packing and shipping for delivery, programming and testing for developing a software module, etc. Maintaining operations are the same for all activities. They include:

- updating the information contained in the relevant orgobject,
- correcting the plan,
- logging the preceding state of the orgobject.

An orgsystem assists a worker to complete both the external operations and the maintaining ones.

1. External operations. Level of help which is possible to offer for completing the external operations depends on the type of activity. For example, programming and testing of a software module are usually performed inside the computer, and they are already fully computerized. Here, an orgsystem should just integrate the existing tools for software development, e.g. editors, debuggers, etc., so that a proper tool is invoked when a user chooses to execute these operations. Packing and shipping are not that easily computerized, not now anyway.

   But even there, an orgsystem can be helpful to some extent by, e.g., making up a packing list. It's important to give a hand in completing the external operations for each kind of activities.

   There's a risk otherwise. If some activity is left without the orgsystem's assistance, a worker who completes it can easily forget to make the appropriate changes in the orgobject concerned. In that case, the completed activity will still remain on the list of planned activities and the orgsystem will keep reminding the worker to complete it. There is also a danger that the same activity will be completed several times.

2. Updating. Modification of an orgobject can often be done on the basis of the information collected in the

process of executing the external operations. For example, an "order" orgobject contains the information on the quantities of the goods already delivered. This information should be updated after each separate delivery. The new quantities can be easily calculated based on the packing list that was made at the previous step, which permits an orgsystem to update the orgobject without assistance from the users.

3. When correcting a plan, a worker is prompted by the system on the appropriate activities to plan next; in simple cases the plan is corrected by the system itself. This is possible, as an orgsystem possesses two type of knowledge:
   - on the working procedures used in the company, which helps to plan new activities, and
   - on division of responsibilities between different divisions, sections, and workers, which permits to correctly assign new activities.
4. Logging includes two operations:
   - saving the old state of the orgobject, and
   - making a report on the activity completed.

Saving the old state of an orgobject is done by an orgsystem without any user assistance, but an activity report needs a human participation.

Even there, an orgsystem helps by automatically supplying the information on what activity has been executed, by whom and when. The rest of the report, e.g., comments, is of course the responsibility of the worker.

User-interface

Conventional computer systems are designed as a set of functions operating on a common database, the main facility of the user-interface being multilevel menus. This type of the user-interface provides the user with a quick access to a function he/she wants to complete.

It reflects the objective of a conventional computer system which is to help workers to cope with single activities like updating information, printing a report, etc. An orgsystem objectives are much wider, which brings about the need for a completely different kind of user-interface. An orgsystem's user-interface permits end-users to freely choose between the object-oriented and activity-oriented way of working with orgobjects, as well as easily switch from one to the other.

The object-oriented approach is applied when a user wants to work with a particular orgobject for a longer time. In this case, he/she may need to look at the object's current state and its history, as well as to plan and execute various activities involving the orgobject. The activity-oriented approach is applied when a user wants to complete the same activity for a number of orgobjects. In this case, the dialogue designed for a given activity is repeated for all relevant orgobjects. The object-oriented way is particularly useful when one worker is responsible for many activities involving an orgobject. It is also the way that management staff can use when there is a need to evaluate the state of a particular process and to devise a plan for a difficult case. The activity-oriented approach is preferable if a worker is responsible for only one type of activities. It's also the right approach to completing simple activities that do not require much human assistance, e.g., printing an invoice, etc.

Another distinguishing feature of an orgsystem's user-interface is that it maintains personal calendars. A personal calendar is a list of activities assigned to a particular worker. The point is that these activities are included in different orgobjects and the calendar permits a perfect overview of a persons' many tasks. The orgsystem offers a variety of ways to use the calendar. A user can browse through his/her calendar, or some parts of it, e.g., to see all activities planned for a particular day, all activities of a certain type, etc. When browsing, he/she can start the execution of his/her activities (activity-oriented approach), or move to the orgobject where a particular activity belongs and start working with this orgobject in the object-oriented manner.

To maintain its user-friendly character, an orgsystem's user-interface should satisfy a number of general requirements. Most important are the following two:

- easy access to all information required for working with orgobjects. For example, when working with an orgobject representing an order, a user should have access to all information related to the customer who ordered goods: his address, previous contacts with him, etc.;
- consistency. There should be standard procedures for navigating to an orgobject, for getting information (e.g., a company's address), for planning, for starting the execution of activities, etc. These standard procedures should be the same for all types of orgobjects and activities.

Joys and Hardships of an Orgsystems Developer

There are, naturally, technical problems to solve in the development of an orgsystem. The system requirements discussed in the previous section must be met. However, an orgsystem designer's greatest problem is that he starts the development in an environment initially not based on the Pc-management, which makes both design and implementation of an orgsystem far from trivial tasks.

Orgsystems Design

An orgsystem designer should begin with:

- identifying the company's operational goals,
- figuring out what processes are used to achieve them, and
- designing orgobjects to represent these processes.

His/her next task is to review all the working procedures and tailor them to fit the Pc-management scheme (by adding maintaining operations to each activity).

This is often a tough job, as there are seldom some written descriptions of the working procedures, and if they exist, they are far from complete. The only way to cope with the job is to try and get the missing information from the company's workers. The workers would, naturally, know nothing about orgobjects, but they know their job.

The conditions in which an orgsystem designer works are similar to those of a linguist who studies a language that exists only in the spoken form. Linguists have special methods permitting them to get the necessary information from the native speakers without teaching them any linguistic notions. Moreover, it's considered a wrong practice to teach informants linguistics, as it may only spoil them.

An orgsystems designer needs similar methods that would permit him to redesign the company's working procedures without introducing the workers into the world of orgobjects, distributed planning, etc. We believe that rapid prototyping is the right method.

As soon as a designer has identified the company's operational goals and processes, and designed the orgobjects to represent them, he/she should make a prototype of the system and let the future users test it. To be able to use prototyping, an orgsystem designer needs appropriate application development tools.

These tools should allow him to quickly produce a sketch of the system that has "look-and-feel" of a real system, but lacks processing routines and database access. It's this sketch that we call the prototype of the system. Working with it, a user can navigate among orgobjects in the same way as he would do that when the orgsystem is ready. He can modify existing orgobjects, create new ones, and see how to start different activities.

But he can't save the information or see the results of the completed activities. After the future users have accepted the prototype, the designer can stepwise add database access and processing routines, which would be also done with the help of the above mentioned application development tools.

Orgsystems Implementation

Implementing an orgsystem means introducing the Pc-management in a non-Pc-management environment. This may be achieved in one of two ways:

- by substituting all the old working procedures in the company at once, or
- by gradual introduction of the new working procedures.

The first approach may suit small companies whose workers often switch from one activity type to another. An orgsystem would help to do these switches very quickly, and it would help the workers, who usually have a lot of different things to do, to preserve the order in their affairs.

The staff of a small company would easily understand the advantages of using all facilities provided by an orgsystem: object-and activity-oriented ways of working, personal calendars, easy access to the history, etc. However, in case of large companies, the second approach may be the best choice. Large companies usually, have a lot of workers who are involved only in one or several activities for each process.

These workers may believe that an orgsystem is too complex for their simple tasks. It would be difficult for them to see the advantages of the object-oriented user-interface, and their earlier experience of traditional computer systems can only make the things worse. Luckily, an orgsystem provides a means for working in the activity-oriented manner, which would put the workers competing simple activities at ease. There would be no problem to teach them to use the orgsystem in the activity-oriented way, because it resembles their old manner of doing things. Later, the workers could be taught the object-oriented way as well, which would give them better possibilities to take the initiative and find solutions for difficult cases.

But even if most of the office workers continue to use the activity-oriented approach, there would always be some key people who benefit from the object-oriented approach, e.g., management staff.

What Makes our Systems Work?

The main ideas of the Pc-management originate from our previous research work on the CHAOS project (CHAOS stands for Concurrent Human-Assisted Object Systems). The project's objective was to work out a formal model for describing distributed interactive systems.

This model is based on the notions of objects and connectors. Objects are used to represent the elements of the "real world", (e.g. people, companies, projects, etc.), whereas connectors are the active elements of the system whose task is to make changes in the objects. A connector may be thought of as a little computer connected to one or several objects. As soon as some of these objects change, the connector changes all the other objects to restore the consistency of the system.

Thus defined, our model has a purely reactive nature, i.e. changes in objects are made as a reaction to changes in other objects. But objects in our model can be complex, i.e. they themselves can contain connectors, which means that a reaction can result in adjusting the system configuration to changes in the environment. The CHAOS model fitted the management field so well that all we had to do was to use another set of terms. Thus, complex objects became orgobjects, connectors became planned activities, and the principle of reactive reconfiguration of the system was called dynamic and distributed planning. Some of the results of applying the CHAOS model to management field were virtually the same as those from the research works based on the theory of planning. However, being more general than the theory of planning, our model provides a better framework for management automation as it covers all aspects of management not only the issues of planning.

The CHAOS model is abstract, but the approach taken in the DealDriver project was very pragmatic. The objective of the project was to create a working system, not to speculate on the management automation issues. This project differs in many ways from similar research projects. Below we list the most important differences:

1. Computer environment. We worked with PC computers under MS DOS in stand-alone and network versions, whereas research projects are often completed on Unix-based workstations. We used text-based terminals, not a graphic-based windowing environment with a mouse, icons, etc. This environment was chosen because it was the one an average company could easily afford.
2. Development tools. Research workers often choose programming languages popular among computer scientists like Lisp, Prolog, Smalltalk, etc. These languages have a sound theoretical basis (e.g., function theory, logic, etc.), but require a lot of programming when they are used for the development of an application. We made a point of getting the maximum available help with programming by employing commercially available application development tools. We chose JAM from JYACC as a front-end tool, and Btrieve from Novell as a record manager. These tools were of great help to us, as we had limited resources for completing the project (in terms of time and manpower).
3. Design principles. Researchers are often far too interested in the technical issues, such as methods of software design and programming, etc. We concentrated on user-interface issues instead. Our only principle of programming was: a program should work and permit to easily make necessary changes. All programming was done in C-language, and though our system was object-oriented in a very high degree, we didn't use any object-oriented extension to C.

Thus, two factors contributed to the successful completion of the DealDriver project:

- the use of a powerful abstract model, and
- a pragmatic approach to system development, and we strongly believe that both of them are obligatory for the development of a computer system of a totally new kind.

We are also convinced that there is no need to wait 10-20 years, which it usually takes for new research ideas to be implemented in application systems. New ideas can be implemented today and with the means available now.

ORGANIZING PROCESS

In cases of management transfer, the estalishment process focuses on a level of user organization where no organization presently exists, that is, at a level of the irrigation network previously managed by the government irrigation agency. Typically this entails organizing federations of user groups at the tertiary level under a secondary-canal association. The challenge of creating a new organization of users is perhaps the most central feature of the management transfer process. The act of management transfer from the agency to the users depends upon a user organization that is capable of assuming those management responsibilities.

Before any organizing of the users is carried out, there needs to be a package of incentives in place for both the users and the agency staff whose jobs would be affected by the transfer program. Such incentives are needed both to make the program work, and to maintain credibility with farmers whose long-term support will be required. If organizing is attempted before an adequate incentive structure is established, the transfer program could well collapse, thus setting the entire program back by several years, as well as causing short-term hardships to those concerned. Thus, if the incentives are not clear and attractive to farmers, the organizing process should be delayed until the incentives are clarified.

First determine:

Who Will do the Organizing?

The first step is to decide on the type of organizers who will work directly with farmers in helping establish the organization. [We use the term "water user association" (WUA) to refer to this new organization, although the term, "WUA" can also refer to organizations at the tertiary level of the system which have always been outside the management control of the government irrigation agency.] In the Philippines, a special cadre of social organizers was recruited and trained by the National Irrigation Administration in the late1970s and early 80s.

These organizers were mostly social workers or social scientists selected for their ability to work easily with farmers in village conditions. They were trained in irrigation management so they could better understand the technical problems of the farmers they were trying to organize. The work of the Philippines social organizers was effective, yet this approach has not been widely replicated by irrigation agencies in other countries. The investment and bureaucratic difficulties involved in recruiting new temporary staff from a different discipline has led many irrigation agencies to try other approaches. In Mexico's transfer program, the National Water Commission's own staff were used along with staff from a sister agency, the Institute for Water Technology (IMTA).

In addition, a few consultants were brought in on a case by case basis. In India, some state irrigation departments have relied on extensionists from the Agriculture Department under the Command Area Development Program. Also in India, several NGOs have been involved in organizing, at the request of the irrigation departments. But the organizers of choice, for most irrigation agencies, will be their own field staff.

These staff are already within the bureaucratic structure of the agency, so the lines of authority are clear, there is little additional expense involved, and these staff are already familiar with the physical systems and with the local farmers. The problems with using irrigation agency field staff for organizing work, however, are considerable. These staff are not necessarily interested in organizing farmers, They have not received any prior training in social work (in most cases), and their superiors have also no training (nor interest) in these tasks. These would-be organizers must be re-trained for their organizing tasks, and just as importantly, their job assignments need to be re-defined to reflect their new role. In addition, their superiors need to be trained and re-oreinted so they understand and appreciate the new role to be played by their field staff.

What Training do the Organizers Need?

Assuming that agency staff will be used for the organizing, and assuming that their professional training has been in irrigation engineering, they would need to be re-tooled as organizers. First of all they would need a thorough understanding of the rationale for PIM, so that they can present a clear message both to the farmers and to their own colleagues within the irrigation agency. Secondly, they will need training in communcation skills (including listening skills) for effective interaction with the users. Thirdly, they will need training in social analysis, including an understanding of social stratification (by caste, ethnicity, or class), kinship, patron-client relations, labour relations, religious factors, political affiliation, land tenure (tenants, share-croppers, owners), etc. And fourthly, they would need training in methods for gathering information from farmers (e.g., participatory rural appraisal) and in methods for organizing farmers.

5

Hospitality and Tourism Management

INTRODUCTION

The concept of *Hospitality Services*, also known as "accommodation sharing", "hospitality exchange" (short "hospex"), and "home stay networks", refers to centrally organized social networks of individuals who trade accommodation without monetary exchange. While this concept could also include house swapping or even time share plans, it has come to be associated mostly with travelers and tourists staying with one another free of charge. Hospitality Club is the direct successor Hospex, the first Internet-based service, operating out of Germany since 2000.

In 1949, Bob Luitweiler founded the first hospitality service called Servas Open Doors as a cross national, non-profit, volunteer run organization advocating interracial and international peace. The next began in 1965 when John Wilcock set up the Traveler's Directory as a listing of his friends willing to host each other when traveling. This later became the Hospitality Exchange in 1988 when Joy Lily rescued the organization from imminent shutdown. CouchSurfing is the largest hospitality exchange organization and was founded in 2004.

Just as all the individual services have their own individual creation stories and organizational histories (often including demise and resurrection), many also have specific niche markets that they cater to including students, activists, religious pilgrims, and even occupational groups like police officers. However, the trend in recent years points to a greater consolidation of users in networks without a specific group, value, or lifestyle affiliation. Since the 1990s, these services have increasingly moved away from using printed catalogs and the telephone, to connecting users via the internet. As of March, 2008 over 1,000,000 people are registered users of these internet networks. In essence, these systems employ reciprocity – users gain access to other users' information only by posting their own. Required fields normally include name and contact information, though newer services encourage users to include more detailed personal material, including likes and dislikes, hopes and dreams, and even photographs. Of course, more information included tends to improve the chances that someone will find them trustworthy enough to host or stay with while traveling. It is very much akin to social networking sites.

TOURISM AND HOSPITALITY

India offers myriad exciting experiences to tourists. The country boasts of the world's highest mountains, miles of coastline with excellent beaches, tropical forests and wildlife, lagoon backwaters, ancient monuments and World Heritage sites, forts and palaces, and of course, the Taj Mahal. The Indian tourism and hospitality industry has thus emerged as one of the key sectors driving the country's growth and is thriving, owing to a huge surge in both business and leisure travel by foreign and domestic tourists.

According to the latest Tourism Satellite Accounting (TSA) research, released by the World Travel and Tourism Council (WTTC) and its strategic partner Accenture, India's travel and tourism industry was estimated to generate approximately US$ 100 billion in 2008. This figure is expected to go up to almost US$ 275.5 billion by 2018, growing at an average of 9.4 per cent over the next ten years.

Moreover, according to the TSA research, travel and tourism is expected to contribute 6.1 per cent to India's national gross domestic product (GDP) and provide almost 40 million jobs by 2018. Significantly, a country brand index (CBI) 2008 survey, conducted by FutureBrand—a leading global brand consultancy—in collaboration with public relations firm Weber Shandwick's Global Travel & Lifestyle Practice, has ranked India second in the value-for-money index.

The rapid growth of India's tourism industry has been instrumental in making South Asia the preferred tourist destination as noted by the UN World Tourism Organisation (UNWTO). In fact, according to the World Travel and Trade Council, demand in tourism in India will continue to grow at a rapid pace. It estimates the demand to grow at an average of 8.8 per cent between 2004 and 2013, making India the world's third fastest-growing tourist market. The boom in the Indian tourism industry has percolated to the rural areas as well. India continues to attract tourists owing to its splendid historical architecture and rich culture along with beautiful beaches and rural tourism.

POTENTIAL INTERPERSONAL CONFLICT OR AWKWARDNESS

There is a chance that guest and host will not get along. Perhaps there will be scheduling or ideological conflicts. Maybe you will find that hosts or visitors have misrepresented themselves. Perhaps the experience will not live up to your expectations. Intense interpersonal communications in advance and a flexibility once you have arrived is your best bet. These experiences require additional planning and courtesy towards the demands of your host. Thus, your living conditions, length of stay, and overall experience will be circumscribed by the living conditions you enter into.

DIGITAL DIVIDE AND DEMOGRAPHIC SEGREGATION

The average user is a young white person who speaks English and lives in a developed nation. While there are many users who do not fit this description, the more different they are, the less likely they will be involved. This is especially true for persons living in the developing world who likely do not have easy access to the fundamental prerequisite for using these services: computers and the Internet. Thus, the sample population found in searches of these databases are really much less diverse than a geographical representation of worldwide users might suggest.

Security

There is a distinct possibility that someone will abuse the system and that innocent users (especially women) will get hurt. All services include disclaimers that require users to waive their rights to hold anyone but themselves responsible for any harm that may come to them in using the system. They advise that the best defense mechanism is to only involve oneself with users that have extensive personal information and interpersonal networks within the system that have been verified by others. It does seem entirely plausible that someone clever and patient enough might be able to invent an entire group of complex user identities and build histories convincing enough to fool even more cautious patrons. Still, the difference between these systems and the other social networking platforms popular nowadays on the web (such as Facebook, MySpace, Tribe, Orkut and LiveJournal) is that any agreement reached through the accommodation sharing medium is contingent on actually meeting other people face-to-face. Other web scams are easier because interpersonal interactions rely so much on putative identities that are never actually verified in the real world. However, this does not diminish the greater risk to physical well being that this kind of traveling by definition must entertain. The best advice is to meet unknown persons in public spaces first, and try to meet some of their acquaintances in person before agreeing to a hospitality exchange.

Example Networks

There are countless websites that serve the idea of hospitality service, with new ones appearing as this phenomenon becomes more popular. While this page is not intended to be a directory listing, here is a small sample of the well-established and long-standing networks:

- CouchSurfing - A very active network with over 700 thousand members in more than 200 countries
- Hospitality Club - A very active network with over 390 thousand members in more than 200 countries
- Servas International - human rights and global peace oriented since 1949. A relatively small network now with over 15,000 members with a very long history.

MOTELS

A motel (motor-ist's hotel) is a hotel which is for a short stay, usually for a night, whilst you are on a long journey. Has direct access from your room to your vehicle so you can go on.

World Record Setting Hotels

Largest

In 2006, Guinness World Records listed the First World Hotel in Genting Highlands, Malaysia as the world's largest hotel with a total of 6,118 rooms.

Oldest

According to the Guinness Book of World Records, the oldest hotel still in operation is the Hoshi Ryokan, in the Awazu Onsen area of Komatsu, Japan which opened in 717.

Tallest

Burj Al Arab is the tallest building used exclusively as a hotel. However, the Rose Tower, also in Dubai, which has already topped Burj Al Arab's height at 333 m (1,090 ft), will take away this title upon its opening.

Living in Hotels

A number of public figures have notably chosen to take up semi-permanent or permanent residence in hotels.

- Actor Richard Harris lived at the Savoy Hotel while in London. Hotel archivist Susan Scott recounts an anecdote that when he was being taken out of the building on a stretcher shortly before his death he raised his hand and told the diners "it was the food".

Hotel Manager

A **hotel manager** or **hotelier** is a person who handles the everyday function and management of a hotel.

Larger hotels often have management teams, instead of individual managers, where each member of the group begins to specialize on a certain area of interest.

Occupational Tasks

Some of the responsibilities of a hotel manager include:

- organizing and directing the hotel's services
    - concierge
    - reception
    - reservations
    - catering
    - housekeeping
- controlling budget and formulating financial plans
- promoting the business
    - marketing
    - advertising
- Achieving profits and expenses
- meeting with customers, contractors and suppliers
- hiring, training, reviewing and overseeing staff members
- attending to problems or customer complaints and comments
- addressing maintenance and upkeep
- seeing to accommodations
    - furniture
- meeting safety, health and licensing regulations
    - security

MOTEL

Entering dictionaries after World War II, the word **motel**, a portmanteau of *motor* and *hotel* or *motorists' hotel,* referred initially to a type of hotel consisting of a single building of connected rooms whose doors faced a parking lot and, in some circumstances, a common area; or a series of small cabins with common parking. As the United States highway system began to develop in the 1920s, long distance road journeys became more common and the need for inexpensive, easily accessible overnight accommodation sited close to the main routes, led to the growth of the motel concept. The motel concept originated with the Motel Inn of San Luis Obispo, constructed in 1925 by Arthur Heineman. In conceiving of a name for his hotel Heineman abbreviated *motor hotel* to *mo-tel.*

Unlike their predecessors, auto camps and tourist courts, motels quickly adopted a homogenized appearance. They are typically constructed in an 'I'- or 'L'- or 'U'-shaped layout that includes guest rooms, an attached manager's office, a small reception and, in some cases, a small diner. Post-war motels sought more visual distinction, often featuring eye-catching neon signs which employed themes from popular culture, ranging from Western imagery of cowboys and Indians to contemporary images of spaceships and atomic era iconography.

In their early years, motels were "mom-and-pop" facilities on the outskirts of a town. They attracted the first "road warriors" as they crossed the United States in their new automobiles.

Motels differ from hotels in their common location along highways, as opposed to the urban cores favored by hotels, and their orientation to the outside (in contrast to hotels whose doors typically face an interior hallway). Motels almost by definition include a parking lot, while older hotels were not built with automobile parking in mind. With the 1952 introduction of Kemmons Wilson's Holiday Inn, the mom-and-pop motels of that era went into decline. Eventually, the emergence of the interstate highway system, along with other factors, led to a blurring of the motel and the hotel, though family-owned motels with as few as five rooms may still be found, especially along older highways.

Long-term

Motels with low rates sometimes serve as housing for people who are not able to afford an apartment or have recently lost their home and need somewhere to stay until further arrangements are made. Motels catering to long-term stays often have kitchenettes.

Short-time

In most countries of Latin America and some countries of East Asia, motels are also known as short-time hotels, and offer a short-time or "transit" stay with hourly rates primarily intended for people having sexual liaisons and not requiring a full night's accommodation. In Mexico love hotel equivalents are known as "Motel de paso" (Passing Motel) (even if they are actually meant mostly for pedestrian access). In Colombia, Venezuela and Brazil, motels are used by people for sexual intercourse only. In Argentina these establishments are called *albergue transitorio* ("temporary lodging"), though known as *telo* in vesre-slang. In Panama love hotels are known as Push Bottoms. In Paraguay, similarly to Brazil and Colombia, motels may charge only by the hour and are also popularly known as *reservados*. In Singapore, cheap hotels often offer a slightly more euphemistic "transit" stay for short-time visitors. In Manila, a campaign against the hotels, believed by religious conservatives to contribute to social decay in the predominantly Roman Catholic country, ended with the city banning hotels from offering stays of very short duration. As of December 2006 there are still many short time hotels in operation. In Belgium and France, these establishments are known as *hôtels de passe*. In Chile, they are known as *moteles parejeros* (coupling motels), and many of them offer hourly rates. In the United States and Canada, some ordinary motels in low income areas—often called *no-tell motels* or *hot sheet motels*—play a similar role to love hotels.

Films

The Bates Motel is an important part of *Psycho*, a 1959 novel by Robert Bloch and the 1960 Alfred Hitchcock film of the same name. Film sequels *Psycho II* and *Psycho III* feature the motel as does the 1987 television movie *Bates Motel*.

Legal Issues

Motels have also served as a haven for fugitives of the law. In the past, the anonymity and the ability to move around easily between motels in different regions by dropping in and checking out with a simple registration process allowed fugitives to remain ahead of the law. However, several advances have reduced the capacity of motels to serve this purpose. Crcard transactions, which in the past were more easily approved and took days to report, are now approved or declined on the spot, and are instantly recorded in a database, thereby allowing law enforcement access to this information. This system was implemented in 1993 after the abduction and murder of Donna Martz, whose crcard was used by her killers following her death to purchase food, gasoline, and to pay for overnight motel stays . The story of Martz's disappearance, leading to the development of this system, was described on The FBI Files. Laws in many places now require registering guests to present a government-issued photo ID, especially when paying with cash. Local law enforcement agencies frequently check motels when they suspect a wanted individual may be staying in their jurisdiction.

RESORT

A **resort** is a place used for relaxation or recreation, attracting visitors for holidays or vacations. Resorts are places, towns or sometimes commercial establishment operated by a single company. Such a self-contained resort attempts to provide for most of a vacationer's wants while remaining on the premises, such as food, drink, lodging, sports, entertainment, and shopping. The term "resort" sometimes is misused to identify a hotel that does not provide the other amenities required of a full resort. However, a hotel is frequently a central feature of a resort, such as the Grand Hotel at Mackinac Island, Michigan. A resort is not merely a commercial establishment operated by a single company, although in the late twentieth century this sort of facility became more common.

Towns that contain resorts—or where tourism or vacationing is a major part of the local activity—are often called resort towns. Towns such as Sochi in Russia, Sharm el Sheikh in Egypt, Barizo of Spain, Cortina d'Ampezzo of Italy, Druskininkai of Lithuania, Nice or French Riviera of France or Newport, Rhode Island or St. Moritz, Switzerland, or larger regions, like the Adirondack Mountains or the Italian Riviera are well known resorts. The Walt Disney World Resort is a prominent example of a modern, self-contained commercial resort. Resorts exist throughout the world, increasingly attracting visitors from around the globe. Thailand, for instance, has become a popular destination. Resorts are especially prevalent in Central America and the Caribbean. Closely related to resorts are convention and large meeting sites. Generally these occur in cities where special meeting halls, together with ample accommodations as well as varied dining and entertainment are provided.

Types of Resort

Resort at a Destination

A commercial establishment at a resort destination such as a recreational area, a scenic or historic site, a theme park, a gaming facility or other tourist attraction competes with other businesses at that destination.. Examples would be hotels in and around Walt Disney World, resorts in St. Martin in the Caribbean, and establishments at Aspen, Colorado in the USA.

Destination Resort

A destination resort is a resort that contains, in and of itself, the necessary guest attraction capabilities—that is to say that a destination resort does not need to be near a destination (town, historic site, theme park, or other) to attract its public. Consequently, another characteristic of a destination resort is that it offers food, drink, lodging, sports, entertainment, and shopping within the facility so that guests have no need to leave the facility throughout their stay. Commonly these facilities are of higher quality than would be expected if one were to stay at a hotel or eat in a town's restaurants. Some examples are Atlantis in the Bahamas, Costa do Sauípe in the Northeastern Brazil, Laguna Phuket in Thailand and Sun City near Johannesburg in South Africa.

All-inclusive Resort

An all-inclusive resort is a resort that, besides providing all of the common amenities of a resort, charges a fixed price that includes most or all items. At a minimum, most inclusive resorts include lodging, unlimited food, drink, sports activities, and entertainment for the fixed price. In recent years, the number of resorts offering "all-inclusive" amenities has decreased dramatically; in 1961, over half offered such plans and in 2007, less than ten percent do so.

Historical Resorts

A famous resort of the ancient world was Baiae, Italy, popular over 2,000 years ago. Capri, an island near Naples, Italy, has attracted visitors since Roman times.

Another famous historical resort was Monte Ne near Rogers, Arkansas, which was active in the early 20th century. At its peak more than 10,000 people a year visited its hotels. It closed in the 1930s, and was ultimately submerged under Beaver Lake in the 1960s.

TOURISM PLANNING

Tourism is one of many activities in a community or region that requires planning and coordination. This bulletin provides a simple structure and basic guidelines for comprehensive tourism planning at a community or regional level. Planning is the process of identifying objectives and defining and evaluating methods of achieving them. By comprehensive planning we mean planning which considers all of the tourism resources, organizations, markets, and programs within a region. Comprehensive planning also considers economic, environmental, social, and institutional aspects of tourism development.

FOREIGN TOURIST ARRIVALS

Estimates of foreign tourist arrivals (FTAs) and foreign exchange earnings (FEE) (on the basis of data received from major airports) are important indicators of the tourism sector.

FTA figures for 2008 were 5.37 million against 5.08 million in 2007, showing a 6-8 per cent rise over 2007, indicating that despite the global financial meltdown and the recent terrorist attacks, the number of tourists coming to India have gone up. In fact, the Indian growth rate of 5.6 per cent for international tourist arrivals exceeded the United Nations World Tourism Organisation's (UNWTO) forecast of a growth rate of 2-3 per cent for international tourist arrivals in the world for 2008.

According to figures released by the Tourism Ministry, FEE from this sector posted a rise of 8 per cent at US$ 11.5 billion in 2008 as against US$ 10.70 billion registered in 2007.

SERVICE OF THE HOTEL

A *hotel* is an establishment that provides paid lodging on a short-term basis. The provision of basic accommodation, in times past, consisting only of a room with a bed, a cupboard, a small table and a washstand has largely been replaced by rooms with modern facilities, including en-suite bathrooms and air conditioning or climate control.

Additional common features found in hotel rooms are a telephone, an alarm clock, a television, and Internet connectivity; snack foods and drinks may be supplied in a mini-bar, and facilities for making hot drinks. Larger hotels may provide a number of additional guest facilities such as a restaurant, a swimming pool or childcare, and have conference and social function services.

Some hotels offer meals as part of a room and board arrangement. In the United Kingdom, a hotel is required by law to serve food and drinks to all guests within certain stated hours; to avoid this requirement it is not uncommon to come across *private hotels* which are not subject to this requirement. In Japan, capsule hotels provide a minimized amount of room space and shared facilities.

In Australia and Canada, hotel may also refer to a pub or bar. In India, the word may also refer to a restaurant since the best restaurants were always situated next to a good hotel.

Etymology

The word *hotel* is derived from the French *hôtel* (coming from *hôte* meaning *host*), which referred to a French version of a townhouse or any other building seeing frequent visitors, rather than a place offering accommodation. In contemporary French usage, *hôtel* now has the same meaning as the English term, and *hôtel particulier* is used for the old meaning. The French spelling, with the circumflex, was also used in English, but is now rare. The circumflex replaces the 's' found in the earlier *hostel* spelling, which over time took on a new, but closely related meaning. Grammatically, hotels usually take the definite article - hence "The Astoria Hotel" or simply "The Astoria".

Classification

The cost and quality of hotels are usually indicative of the range and type of services available. Due to the enormous increase in tourism worldwide during the last decades of the 20th century, standards, especially those of smaller establishments, have improved considerably. For the sake of greater comparability, rating systems have been introduced, with the one to five stars classification being most common and with higher star ratings indicating more luxury. Hotels are independently assessed in traditional systems and these rely heavily on the facilities provided. Some consider this disadvantageous to smaller hotels whose quality of accommodation could fall into one class but the lack of an item such as an elevator would prevent it from reaching a higher categorization. In some countries, there is an official body with standard criteria for classifying hotels, but in many others there is none. There have been attempts at unifying the classification system so that it becomes an internationally recognized and reliable standard but large differences exist in the quality of the accommodation and the food within one category of hotel, sometimes even in the same country. The American Automobile Association (AAA) and their affiliated bodies use diamonds instead of stars to express hotel and restaurant ratings levels.

Historic Hotels

Some hotels have gained their renown through tradition, by hosting significant events or persons, such as Schloss Cecilienhof in Potsdam, Germany, which derives its fame from the Potsdam Conference of the World War II allies Winston Churchill, Harry Truman and Joseph Stalin in 1945. The Taj Mahal Palace & Tower in Mumbai is one of India's most famous and historic hotels because of its association with the Indian independence movement.

Some establishments have given name to a particular meal or beverage, as is the case with the Waldorf Astoria in New York City, United States where the Waldorf Salad was first created or the Hotel Sacher in Vienna, Austria, home of the Sachertorte. Others have achieved fame by association with dishes or cocktails created on their premises, such as the Hotel de Paris where the crêpe Suzette was invented or the Raffles Hotel in Singapore, where the Singapore Sling cocktail was devised.

A number of hotels have entered the public consciousness through popular culture, such as the Ritz Hotel in London, UK, through its association with Irving Berlin's song, 'Puttin' on the Ritz'. The Algonquin Hotel in New York City is famed as the meeting place of the literary group, the Algonquin Round Table, and Hotel Chelsea, also in New York City, has been the subject of a number of songs and the scene of the stabbing of Nancy Spungen (allegedly by her boyfriend Sid Vicious). The luxurious Grand Hotel Europe in Saint Petersburg, Russia achieved fame with its inclusion in the James Bond film GoldenEye.

Unusual Hotels

Many hotels can be considered destinations in themselves, by dint of unusual features of the lodging or its immediate environment:

Treehouse Hotels

Some hotels are built with living trees as structural elements, for example the Costa Rica Tree House in the Gandoca-Manzanillo Wildlife Refuge, Costa Rica; the Treetops Hotel in Aberdare National Park, Kenya; the Ariau Towers near Manaus, Brazil, on the Rio Negro in the Amazon; and Bayram's Tree Houses in Olympos, Turkey.

Cave Hotels

Desert Cave Hotel in Coober Pedy, South Australia and the Cuevas Pedro Antonio de Alarcón (named after the author) in Guadix, Spain, as well as several hotels in Cappadocia, Turkey, are notable for being built into natural cave formations, some with rooms underground.

Capsule Hotels

Capsule hotels are a type of economical hotel that are found in Japan.

Ice and Snow Hotels

The Ice Hotel in Jukkasjärvi, Sweden, and the Hotel de Glace in Duschenay,- Canada, melt every spring and are rebuilt each winter; the Mammut Snow Hotel in Finland is located within the walls of the Kemi snow castle; and the Lainio Snow Hotel is part of a snow village near Ylläs, Finland.

Garden Hotels

Garden hotels, famous for their gardens before they became hotels, include Gravetye Manor, the home of garden designer William Robinson, and Cliveden, designed by Charles Barry with a rose garden by Geoffrey Jellicoe.

Underwater Hotels

Some hotels have accommodation underwater, such as Utter Inn in Lake Mälaren, Sweden. Hydropolis, under construction in Dubai, will have suites on the bottom of the Persian Gulf, and Jules Undersea Lodge in Key Largo, Florida requires scuba diving to access its rooms.

Other Unusual Hotels

- The Library Hotel in New York City is unique in that each of its ten floors are assigned one category from the Dewey Decimal System.
- The Burj al-Arab hotel in Dubai, United Arab Emirates, built on an artificial island, is structured in the shape of a boat's sail.
- The former ocean liner RMS *Queen Mary* in Long Beach, California uses its first-class staterooms as a hotel.
- The Jailhotel Löwengraben in Lucerne, Switzerland is a converted prison now used as a hotel.
- The Luxor, a hotel and casino on The Las Vegas Strip in Paradise, Nevada, United States due to its pyramidal structure.
- The Liberty Hotel in Boston used to be the Charles Street Jail.

Benefits

Monetary Savings

Staying in private homes means that travelers can save lots of money on accommodation that they would usually be spending on hotels or hostels. Used over a long period of time (2 to 4 weeks), this strategy can cut overall travel budgets in half, or even more combined with hitchhiking. These savings can then be passed on towards more generously patronizing local establishments or simply staying abroad for longer periods of time.

Local Economic Sustainability

Many tourist vacations today are sold in package form, often including flights, hotels, rental cars, sightseeing tours, and coupons for chain restaurants and bars. While this makes purchasing more convenient, it also puts more money in the hands of large multinational corporations exploiting the synergy strategy of marketing their products in the context of their subsidiary companies operating in other markets.

Many years ago, this might have been termed *collusion*; today, however, it is the norm. This comes at the expense of locally owned independent businesses. Accommodation sharing helps to break apart this monopoly and hopefully redirects some of the tourist revenue back to the local or national economy.

Ecological Sustainability

While this is especially important in more rural travel venues where hotels are often built in very picturesque, though fragile environments, every night stayed at a local's home means that much less demand for such hotel rooms. Also, if accommodation sharing does in fact increase the length of average stays, it may reduce the amount of trips to and from different locations and back home again, thus reducing the overall fuel expenditures in the process.

Local Contact

Ostensibly, one of the primary reasons we travel is to experience what life is like for people living in other countries. Making interpersonal connections and fostering understanding of different cultures may in the long run also be important to international relations.

However, even in our increasingly globalized world, supposedly rife with diversity, in many popular travel destinations, we find tourists milling around "tourist enclaves", where the companies they patronize back home have set up shop to cater to their desires while they are abroad. Sociologist George Ritzer has referred to this phenomenon as the "McDonaldisation of society" and the more recently, the "globalization of nothing".

The location of hotels near these centers only fosters more convenient envelopment of the tourist money. During hospitality exchanges, hosts want to show off their local knowledge and exciting "off the map" venues. Not only may travelers get a distinctly different experience, but they will also get a feel for the everyday lives of local residents.

Reciprocity

These systems foster richer and more convenient travel experiences not so much on the premise of altruism, but on the basis of social exchange theory. Implicit in the agreement to host travelers is the ability to ask to be hosted by them in the future. If one enjoys having interesting guests in their home, this works out well for both parties. It works comparatively better if you are visited by travelers from a locale you find particularly attractive.

Thus, hosting someone from New York City in Gainesville, Florida seems to be an unbelievable opportunity. Moreover, if you are a Westerner visiting someone in a developing country, your stay might be the only way that this individual or family could afford a trip to a rich nation. This may mean more than just a relaxing vacation for such disadvantaged parties.

Authenticity and Adventure

Tourism has always searched for these two qualities, but much like Midas and his golden touch, the reach of tourism has to a large extent destroyed the opportunity to encounter them in most places.

Unluckily, the experience has been thoroughly commodified by everyone who wanted to secure their opportunity to make a profit in the process. Accommodation sharing offers a way out of this bind and a viable alternative to having one's desires manipulated by corporate conglomerates who never had the best interests of the place or the people foremost in their minds.

Drawbacks

Lack of Guarantee

There is no contractual agreement between users in these systems. Reservations are made, but if they are for some reason broken, there is no higher authority to which one could plead for a refund or other compensation.

The only repercussion will be the poor rating you give that user and your only consolation will be that your warning will deter others from visiting or hosting them. For those who feel insecure unless their travel arrangements are written in stone before departure, this system will not be comforting.

HOSPITALITY IN TOURISM AND MANAGEMENT

The National University of Management (NUM) was founded in 1983 as the Economics Science Institute (ESI), and until 1991 received assistance from the National Economics University in Hanoi, Vietnam. During this period, students were enrolled in a five-year undergraduate program with the Vietnamese language serving as the main language of instruction. The curriculum, set by the visiting faculty from Hanoi, included major fields in Finance, Commerce, Agriculture, Industry, and Socialist Planning.

With the opening up of Cambodia to the international community during the early 1990's. The ESI was renamed the Faculty of Business (FOB). Initial support for the FOB was provided by the Asia Foundation and later through a three years USAID grant (1994 to 1997) by the Georgetown University and the University of Sanfrancisco.

This support provided teacher training, institutional development, and encouraged transformation of the curriculum along the lines of an international or American style business school. Marketing and Accounting majors were introduced during this period, and the length of the undergraduate program was reduced from five to four years of study. Commercial law course were also added to the curriculum by the University of San Francisco Law school.

This support provided teacher training, institutional development, and encouraged transformation of the curriculum along the lines of an international or American style business school.

Marketing and Accounting majors were introduced during this period, and the length of the undergraduate program was reduced from five to four years of study. Commercial law course were also added to the curriculum by the University of San Francisco Law school.

In 2004, the FOB was transformed into the National University of Management (NIM) and program offerings were expanded to include the fields of Tourism and Hospitality Management, Finance & Banking and MIS. NUM also opened the first MBA program in Cambodia in cooperation with the University Utara Malaysia (UUM), which is s State sponsored university located in Northern Malaysia. NUM also maintains a five year faculty exchange and research program with the University of Antwerp.

Belgium and has just recently opened a Center for Entrepreneurship and Development in partnership with Fisk University (Nashville,U.S) and Tennessee State University, sponsored by UNCF/USAID.

Currently, more than 10,000 students attend courses at NUM's main campus in Phnom Penh. NUM also operates a full Bachelor of Business Administration degree program in Battambang with more than 700 students attending courses at NUM 's provincial campus.

According to the World Travel and Tourism Council (1997), the economics of the 21st century will be dominated by three industries: telecommunications, information technology and tourism. The travel and tourism industries have grown by 500% in the last 25 years and it is estimated that by the year 2007 tourists will spend US$884 billion in foreign countries on tourism related activities. Travel and tourism represents a broad range of related industries. The growth of these industries has opened up many new job opportunities for graduates in areas such as:

- hotels
- restaurants
- retailing
- transportation
- travel agencies
- tour companies
- tourist attractions
- leisure, recreation and sport
- cultural industries

It is interesting to realise that in 1997 travel and tourism provides 10.5% of the total world employment, with up to 25% of all employment, in some areas, such as the Caribbean. It has been estimated that, by 2007, more than 100 million people worldwide will be employed in this sector. Because of this, tourism is now seen to be of importance to most countries of the world. During this time, the nature of tourism has developed in scope and direction, away from traditional activities, such as the sunshine sand and sea holidays to a wide range of new activities such as cultural tourism, adventure tourism, sports and leisure activities and eco-tourism.

Hospitality and Tourism Management (HTM) is a major in a Bachelors of Science in Business Administration. Graduate students graduate with a Masters of Business Administration, a Masters or Science, or a Doctorate of Philosophy in Hospitality and Tourism Management. It is a focus that is studied by individuals that are intending to work in the Hospitality Industry, examples of which are; Hotels, Resorts, Casinos, and Restaurants. Within the HTM concentration there is generally:

- Food Management and Operations (Examples: Food Science, Food Selection and Preparation, Food and Beverage Operations)
- Lodging Operations (Examples: Hotel Operations, Lodging Management, Financial Management and Cost Control for Hospitality Organizations)

- Global Tourism (Examples: Travel and Tourism Management, Tourism Analysis, Hospitality and Research Methods)
- Event Management (Examples: Hospitality Sales, Catering Management, Hospitality Marketing Management)

Several large corporations such as Marriot, Hyatt, Wyndham and Hilton Hotels have summer internships/manager in training programs for students majoring in Hospitality and Tourism Management, to help students get valuable work experience.

National University of Management

N.U.M. is the leading university in providing educational training to all people in the areas of Management, Economics, Commerce, IT, Business Law, Tourism, and Foreign languages accompanied by research and development in response to the needs of job market today.

Mission: The mission of N.U.M. is to serve the country through educational training by providing graduates with academic excellence, wisdom, morality, and good responsibility in the society. With the vision above, NUM is trying its best to:

- Train students with their day-to-day work for their job satisfaction.
- Illustrate the reality of conflicts and resolutions in terms of managers entrepreneurs.
- Provide opportunities for all levels of people to improve their knowledge and ability through part-time training.

Careers in Hospitality and Tourism Management

Given the potential for interesting and rewarding careers in these industries many young people are looking for suitable courses which will help prepare them for careers in management within the tourism and hospitality industries.

The UK higher education system has a well developed range of courses, at all levels from Higher National Diploma, BA or BSc degrees and MA/MSc/MBA Masters courses and using alternative methods of studying, (including full-time, part-time and distance learning).

When looking at courses in hospitality and tourism, there can seem to be a bewildering variety of course titles covering the main employment areas of travel, tourism, hotels and restaurants. Typical titles include:

For hotels and restaurant management:

- hospitality management
- international hospitality management
- hotel and catering management

For travel and tourism:

- tourism management
- tourism studies
- travel and tourism

There are also joint degrees where it is possible to study combinations of subjects, such as tourism and hospitality, tourism and leisure, hospitality and marketing. Most undergraduate courses (HND/BSc/BA) will include a period of work experience as part of the course, varying in length from 6 months to one year.

This work experience is seen to be a central part of the course, where the student gets the opportunity to practise what they have learned in college or university. Employers also see great value in this work experience when considering the employment of graduates. Given the international nature of these industries, another valuable part of any course is the study of languages.

Most courses in hospitality and tourism provide access to language courses, either as core components or as options. Courses at Masters level are becoming increasingly important in tourism and hospitality. These Masters level courses are useful to two groups of people:

- those who have completed a degree course in a subject other than hospitality or tourism but who are looking at ways of getting employment in the industry;
- those who have a degree or sub-degree qualification in hospitality or tourism together with significant management experience within the hospitality or tourism industries and who wish to develop themselves

to a higher level or to seek a more senior position in industry. There are many Masters courses in Hospitality Management, Hotel and Catering Management and Tourism Management in universities and colleges in the UK.

In addition to the above courses, there are also more specialised Masters courses in Tourism covering areas such as Cultural Tourism, Tourism Marketing, Tourism Planning, Museum Management, Heritage Management, Cultural Tourism and Sustainable Tourism: these are suitable for people who have an interest in employment in a specific sector of the industry.

Within the UK there are many university and college courses to choose from, but each course will have its own unique characteristics. Before applying, you should think carefully about the type of career you want: if it is in a hotel are you interested in restaurant management or rooms division management? Do you see yourself as a practical hands-on person or someone who is happier to work behind the scenes in a desk based job? Do you aspire to become a general manager of a hotel which is part of one of the major worldwide groups, or do you want to manage your own operation? Are you more interested in one of the functional management areas, such as marketing, human resources, conferences.

FUTURE TRENDS

The substantial growth of the tourism activity clearly marks tourism as one of the most remarkable economic and social phenomena of the past century. The number of international arrivals shows an evolution from a mere 25 million international arrivals in 1950 to an estimated 806 million in 2005, corresponding to an average annual growth rate of 6.5%.

During this period, development was particularly strong in Asia and the Pacific (13% on average a year) and in the Middle East (10%) while the Americas (5%) and Europe (6%), grew at a slower pace and slightly below the world's average growth.

New destinations are steadily increasing their market share while more mature regions such as Europe and the Americas tend to have less dynamic growth. Europe's world share declined by over 10 percentage points since 1950 whereas the Americas lost 13 percentage points.

Though the Americas' performance has been most affected by the declines suffered in the past years, the fact is that its annual average growth rate for the period 1950-2000 was 5.8%, also bellow the average for the world (6.8%). Europe and the Americas were the main tourist-receiving regions between 1950 and 2000. Both regions represented a joint market share of over 95 per cent in 1950, 82% forty years later and 76% in 2000.

6

Tourism Market Segments

In a general tourism plan, some clear target tourism market segments should be identified (See Table 3). You might begin by defining the market area from which you will draw most of your visitors. The size of your market area depends upon the uniqueness and quality of your "product", transportation systems, tastes and preferences of surrounding populations, and your competition. Identifying the market area will help target information and promotion and define transportation routes and modes, competition, and characteristics of your market.

Next, divide your travel market into the following trip length categories:

- day trips from a 50 mile radius,
- day trips from 50 to 200 miles away,
- pass-through travelers,
- overnight trips of 1 or 2 nights (most likely weekends), and
- extended overnight vacation trips.

After you have an idea of your market area and kinds of trips you will be serving, begin defining more specific market segments like vehicle campers, downhill skiers, sightseers, family vacationers, single weekenders, and the like. These segments can be more clearly tied to particular resources, businesses, and facilities in your community.

What kinds of products and services are likely to attract each of these groups? Tourist needs as well as their impact on the local community are quite different for day tourists versus overnight tourists. Areas catering primarily to weekend traffic will experience large fluctuations in use. In deciding the relative importance of these different segments, communities need to assess both their ability to provide required services (do you have enough rooms?), as well as the demand for different types of trips relative to the supply and your competition.

THE ENVIRONMENT: A tourism plan is significantly affected by many factors in the broader environment. Indeed, one of the complexities of tourism planning is the number of variables that are outside of the control of an individual tourism business or community. These include such things as tourism offerings and prices at competing destinations, federal and state policy and legislation, currency exchange rates, the state of the economy, and weather. These factors are discussed more fully in Extension bulletin E-1959 as part of the market environment analysis.

Local populations also must be considered in tourism planning. As they compete with tourists for resources, they can be significantly affected by tourism activity, and they are an important source of support in getting tourism plans implemented. A survey of local residents can be conducted to assess community attitudes toward tourism development, identify impacts of tourism on the community, and obtain local input into tourism plans. Public hearings, workshops, and advisory boards are other ways to obtain public involvement in tourism planning. Local support and cooperation is important to the success of tourism programs and should not be overlooked.

Table. Tourism Market Segments

I. Geographic market areas

II. Trip categories

Day Trips:

- short-within 50 miles
- long-up to 200 miles

Pass through traffic:

- day visitors
- overnight stays

Overnight Trips:

- weekend
- vacation

III. Activity or trip purpose

Outdoor Recreation:

- Water-based Activity:
  - — Boating: sail, power, cruise, row, canoe, water ski
  - — Swimming: pool, beach, sunbathing, scuba
  - — Fishing: charter, sport, from pier, boat, shore, ice
- Land-based Activity:
  - — Camping: backpacking, primitive, developed
  - — Hiking: climbing, beachcombing, spelunking
  - — Hunting
  - — Skiing: downhill, cross country
  - — Snowmobiling
  - — Bicycling
  - — Horseback riding
  - — Picnicking
- Air-based Activity:
  - — Airplane rides, hang gliding, ballooning, parachuting
- General:
  - — Nature study
  - — Photography or landscape painting
  - — Viewing natural scenery

Sightseeing & Entertainment:

- Visiting particular sites or areas:
  - — historic or pre-historic
  - — cultural
  - — amusements
  - — scenic

- Attending particular events, shows, or demonstrations:
  - — ethnic festivals
  - — sporting events
  - — performances
  - — agricultural fair or festival
  - — boat show
  - — shopping

Other Primary Purpose for Trip:

- Visiting Friends & Relatives
- Convention & Business/Pleasure

STEP THREE: Generating Alternatives. Generating alternative development and marketing options to meet your goals requires some creative thinking and brainstorming. The errors made at this stage are usually thinking too narrowly or screening out alternatives prematurely. It is wise to solicit a wide range of options from a diverse group of people. If tourism expertise is lacking in your community, seek help and advice outside the community.

Tourism planning involves a wide range of interrelated development and marketing decisions. The following development questions will get you started:

- How much importance should be assigned to tourism within a community or region?
- Which general community goals is tourism development designed to serve?
- Which organization(s) will provide the leadership and coordination necessary for community tourism planning? What are the relative roles of public and private sectors?

Tourism marketing decision questions include (Extension bulletin E-1959):

- Segments: Which market segments should be pursued; geographic markets, trip types, activity or demographic subgroups?
- Product: What kinds of tourism products and services should be provided? Who should provide what?

- Place: Where should tourism facilities be located?
- Promotion: What kinds of promotion should be used, by whom, in which media, how much, when? What community tourism theme or image should be established? (See Extension bulletins E-1939, E-1957, E-1940, E-1938, E-2005)
- Price: What prices should be charged for which products and services. Who should capture the revenue? (See Extension bulletin E-1999)

STEP FOUR: Evaluating Alternatives. Tourism development and marketing options are evaluated by assessing the degree to which each option will be able to meet the stated goals and objectives.

There are usually two parts to a systematic evaluation of tourism development and marketing alternatives: (1) Feasibility analysis, and (2) Impact assessment. These two tasks are interrelated, but think of them as trying to answer two basic questions: (1) Can it be done?, and (2) What are the consequences? A decision to take a specific action must be based both on feasibility and desirability.

FEASIBILITY ANALYSIS: First, screen alternatives and eliminate those that are not feasible due to economic, environmental, political, legal, or other factors. Evaluate the remaining set of alternatives in more detail, paying particular attention to the market potential and financial plan.

Make a realistic assessment of your community's ability to attract and serve a market segment or segments. This requires a clear understanding of the tourism market in your area and how this market is changing. Also carefully identify your competition and evaluate your advantages and disadvantages compared to the competition.

Plan toward the future because it takes time to implement decisions and for your actions to take effect. Therefore, look at the likely market and competition for several years to come. Review forecasts for the travel market in your area, if available. Careful tracking of tourism trends in your own community can help identify changes in the market that you will have to adapt to. (See Extension bulletins E-1959 and E-1992 for more details on feasibility and marketing.)

IMPACT ASSESSMENT: When evaluating alternative development and marketing strategies it is important to understand the impacts, both positive and negative, of proposed actions. Table 4 presents a classification of economic, environmental, and social impacts associated with tourism development. The types of impacts and their importance vary across different communities and proposed actions. Generally, the size, extent, and nature of tourism impacts depend upon:

- volume of tourist activity relative to local activity
- length and nature of tourist contacts with the community
- degree of concentration/dispersal of tourist activity in the area
- similarities or differences between local populations and tourists
- stability/sensitivity of local economy, environment, and social structure
- how well tourism is planned, controlled, and managed.

Look at both the benefits and costs of any proposed actions (See Extension bulletin E-1937). While tourism development can increase income, revenues, and employment, it also involves costs. Evaluate benefits and costs of tourism development from the perspectives of local government, businesses, and residents.

Table. Impacts Of Tourism

Economic Impacts:

- Sales, revenue, and income
- Employment
- Fiscal impact-taxes, infrastructure costs
- Prices
- Economic base & structure

Environmental Impacts:

- Lands
- Waters
- Air
- Infrastructure
- Flora & fauna

Social Impacts:

- Population structure & distribution
- Values & attitudes
- Education
- Occupations
- Safety & security
- Congestion & crowding
- Community spirit & cohesion
- Quality of life

IMPACTS ON LOCAL GOVERNMENT

Local government provides most of the infrastructure and many of the services essential to tourism development, including highways, public parks, law enforcement, water and sewer, garbage collection and disposal. Evaluate tourism decisions with a clear understanding of the capacity of the local infrastructure and services relative to anticipated needs, and take into account both the needs of local populations and tourists.

A fiscal impact analysis evaluates the impact of tourism on the community's tax base and local government costs. It entails predicting the additional infrastructure and service requirements of tourism development, estimating their costs, deciding who will pay for/provide them, and how. Will tourism generate increased local government revenue through fees and charges, local sales or use taxes, increased property values or property tax rates, or larger local shares of federal and state tax revenues?

Impacts on Business and Industry Businesses that are directly serving tourists benefit from sales to tourists. Through secondary impacts, tourism activity also benefits a wide range of businesses in a community. For example, a local textile industry may sell to a linen supply firm that serves hotels and motels catering primarily to tourists. A local forest products industry sells to a lumberyard where local woodcarvers or furniture makers buy their supplies. They in turn sell to tourists through various retail outlets. All of these businesses benefit from tourism. If most products and services for tourists are bought outside of the local area, much of the tourist spending "leaks" out of the local economy. The more a community is "self-sufficient" in serving tourists, the larger the local impact.

Impacts on Residents

Local residents may experience a broad range of both positive and negative impacts from tourism development. Tourism development may provide increased employment and income for the community. Although tourism jobs are primarily in the service sectors and are often seasonal, part time, and low-paying, these characteristics, are neither universal nor always undesirable. Residents may value opportunities for part time and seasonal work. In particular, employment opportunities and work experiences for students or retirees may be desired.

Residents may also benefit from local services that otherwise would not be available. Tourism development may mean a wider variety of retailers and restaurants, or a better community library. It may also mean more traffic, higher prices, and increases in property values and local taxes. The general quality of the environment and life in the community may go up or down due to tourism development. This depends on the nature of tourism development, the preferences and desires of local residents, and how well tourism is planned and managed.

STEPS FIVE AND SIX:Implementation, and Monitoring and Evaluation. We will not attempt a complete discussion of decisionmaking, plan implementation, and monitoring, but these are critical steps in the success of a tourism plan. A set of specific actions should be prescribed with clearly defined responsibilities and timetables. Monitor progress in implementing the plan and evaluate the success of the plan in meeting its goals and objectives on a regular basis. Plans generally need to be adjusted over time due to changing goals, changing market conditions, and unanticipated impacts. It is a good idea to build monitoring and evaluation systems into your planning efforts.

TWO SIDES OF TOURISM PLANNING

Tourism planning has evolved from two related but distinct sets of planning philosophies and methods. On the one hand, tourism is one of many activities in an area that must be considered as part of physical, environmental, social, and economic planning. Therefore, it is common to find tourism addressed, at least partially, in a regional land use, transportation, recreation, economic development, or comprehensive plan. The degree to which tourism is addressed in such plans depends upon the relative importance of tourism to the community or region and how sensitive the planning authority is to tourism activities.

Tourism may also be viewed as a business in which a community or region chooses to engage. Individual tourism businesses conduct a variety of planning activities including feasibility, marketing, product development, promotion, forecasting, and strategic planning. If tourism is a significant component of an area's economy or development plans, regional or community-wide marketing plans are needed to coordinate the development and marketing activities of different tourism interests in the community.

A comprehensive approach integrates a strategic marketing plan with more traditional public planning activities. This ensures a balance between serving the needs and wants of the tourists versus the needs and wants of local residents. A formal tourism plan provides a vehicle for the various interests within a community to coordinate their activities and work toward common goals. It also is a means of coordinating tourism with other community activities.

STEPS IN THE PLANNING PROCESS

Like any planning, tourism planning is goal-oriented, striving to achieve certain objectives by matching available resources and programs with the needs and wants of people. Comprehensive planning requires a systematic approach, usually involving a series of steps. The process is best viewed as an iterative and on-going one, with each step subject to modification and refinement at any stage of the planning process.

There are six steps in the planning process:

1. Define goals and objectives.
2. Identify the tourism system.

(a) Resources

(b) Organizations

(c) Markets

3. Generate alternatives.
4. Evaluate alternatives.
5. Select and implement.
6. Monitor and evaluate.

STEP ONE: Defining Goals and objectives. Obtaining clear statements of goals and objectives is difficult, but important. Ideally, tourism development goals should flow from more general community goals and objectives. It is important to understand how a tourism plan serves these broader purposes. Is the community seeking a broader tax base, increased employment opportunities, expanded recreation facilities, better educational programs, a higher quality of life? How can tourism contribute to these objectives?

If tourism is identified as a means of serving broader community goals, it makes sense to develop plans with more specific tourism development objectives. These are generally defined through a continuing process in which various groups and organizations in a community work together toward common goals. A local planning authority, chamber of commerce, visitors bureau, or similar group should assume a leadership role to develop an initial plan and obtain broad involvement of tourism interests in the community. Public support for the planning process and plan is also important.

Having a good understanding of tourism and the tourism system in your community is the first step toward defining goals and objectives for tourism development. The types of goals that are appropriate and the precision with which you are able to define them will depend upon how long your community has been involved in tourism and tourism planning.

In the early stages of tourism development, goals may involve establishing organizational structures and collecting information to better identify the tourism system in the community. Later, more precise objectives can be formulated and more specific development and marketing strategies evaluated.

STEP TWO: Identifying Your Tourism System When planning for any type of activity, it is important to first define its scope and characteristics. Be clear about exactly what your plan encompasses. A good initial question is, "What do you mean by tourism?" Tourism is defined in many ways. Generally, tourism involves people traveling outside of their community for pleasure. Definitions differ on the specifics of how far people must travel, whether or not they must stay overnight, for how long, and what exactly is included under traveling for "pleasure". Do you want your tourism plan to include day visitors, conventioneers, business travelers, people visiting friends and relatives, people passing through, or seasonal residents? Which community resources and organizations serve tourists or could serve tourists? Generally, tourists share community resources with local residents and businesses. Many organizations serve both tourists and locals. This complicates tourism planning and argues for a clear idea of what your tourism plan entails. You can begin to clarify the tourism system by breaking it down into three subsystems:

(1) tourism resources,

(2) tourism organizations, and

(3) tourism markets.

An initial task in developing a tourism plan is to identify, inventory, and classify the objects within each of these subsystems.

TOURISM RESOURCES are any (1) natural, (2) cultural, (3) human, or (4) capital resources that either are used or can be used to attract or serve tourists. A tourism resource inventory identifies and classifies the resources available that provide opportunities for tourism development. Conduct an objective and realistic assessment of the quality and quantity of resources you have to work with. Table I provides a suggested classification to help obtain a broad and organized picture of your tourism resources.

TOURISM ORGANIZATIONS combine resources in various proportions to provide products and services for the tourist. Table 2 is a partial list and classification of organizations that manage or coordinate tourism-related activities. It is important to recognize the diverse array of public and private organizations involved with tourism.

The most difficult part of tourism planning is to get these groups to work toward common goals. You should develop a list of these organizations within your own community and obtain their input and cooperation in your tourism planning efforts. Setting up appropriate communication systems and institutional arrangements is a key part of community tourism planning.

Table: Tourism Resources

Natural Resources

- Climate-seasons
- Water resources-lakes, streams, waterfalls
- Flora-forests, flowers, shrubs, wild edibles
- Fauna-fish & wildlife
- Geological resources-topography, soils, sand dunes, beaches, caves, rocks & minerals, fossils
- Scenery-combinations of all of the above

Cultural Resources

- Historic buildings, sites
- Monuments, shrines
- Cuisine
- Ethnic cultures
- Industry, government, religion, etc.
- Anthropological resources
- Local celebrities

Human Resources

- Hospitality skills
- Management skills
- Seasonal labor force
- Performing artists-music, drama, art, storytellers, etc.
- Craftsman and artisans

- Other labor skills from chefs to lawyers to researchers
- Local populations

Capital

- Availability of capital, financing
- Infrastructure-transportation roads, airports, railroads, harbors & marinas, trails & walkways
- Infrastructure: utilities water, power, waste treatment, communications

Table: Tourism Management organizations and Services

Off-Site: Coordination, planning, technical assistance, research, regulation:

- Federal & state departments of commerce, transportation, & natural resources
- Federal, state, regional, & local tourism associations
- Educational organizations & consultants, e.g., Travel & Tourism Research Association; U.S. Travel Data Center; Travel Reference Center, Univ. of Colorado, Boulder; Travel, Tourism, & Recreation Resource Center, Michigan State University.
- Travel information & reservation services

On-Site: development, promotion and management, of tourism resources:

- Federal agencies, NB. departments of commerce, transportation, & land management agencies
- State agencies, NB. departments of commerce, transportation, & land/facility management agencies
- Local government organizations, e.g., visitor information, chamber of commerce, convention & visitor's bureaus, parks
- Businesses:
  - Accommodations: Hotels, motels, Lodges, resorts, bed & breakfast cabins & cottages, Condominiums, second homes, Campgrounds

- — Food & Beverage: Restaurants, Grocery, Bars, nightclubs, Fast food, Catering services
- — Transportation: Air, rail, bus; Local transportation: taxi, limo, Auto, bicycle, boat rental; Local tour services
- — Information: Travel agencies, Information and reservation services, Automobile clubs
- — Recreation Facilities & Services: Winter sports: ski, skating, snowmobile areas; Golf courses, miniature golf; Swimming pools, water slides, beaches; tennis, handball, racquetball courts, bowling alleys; Athletic clubs, health spas; Marinas, boat rentals and charters; hunting & fishing guides; Horseback enterprises; Sporting goods sales & rentals
- — Entertainment: Nightclubs, amusement parks, spectator sport facilities; Gambling facilities: casinos, horse racing, bingo; video arcades; art galleries and studios, craft shops, studios, demonstrations; performing arts: theater, dance, music, film; historic & prehistoric sites; museums: art, history, science, technology; arboreta, zoos, nature centers,
- — Special festivals and events
- — Support services: Auto repair, gasoline service stations; boat & recreation vehicle dealers and service; retail shops: sporting goods, specialties, souvenirs, clothing; health services: hospitals, clinics, pharmacies; laundry and dry cleaning; beauty & barber shops; babysitting services; pet care; communications: newspaper, telephone; banking and financial services

TOURISM MARKETS: Tourists makeup the third, and perhaps most important subsystem. Successful tourism programs require a strong market orientation. The needs and wants of the tourists you choose to attract and serve must be the focus of much of your marketing and development activity. Therefore, it is important to clearly understand which tourism market segments you wish to attract and serve. Tourists fall into a very diverse set of categories with quite distinct needs and wants. You should identify the different types of tourists, or market segments that you presently serve or would like to serve. This may involve one or more tourism market surveys.

A visitor survey identifies the size and nature of the existing market and asks the following questions:

- What are the primary market segments you presently attract?
- Where do they come from?
- What local businesses and facilities do they use?
- What attracted them to the community?
- How did they find out about your community?
- How satisfied are they with your offerings?

A market survey (usually a telephone survey) also can be conducted among households in regions from which you wish to attract tourists. This type of study helps identify potential markets, and means of attracting tourists to your area.

CONCLUDING REMARKS

Successful tourism planning and development means serving both tourists and local residents. The bulletins in this series stress the importance of a market orientation for attracting and serving tourists. This market orientation must be balanced with a clear view of how tourism serves the broader community interest and an understanding of the positive and negative impacts of tourism development.

Remember, tourism should serve the community first and the tourist second. Tourism development must be compatible with other activities in the area and be supported by the local population. Therefore, the tourism plan should be closely coordinated with other local and regional planning efforts, if not an integral part of them.

7

Government Promotion of Tourism

INTRODUCTION

Under the scheme, tourists are given the opportunity see the rural areas of Himachal, enjoying their stay in comfortable home-stay accommodations. Every Home Stay Unit owner shall get the unit registered with the state department of tourism and the owner of the Home Stay Unit would charge the rates approved by the department. Under the 'Vibrant Gujarat' programme, the Gujarat government plans to actively market the tourism sector and is expecting an inflow of US$ 20.22 billion in the next five years as investment.

The government is planning to introduce an investor tourism policy for the same. With a 1,650-km coastline, the state has big plans of developing beaches in regions like Kutch and Mandvi on similar lines like those in Kerala and Goa. At the Vibrant Gujarat Global Investors' Summit, memorandums of understanding (MoUs) worth US$ 9.10 billion for hotels, convention centres, resorts, and adventure tourism in the state, were signed. Apart from various tourism destinations, the governments also plan to market festivals such as Navrathri and the International Kite Festival. The government has singled out 37 destinations for tourism development and over the last two years, over 600 projects in 300 tourist destinations have been developed with an investment of US$ 20.22 million. Amongst them, the government is planning to promote Kutch as an aqua-tourism destination for not only bringing in leisure travellers, but also travellers in the Meeting, Incentive, Conference and Exhibition (MICE) segment. Amidst fears of global meltdown likely to impact the tourism sector in India, the government is trying to woo tourists.

NATURAL RESOURCE MANAGEMENT

Natural resource management can be utilized as a specialized tool for the development of eco-tourism. There are several places throughout the world where the amount of natural resources are abundant.

But, with human encroachment and habitats these resources are depleting. Without knowing the proper utilization of certain resources they are destroyed and floral and faunal species are becoming extinct. Ecotourism programmes can be introduced for the conservation of these resources. Several plans and proper management programmes can be introduced so that these resources remain untouched. Several organizations, NGO's, scientists are working on this field. Natural resources of hill areas like Kurseong in West Bengal are plenty in number with various flora and fauna, but tourism for business purpose poised the situation. Researcher from Jadavpur University presently working in this area for the develeopment of eco-tourism which can be utilized as a tool for natural resource management.

Tour operators, travel agencies & retailers

Some companies specialise in ecotourism, designing their trips to be environmentally, culturally and socially friendly. Companies such as Intrepid Travel, Frontier, and Marine Conservation Society, Peregrine Adventures, World Expeditions, Explore Worldwide and Exodus offer trips catering for the thoughtful traveller. Some tour operators are keenly aware of the impacts that they may have on specific areas and rotate clients around to different sites for snorkeling, bird watching, and other activities. Others are just beginning to see the advantage of "green" travel destinations.

HERITAGE TOURISM

Cultural heritage tourism (or just heritage tourism) is a branch of tourism oriented towards the cultural heritage of the location where tourism is occurring. Culture has always been a major object of travel, as the development of the Grand Tour from the 16th century onwards attests.

In the 20th century, some people have claimed, culture ceased to be the objective of tourism: tourism is now culture. Cultural attractions play an important role in tourism at all levels, from the global highlights of world culture to attractions that underpin local identities. (Richards, 1996)

According to the Weiler and Hall, culture, heritage and the arts have long contributed to appeal of tourist destination. However, in recent years 'culture' has been rediscovered as an important marketing tool to attract those travellers with special interests in heritage and arts. According to the Hollinshead, cultural heritage tourism defines as cultural heritage tourism is the fastest growing segment of the tourism industry because there is a trend toward an increase specialization among tourists. This trend is evident in the rise in the volume of tourists who seek adventure, culture, history, archaeology and interaction with local people.

Cultural heritage tourism is important for various reasons; it has a positive economic and social impact, it establishes and reinforces identity, it helps preserve the cultural heritage, with culture as an instrument it facilitates harmony and understanding among people, it supports culture and helps renew tourism (Richards, 1996). Putangina Cultural heritage tourism has a number of objectives that must be met within the context of sustainable development such as; the conservation of cultural resources, accurate interpretation of resources, authentic visitors experience, and the stimulation of the earned revenues of cultural resources. We can see, therefore, that cultural heritage tourism is not only concerned with identification, management and protection of the heritage values but it must also be involved in understanding the impact of tourism on communities and regions, achieving economic and social benefits, providing financial resources for protection, as well as marketing and promotion. (J. M. Fladmark, 1994)

Heritage tourism involves visiting historical or industrial sites that may include old canals, railways, battlegrounds, etc. The overall purpose is to gain an appreciation of the past. It also refers to the marketing of a location to members of a diaspora who have distant family roots there.

Decolonization and immigration form the major background of much contemporary heritage tourism. Falling travel costs have also made heritage tourism possible for more people.

Another possible form involves religious travel or pilgrimages. Many Catholics from around the world come to the Vatican and other sites such as Lourdes or Fátima. Large numbers of Jews have both visited Israel and emigrated there. Many have also gone to Holocaust sites and memorials. Islam commands its followers to take the *hajj* to Mecca, thus differentiating it somewhat from tourism in the usual sense, though the trip can also be a culturally important event for the pilgrim.

Heritage Tourism can also be attributed to historical events that have been dramatised to make them more entertaining. For example a historical tour of a town or city using a theme such as ghosts or vikings.

OUTBOUND TOURISTS

A booming economy and increase in disposable income has led to a massive growth in the number of Indians travelling abroad.

Indian outbound tourist flow is expected to increase at a CAGR of 13.30 per cent during 2008-2012, according to a new report titled, 'Indian Tourism Industry Analysis', by RNCOS, a leading market research and information analysis company.

Similarly, Euromonitor International estimates the outgoing tourism expenditure from India to grow to US$ 21 million by 2011, representing a growth rate of over 25.7 per cent between 2006 and 2011.

Medical Tourism

'First World treatment' at Third World prices' is how industry sources define medical tourism in India. Although India is a recent entrant into medical tourism, it is fast catching up. According to a study by McKinsey and the Confederation of Indian Industry (CII), medical tourism in India could become a US$ 2 billion industry by 2012 (from US$ 350 million in

2006). Credit Suisse estimates medical tourism to be growing at about 25-30 per cent annually. Indian hospitals are fast becoming the first choice for an increasing number of foreign tourists, and as per a Credit Suisse estimate, nearly 180,000 medical tourists were treated in India in 2004.

The key selling points of the medical tourism industry are its cost effectiveness and its combination with the attractions of tourism. Many travel agents are now selling combined packages of treatment and vacation. India has some of the best hospitals and treatment centres which are well equipped and are at par with those in the US, UK and Europe with costs that are a fraction–only a tenth and sometimes even a sixteenth–of the cost in the West.

Hospitality

The boom in India's tourism industry and the surge in tourist inflow to the country have percolated to other associated sectors like hospitality. The revenues for the Indian hotel and restaurant industry in the year 2006-07 exceeded US$ 118.85 million, an increase of nearly 22 per cent over the previous year. The industry is poised for rapid growth and is projected to be well worth over US$ 158.49 million by the year 2010.

And with the continuing surge in tourist inflow, this sector is likely to offer tremendous opportunity for investors. For example, while the estimated number of required hotel rooms is around 240,000, the current availability is just 90,000 rooms-leaving a shortfall of 150,000 rooms to be provided. India's hospitality sector is expected to see around 40 international hotel brands by 2011, according to a report by Ma Foi Management Consultants. Moreover, the sector is expected to provide over 400,000 jobs.

Along with these large-scale expansion plans, international hotel asset management companies are also likely to enter India. Several global hotel chains see immense investment opportunities in the sector with global chains like Hilton, Marriott International, Berggruen Hotels, Cabana Hotels, Premier Travel Inn (PTI), InterContinental Hotels group and Hampshire amongst others having announced major investment plans in India with others likely to follow suit. With land prices coming down and a huge opportunity for quality hotels in India, many global hotel players are announcing new projects in India. According to Rashes Shah, analyst with brokerage firm, ICICI Direct,"International hotel majors have a long-term view of India. Most properties will become operational only around 2012 by which time the market is expected to bounce back. Most of them also have enough cash to buy land."

Emerging Trends

Hotels are no longer satisfied with the plain-vanilla room concept but are now getting ready for alternate hospitality formats such as residential hotels, destination resorts, condo hotels, vacation ownership and private residents' club.

- Four Seasons is developing a destination resort in Puthenkayal, Kerala, which will have 75 villas and also 20 branded, luxury private residences. The resort will be operational by 2012.
- Nearly 11 per cent of the hotel demand in the country is from long-stay guests. The Leela Group is looking at tapping this market. Its property in Gurgaon will have 90 apartments called 'The Residence', aimed at long-stay guests.
- India's largest real estate player, DLF, is building India's first residential hotel in Goa with the Hilton Group. DLF plans to invest US$ 2 billion to have six hotels on a similar format in the next five years.

International Recognition

India's booming tourism sector has not only witnessed international investments but also achieved international accolades with its increasing appeal as the leading global tourist destination.

The government has been instrumental in making tourism a priority sector. Its efforts have borne fruits with a series of international recognition and awards.

- India has been elected to head the UN World Tourism Organisation (UNWTO), the highest policy making world tourism body represented by 150 countries.

- The world's leading travel and tourism journal, Conde Nast Traveller, has ranked India as the 'numero uno' travel destination in the world.
- India was adjudged Asia's leading destination at the regional World Travel Awards (WTA).
- India's Taj Mahal continues to figure in the Seven Wonders of the World.
- Bangalore-based Leela Palace Kempinski was voted the favourite business hotel in the world in a Readers' Choice Awards by Conde Nast Traveller in 2007.
- India bagged the World's leading Destination Marketing Award for the Incredible India campaign in 2007.
- According to the country brand index (CBI) 2008 survey, conducted by FutureBrand - a leading global brand consultancy - in conjunction with public relations firm Weber Shandwick's Global Travel & Lifestyle Practice, India ranks second in value-for-money index.

Government Initiatives

To unlock the huge potential in this sector, the government has taken various initiatives for the development of this sector.

- Launch of Incredible India campaign to promote tourism both in domestic and international markets.
- Recognition of spare rooms available with various house owners by classifying these facilities as 'Incredible India Bed and Breakfast Establishments', under 'Gold' or 'Silver' category.
- A new category of visa, 'Medical Visa' ('M'-Visa), has been introduced which can be given to foreign tourists coming into India for medical tourism.
- Ministry of Tourism has tied up with United Nations Development Programme (UNDP) to promote rural tourism.
- Companies in the hotels sector can now raise external commercial borrowings (ECBs) under the automatic

route and utilise the proceeds for both foreign currency and/or rupee capital expenditure.

The Road Ahead

With India being on the global tourist map and an increasing number of people coming to India for tourism or business, hotels are looking at expansion in a major way.

- The US-based Hilton Hotels Corporation will be launching its upscale brand, Doubletree, in India. Its 182-room hotel in Gurgaon is scheduled to open in 2010.
- Global Hyatt Corporation plans to add 20 properties in India over the next four years, with a presence in Tier 2 and 3 cities as well.
- Marriott International Inc is also planning to open seven hotels in 2009, which entails 1,561 new rooms. An additional 14 (previously announced) hotels are likely to be commissioned by 2012.
- InterContinental Hotels Group will be developing 22 additional hotels to its current portfolio of 13 hotels, within the next few years. These will be built under its three brands — InterContinental Hotels & Resorts, Crowne Plaza Hotels & Resorts and Holiday Inn Hotels & Resorts.
- The Taj Hotels Resorts and Palaces, in a joint venture with CC Africa, a leading safari operator and ecotourism company from Africa - is opening two safari lodges in Madhya Pradesh at Panna and Kanha National Parks. It already has a safari lodge each at Bandhavgarh and Pench National Parks.
- EIH, which owns the Oberoi and Trident group of hotels, is looking at opening 10 hotels in India and abroad in the next three years. These include a luxury Oberoi Hotel in Gurgaon to be opened in 2009, a 320-room Trident hotel at the Bangalore International Airport to be opened in 2010, and two hotels to be opened in Hyderabad in 2010.
- Hotels in Hyderabad are on an expansion spree and 4,000 rooms will be added in the next couple of years.

Around 20 major properties including that of Park Hyatt, Trident, Marriott, Leela and Taj among others will effectively double the current capacity of 4,000 rooms across all types of hotels.

The government is promoting 2009 as the 'Visit India Year'. The idea behind the scheme is that those who visit India in 2009 would subsequently experience India's rural tourism, eco tourism, adventure tourism, and wellness tourism in specially designed packages in 2010 and 2011. The reduced rates would also make India an inexpensive tourist destination.

Apart from leisure travel, the new emerging target areas would be business travel, domestic travel, medical tourism and the mid-market segment.

CULINARY TOURISM

Judging by the surge since 2001 in the number of times "culinary tourism" has appeared as a subject matter or in a session title in tourism industry conferences and programs, we can see that **Culinary Tourism** is valued by tourism industry professionals as one of the most popular niches in the world's tourism industry. This makes sense, given recent consumer focus on healthy and organic eating, culinary/food pedigrees, and the simple fact that all travelers must eat. Not every visitor goes shopping or visits museums, but all travelers eat. For anyone who doubts, look at the increase in cooking shows featured on The Travel Channel Anthony Bourdain No Reservations or travel shows featured on The Food Network Rachel Ray's $40 a Day series, as examples.

Culinary Tourism is defined as the pursuit of unique and memorable eating and drinking experiences, according to the International Culinary Tourism Association. Culinary Tourism differs from agritourism in that culinary tourism is considered a subset of cultural tourism (cuisine is a manifestation of culture) whereas agritourism is considered a subset of rural tourism, according to Culinary Tourism: The Hidden Harvest. That said, culinary tourism and agritourism are inextricably linked, as the seeds of cuisine can be found in agriculture. Culinary Tourism is not just experiences of the highest caliber - that would be gourmet tourism. This is perhaps best illustrated by the notion that Culinary Tourism is about what is "unique and memorable, not what is necessarily pretentious and exclusive". Similarly, wine tourism, beer tourism and spa tourism are also regarded as subsets of culinary tourism.

DARK TOURISM

Dark tourism (also **black tourism** or **grief tourism**) is tourism involving travel to sites associated with death and suffering. **Thanatourism**, derived from the Ancient Greek word *thanatos* for the personification of death, is associated with dark tourism but refers more specifically to violent death; it is used in fewer contexts than the terms dark tourism and grief tourism.

This includes castles and battlefields such as Culloden near Inverness, Scotland; sites of disaster, either natural or man made such as Ground Zero in New York; prisons now open to the public such as Beaumaris Prison in Anglesey, Wales; and purpose built centers such as the London Dungeon.

One of the most notorious destinations for dark tourism is the Nazi extermination camp at Auschwitz in Poland, Chernobyl site in ex USSR or Bran Castle, Poienari Castle in Romania.

8

Eco and Disaster Tourism

INTRODUCTION

Ecotourism, responsible tourism, jungle tourism and sustainable development have become prevalent concepts since the late 1980s, and ecotourism has experienced arguably the fastest growth of all sub-sectors in the tourism industry. The popularity represents a change in tourist perceptions, increased environmental awareness, and a desire to explore natural environments. Such changes have become as much a statement affirming one's social identity, educational sophistication, and disposable income as it has about preserving the Amazon rainforest or the Caribbean reef for posterity.

Ecotourism is travel to fragile, pristine, and usually protected areas that strives to be low impact and (often) small scale. It helps educate the traveler; provides funds for conservation; directly benefits the economic development and political empowerment of local communities; and fosters respect for different cultures and for human rights. As defined by the co-founder of the Center for Responsible Travel, Martha Honey, Ph.D., in her book *Ecotourism and Sustainable Development, Second Edition: Who Owns Paradise?*. Most serious studies of ecotourism including several University programs now use this as the working definition.

Ecotourism (also known as **ecological tourism**) is a form of tourism, that appeals to ecologically and socially conscious individuals. Generally speaking, ecotourism focuses on volunteering, personal growth and learning new ways to live on the planet. It typically involves travel to destinations where flora, fauna and cultural heritage are the primary attractions. Ecotourism is a conceptual experience, enriching those who delve into researching and understanding the environment around them. It gives us insight into our impacts, as human beings and also a greater appreciation of our own natural habitats.

Responsible ecotourism includes programs that minimize the negative aspects of conventional tourism on the environment and enhance the cultural integrity of local people. Therefore, in addition to evaluating environmental and cultural factors, an integral part of ecotourism is the promotion of recycling, energy efficiency, water conservation and creation of economic opportunities for the local communities.

Criteria

Ecotourism is a form of tourism that involves traveling to tranquil and unpolluted natural areas. According to the definition and principles of ecotourism established by The International Ecotourism Society (TIES) in 1990, ecotourism is "Responsible travel to natural areas that conserves the environment and improves the well-being of local people." (TIES, 1990). Martha Honey, expands on the TIES definition by describing the seven characteristics of ecotourism, which are:

- Involves travel to natural destinations.
- Minimizes impact.
- Builds environmental awareness.
- Provides direct financial benefits for conservation.
- Provides financial benefits and empowerment for local people.
- Respects local culture.
- Supports human rights and demographic movements.

Ideally, ecotourism should satisfy several criteria, such as:

- Conservation of biological diversity and cultural diversity through ecosystem protection
- Promotion of sustainable use of biodiversity, by providing jobs to local populations

- Sharing of socio-economic benefits with local communities and indigenous peoples by having their informed consent and participation in the management of ecotourism enterprises
- Tourism to unspoiled natural resources, with minimal impact on the environment being a primary concern.
- Minimization of tourism's own environmental impact
- Affordability and lack of waste in the form of luxury
- Local culture, flora and fauna being the main attractions

For many countries, ecotourism is not simply a marginal activity to finance protection of the environment, but is a major industry of the national economy. For example, in Costa Rica, Ecuador, Nepal, Kenya, Madagascar and Antarctica, ecotourism represents a significant portion of the gross domestic product and economic activity.

The concept of ecotourism is widely misunderstood and in practice is often used as a marketing tool to promote tourism, which is related to nature. This is an especially frequent malpractice in the realm of Jungle tourism. Critics claim that these greenwashing practices, carried out in the name of ecotourism, often consist of placing a hotel in a splendid landscape, to the detriment of the ecosystem. According to them, ecotourism must above all sensitize people to the beauty and the fragility of nature. They condemn some operators as greenwashing their operations: using the labels of "green" and "eco-friendly", while behaving in environmentally irresponsible ways.

Although academics disagree about who can be classified as an ecotourist and there is precious little statistical data, some estimate that more than five million ecotourists - the majority of the ecotourist population - come from the United States, with others from Western Europe, Canada and Australia.

Currently, there are various moves to create national and international ecotourism accreditaion programs, although the process is also controversial. National ecotourism certification programs have been put in place in countries such as Costa Rica, Australia, Kenya and Sweden.

DISASTER TOURISM

Disaster tourism is the act of traveling to a disaster area as a matter of curiosity. The behavior can be a nuisance if it hinders rescue, relief, and recovery operations.

If not done because of pure curiosity, it can be cataloged as disaster learning.

Hurricane Katrina

Disaster tourism took hold in the Greater New Orleans Area in the aftermath of Hurricane Katrina. There are now guided bus tours to neighborhoods that were severely damaged by storm-related flooding. Some local residents have criticized these tours as unethical, because the tour companies are profiting from the misery of their communities and families. The Army Corps of Engineers has noted that traffic from tour buses and other tourist vehicles have interfered with the movement of trucks and other cleanup equipment on single-lane residential roads. Furthermore, during the first six months after the storm, most of these neighborhoods lacked electricity, phone access, street signs, or access to emergency medical or police assistance. Simply traveling to these neighborhoods was hazardous. For these reasons, organized disaster tours are now banned from two of the most severely damaged areas in the city, the Lower 9th and St. Bernard Parish near the Industrial Canal.

On the other hand, such communities as Gentilly and Lakeview, along the 17th Street Canal, have welcomed organized tour groups as a means to publicize the scale of the destruction and attract more aid to the city. Much of the recovery effort in the New Orleans relies on out-of-state volunteers and donations. Numerous non-profit organization, including Habitat for Humanity International and Catholic Charities, have converged on the city to gut and rebuild homes. There is also a movement by local residents to bring congressmen and other national leaders to the city and view the damage in person, since recovery efforts have been hampered by the failure of many homeowners and businesses to receive claims from their insurance providers.

CRITICISMS

Definitional Problems and Greenwashing

To approach an understanding of the problem, a clear definition must delineate what is, and is not, ecotourism. Ideally, ecotourism satisfies several general criteria, including the conservation of biological diversity and cultural diversity through ecosystem protection, promotion of sustainable use of biodiversity, share of socio-economic benefits with local communities through informed consent and participation, increase in environmental and cultural knowledge, affordability and reduced waste, and minimization of its own environmental impact. In such ways, it contributes to the long term benefits to both the environment and local communities.

However, in the continuum of tourism activities that stretch from conventional tourism to ecotourism proper, there has been a lot of contention to the limit at which biodiversity preservation, local socio-economic benefits, and environmental impact can be considered "ecotourism". For this reason, environmentalists, special interest groups, and governments define ecotourism differently. Environmental organizations have generally insisted that ecotourism is nature-based, sustainably managed, conservation supporting, and environmentally educated.

The tourist industry and governments, however, focus more on the product aspect, treating ecotourism as equivalent to any sort of tourism based in nature. As a further complication, many terms are used under the rubric of ecotourism. Nature tourism, low impact tourism, green tourism, bio-tourism, ecologically responsible tourism, and others have been used in literature and marketing, although they are not necessary synonymous with ecotourism.

The problems associated with defining ecotourism have led to confusion among tourists and academics alike. Definitional problems are also subject of considerable public controversy and concern because of greenwashing, a trend towards the commercialization of tourism schemes disguised as sustainable, nature based, and environmentally friendly ecotourism. According to McLaren, these schemes are environmentally destructive, economically exploitative, and culturally insensitive at its worst. They are also morally disconcerting because they mislead tourists and manipulate their concerns for the environment.

Despite objections, greenwashing continues to grow unabated. The Nature's Sacred Paradise, a theme park in Quintana Roo, Mexico, is responsible for displacing local Mayan communities and illegally keeping endangered species in captivity to attract visitors. The development and success of such large scale, energy intensive, and ecologically unsustainable schemes are a testament to the tremendous profits associated with being labeled as ecotourism.

NEGATIVE IMPACT OF TOURISM

Ecotourism has become one of the fastest-growing sectors of the tourism industry, growing annually by 10-15% worldwide (Miller, 2007). One definition of ecotourism is "the practice of low-impact, educational, ecologically and culturally sensitive travel that benefits local communities and host countries" (Honey, 1999). Many of the ecotourism projects are not meeting these standards.

Even if some of the guidelines are being executed, the local communities are still facing other negative impacts. South Africa is one of the countries that are reaping significant economic benefits from ecotourism, but negative effects - including physical displacement of persons, gross violation of fundamental rights, and environmental hazards - far outweigh the medium-term economic benefits (Miller, 2007). A tremendous amount of money is being spent and human resources continue to be used for ecotourism despite the lack of success, and even more money is put into public relation campaigns to dilute the effects of criticism. Ecotourism channels resources away from other projects that could contribute more sustainable and realistic solutions to pressing social and environmental problems.

"The money tourism can generate often ties parks and managements to eco-tourism" (Walpole et al. 2001). But there is a tension in this relationship because eco-tourism often causes conflict and changes in land-use rights, fails to deliver promises of community-level benefits, damages environments, and has plenty of other social impacts. Indeed many argue repeatedly that eco-tourism is neither ecologically nor socially beneficial, yet it persists as a strategy for conservation and development (West, 2006). While several studies are being done on ways to improve the ecotourism structure, these examples provide rationale for stopping it altogether.

The ecotourism system exercises tremendous financial and political influence. The evidence above shows that at the very least a strong case exists for restraining such activities. Funding could be used for field studies aimed at finding alternative solutions to tourism and the diverse problems Africa faces in result of urbanization, industrialization, and over exploitation of agriculture (Kamuaro, 2007). At the local level ecotourism has become a source of conflict over control of land, resources, and tourism profits. There are many problems with the idea of ecotourism. Environmental, the effects on the local people, and conflicts over profit distribution are only a few of the negative effects of ecotourism. In a perfect world more efforts would be made towards educating tourists of the environmental and social effects of their travels. Very few regulations or laws stand in place as boundaries for the investors in ecotourism. These should be implemented to prohibit the promotion of unsustainable ecotourism projects and materials which project false images of destinations, demeaning local and indigenous cultures.

DIRECT ENVIRONMENTAL IMPACTS

Ecotourism operations occasionally fail to live up to conservation ideals. It is sometimes overlooked that ecotourism is a highly consumer-centered activity, and that environmental conservation is a means to further economic growth.

Although ecotourism is intended for small groups, even a modest increase in population, however temporary, puts extra pressure on the local environment and necessitates the development of additional infrastructure and amenities. The construction of water treatment plants, sanitation facilities, and lodges come with the exploitation of non-renewable energy sources and the utilization of already limited local resources. The conversion of natural land to such tourist infrastructure is implicated in deforestation and habitat deterioration of butterflies in Mexico and squirrel monkeys in Costa Rica. In other cases, the environment suffers because local communities are unable to meet the infrastructure demands of ecotourism. The lack of adequate sanitation facilities in many East African parks results in the disposal of campsite sewage in rivers, contaminating the wildlife, livestock, and people who draw drinking water from it.

Aside from environmental degradation with tourist infrastructure, population pressures from ecotourism also leaves behind garbage and pollution associated with the Western lifestyle.

Although ecotourists claim to be educationally sophisticated and environmentally concerned, they rarely understand the ecological consequences of their visits and how their day-to-day activities append physical impacts on the environment. As one scientist observes, they "rarely acknowledge how the meals they eat, the toilets they flush, the water they drink, and so on, are all part of broader regional economic and ecological systems they are helping to reconfigure with their very activities." Nor do ecotourists recognize the great consumption of non-renewable energy required to arrive at their destination, which is typically more remote than conventional tourism destinations. For instance, an exotic journey to a place 10,000 kilometers away consumes about 700 liters of fuel per person.

Ecotourism activities are, in of itself, issues in environmental impact because they disturb fauna and flora. Ecotourists believe that because they are only taking pictures and leaving footprints, they keep ecotourism sites pristine, but even harmless sounding activities such as a nature hike can be ecologically destructive.

In the Annapurna Circuit in Nepal, ecotourists have worn down the marked trails and created alternate routes, contributing to soil impaction, erosion, and plant damage. Where the ecotourism activity involves wildlife viewing, it can scare away animals, disrupt their feeding and nesting sites, or acclimate them to the presence of people. In Kenya, wildlife-observer disruption drives cheetahs off their reserves, increasing the risk of inbreeding and further endangering the species.

ENVIRONMENTAL HAZARDS

Unfortunately, industrialization, urbanization, and unsustainable agriculture practices have all had serious effects on the environment. Ecotourism is now also playing a role in this depletion. While the term ecotourism may sound relatively benign, one of its most serious impacts is its consumption of virgin territories (Kamuaro, 2007). These invasions often include deforestation, disruption of ecological life systems and various forms of pollution, all of which contribute to environmental degradation. The number of motor vehicles crossing the park increases as tour drivers search for rare species. The number of roads has disrupted the grass cover which has serious effects on plant and animal species. These areas also have a higher rate of disturbances and invasive species because of all the traffic moving off the beaten path into new undiscovered areas (Kamuaro, 2007). Ecotourism also has an effect on species through the value placed on them. "Certain species have gone from being little known or valued by local people to being highly valued commodities. The commodification of plants may erase their social value and lead to overproduction within protected areas. Local people and their images can also be turned into commodities" (West, 2006). Kamuaro brings up a relatively obvious contradiction, any commercial venture into unspoiled, pristine land with or without the "eco" prefix as a contradiction in terms. To generate revenue you have to have a high number of traffic, tourists, which inevitably means a higher pressure on the environment.

Local People

Most forms of ecotourism are owned by foreign investors and corporations that provide few benefits to local communities. An overwhelming majority of profits are put into the pockets of investors instead of reinvestment into the local economy or environmental protection. The limited numbers of local people who are employed in the economy enter at its lowest level, and are unable to live in tourist areas because of meager wages and a two market system.

In some cases, the resentment by local people results in environmental degradation. As a highly publicized case, the

Maasai nomads in Kenya killed wildlife in national parks to show aversion to unfair compensation terms and displacement from traditional lands. The lack of economic opportunities for local people also constrains them to degrade the environment as a means of sustenance. The presence of affluent ecotourists encourage the development of destructive markets in wildlife souvenirs, such as the sale of coral trinkets on tropical islands and animal products in Asia, contributing to illegal harvesting and poaching from the environment. In Suriname, sea turtle reserves use a large portion of their budget to guard against these destructive activities.

Displacement of People

One of the most powerful examples of communities being moved in order to create a park is the story of the Masai. About 70% of national parks and game reserves in East Africa are on Masai land (Kamuaro, 2007). The first undesirable impact of tourism was that of the extent of land lost from the Masai culture. Local and national governments took advantage of the Masai's ignorance on the situation and robbed them of huge chunks of grazing land, putting to risk their only socio-economic livelihood. In Kenya the Masai also have not gained any economic benefits.

Despite the loss of their land, employment favours better educated workers. Furthermore the investors in this area are not local and have not put profits back into local economy. In some cases game reserves can be created without informing or consulting local people, who come to find out about the situation when an eviction notice is delivered (Kamuaro, 2007). Another source of resentment is the manipulation of the local people by their government. "Eco-tourism works to create simplistic images of local people and their uses and understandings of their surroundings. Through the lens of these simplified images, officials direct policies and projects towards the local people and the local people are blamed if the projects fail" (West, 2006). Clearly tourism as a trade is not empowering the local people who make it rich and satisfying. Instead ecotourism exploits and depletes, particularly in African Masai tribes. It has to be reoriented if it is to be useful to local communities and to become sustainable (Kamuaro, 2007).

THREATS TO INDIGENOUS CULTURES

Ecotourism often claims that it preserves and "enhances" local cultures. However, evidence shows that with the establishment of protected areas local people have illegally lost their homes, and most often with no compensation (Kamuaro, 2007). Pushing people onto marginal lands with harsh climates, poor soils, lack of water, and infested with livestock and disease does little to enhance livelihoods even when a proportion of ecotourism profits are directed back into the community. The establishment of parks can create harsh survival realities and deprive the people of their traditional use of land and natural resources. Ethnic groups are increasingly being seen as a "backdrop" to the scenery and wildlife. The local people struggle for cultural survival and freedom of cultural expression while being "observed" by tourists. Local indigenous people also have strong resentment towards the change, "Tourism has been allowed to develop with virtually no controls. Too many lodges have been built, too much firewood is being used and no limits are being placed on tourism vehicles. They regularly drive off-track and harass the wildlife. Their vehicle tracks criss-cross the entire Masai Mara. Inevitably the bush is becoming eroded and degraded" (Kamuaro, 2007).

Mismanagement

While governments are typically entrusted with the administration and enforcement of environmental protection, they often lack the commitment or capability to manage ecotourism sites effectively. The regulations for environmental protection may be vaguely defined, costly to implement, hard to enforce, and uncertain in effectiveness. Government regulatory agencies, as political bodies, are susceptible to making decisions that spend budget on politically beneficial but environmentally unproductive projects. Because of prestige and conspicuousness, the construction of an attractive visitor's center at an ecotourism site may take precedence over more pressing environmental concerns like acquiring habitat, protecting endemic species, and removing invasive ones. Finally, influential groups can pressure and sway the interests of the government to their favor. The government and its regulators can become vested in the benefits of the ecotourism industry which they are supposed to regulate, causing restrictive environmental regulations and enforcement to become more lenient.

Management of ecotourism sites by private ecotourism companies offers an alternative to the cost of regulation and deficiency of government agencies. It is believed that these companies have a self interest in limited environmental degradation, because tourists will pay more for pristine environments, which translates to higher profit. However, theory indicates that this practice is not economically feasible and will fail to manage the environment.

The model of monopolistic competition states that distinctiveness will entail profits, but profits will promote imitation. A company that protects its ecotourism sites is able to charge a premium for the novel experience and pristine environment. But when other companies view the success of this approach, they also enter the market with similar practices, increasing competition and reducing demand. Eventually, the demand will be reduced until the economic profit is zero. A cost-benefit analysis shows that the company bears the cost of environmental protection without receiving the gains. Without economic incentive, the whole premise of self interest through environmental protection is quashed; instead, ecotourism companies will minimize environment related expenses and maximize tourism demand.

The tragedy of the commons offers another model for economic unsustainability from environmental protection, in ecotourism sites utilized by many companies. Although there is a communal incentive to protect the environment, maximizing the benefits in the long run, a company will conclude that it is in their best interest to utilize the ecotourism site beyond its sustainable level. By increasing the number of ecotourists, for instance, a company gains all the economic benefit while paying only a part of the environmental cost. In the same way, a company recognizes that there is no incentive to actively protect the environment; they bear all the costs, while the benefits are shared by all other companies. The result, again, is mismanagement.

Taken together, the mobility of foreign investment and lack of economic incentive for environmental protection means that ecotourism companies are disposed to establishing themselves in new sites once their existing one is sufficiently degraded.

IMPROVING SUSTAINABILITY

Regulation and Accreditation

Because the regulation of ecotourism is poorly implemented or nonexistent, ecologically destructive greenwashed operations like underwater hotels, helicopter tours, and wildlife theme parks are categorized as ecotourism along with canoeing, camping, photography, and wildlife observation. The failure to acknowledge responsible, low impact ecotourism puts these companies at a competitive disadvantage. Many environmentalists have argued for a global standard of accreditation, differentiating ecotourism companies based on their level of environmental commitment. A national or international regulatory board would enforce accreditation procedures, with representation from various groups including governments, hotels, tour operators, travel agents, guides, airlines, local authorities, conservation organizations, and non-governmental organizations.

The decisions of the board would be sanctioned by governments, so that non-compliant companies would be legally required to disassociate themselves from the use of the ecotourism brand. Crinion suggests a Green Stars System, based on criteria including a management plan, benefit for the local community, small group interaction, education value and staff training. Ecotourists who consider their choices would be confident of a genuine ecotourism experience when they see the higher star rating. In addition, environmental impact assessments could be used as a form of accreditation. Feasibility is evaluated from a scientific basis, and recommendations could be made to optimally plan infrastructure, set tourist capacity, and manage the ecology. This form of accreditation is more sensitive to site specific conditions.

Guidelines and Education

An environmental protection strategy must address the issue of ecotourists removed from the cause-and-effect of their actions on the environment. More initiatives should be carried out to improve their awareness, sensitize them to environmental issues, and care about the places they visit.

Tour guides are an obvious and direct medium to communicate awareness. With the confidence of ecotourists and intimate knowledge of the environment, they can actively discuss conservation issues. A tour guide training program in Costa Rica's Tortuguero National Park has helped mitigate negative environmental impacts by providing information and regulating tourists on the parks' beaches used by nesting endangered sea turtles.

SMALL SCALE, SLOW GROWTH AND LOCAL CONTROL

The underdevelopment theory of tourism describes a new form of imperialism by multinational corporations that control ecotourism resources. These corporations finance and profit from the development of large scale ecotourism that causes excessive environmental degradation, loss of traditional culture and way of life, and exploitation of local labor. In Zimbabwe and Nepal's Annapurna region, where underdevelopment is taking place, more than 90 percent of ecotourism revenues are expatriated to the parent countries, and less than 5 percent go into local communities.

The lack of sustainability highlights the need for small scale, slow growth, and locally based ecotourism. Local peoples have a vested interest in the well being of their community, and are therefore more accountable to environmental protection than multinational corporations. The lack of control, westernization, adverse impacts to the environment, loss of culture and traditions outweigh the benefits of establishing large scale ecotourism.

The increased contributions of communities to locally managed ecotourism create viable economic opportunities, including high level management positions, and reduce environmental issues associated with poverty and unemployment. Because the ecotourism experience is marketed to a different lifestyle from large scale ecotourism, the development of facilities and infrastructure does not need to conform to corporate Western tourism standards, and can be much simpler and less expensive. There is a greater multiplier effect on the economy, because local products, materials, and labor are used. Profits accrue locally and import leakages are reduced. However, even this form of tourism may require foreign investment for promotion or start up. When such investments are required, it is crucial for communities for find a company or non-governmental organization that reflects the philosophy of ecotourism; sensitive to their concerns and willing to cooperate at the expense of profit.The basic assumption of the multiplier effect is that the economy starts off with unused resources, for example, that many workers are cyclically unemployed and much of industrial capacity is sitting idle or incompletely utilized. By increasing demand in the economy it is then possible to boost production. If the economy was already at full employment, with only structural, frictional, or other supply-side types of unemployment, any attempt to boost demand would only lead to inflation. For various laissez-faire schools of economics which embrace Say's Law and deny the possibility of Keynesian inefficiency and under-employment of resources, therefore, the multiplier concept is irrelevant or wrong-headed.

As an example, consider the government increasing its expenditure on roads by $one million, without a corresponding increase in taxation. This sum would go to the road builders, who would hire more workers and distribute the money as wages and profits. The households receiving these incomes will save part of the money and spend the rest on consumer goods. These expenditures in turn will generate more jobs, wages, and profits, and so on with the income and spending circulating around the economy.

The multiplier effect arises because of the induced increases in consumer spending which occur due to the increased incomes — and because of the feedback into increasing business revenues, jobs, and income again. This process does not lead to an economic explosion not only because of the supply-side barriers at potential output (full employment) but because at each "round", the increase in consumer spending is less than the increase in consumer incomes. That is, the marginal propensity to consume (mpc) is less than one, so that each round some extra income goes into saving, leaking out of the cumulative process. Each increase in spending is thus smaller than that of the previous round, preventing an explosion.Ecotourism has to be implemented with care.

LGBT TOURISM

Gay tourism or **LGBT tourism** is a form of niche tourism marketed to gay, lesbian, bisexual and transgender (LGBT) people. They are usually open about their sexual orientation and gender identity but may be more or less open when traveling; for instance they may be closeted at home or if they have come out, may be more discreet in areas known for violence against LGBT people. The main components of LGBT tourism is for cities and countries wishing to attract LGBT tourists; people looking to travel to LGBT-friendly destinations; people wanting travel with other LGBT people when traveling regardless of the destination and LGBT travelers who are mainly concerned with cultural and safety issues. The slang term *gaycation* has come to imply a version of a vacation that includes a pronounced aspect of LGBT culture, either in the journey or destination. The LGBT tourism industry includes travel agents, tour companies, cruise lines and travel advertising and promotions companies who market these destinations to the gay community. Coinciding with the increased visibility of LGBT people raising children in the 1990s, an increase in family-friendly LGBT tourism has emerged in the 2000s, for instance R Family Vacations which includes activities and entertainment geared towards couples including same-sex weddings. R Family's first cruise was held aboard Norwegian Cruise Lines's *Norwegian Dawn* with 1600 passengers including 600 children.

Major companies in the travel industry have become aware of the substantial money (also known as the "pink dollar" or "pink pound") generated by this marketing niche, and have made it a point to align themselves with the gay community and gay tourism campaigns. According to a 2000 Tourism Intelligence International report 10% of international tourists were gay and lesbian accounting for more than 70 million arrivals worldwide. This market segment is expected to continue to grow as a result ongoing acceptance of LGBT people and changing attitudes towards sexual and gender minorities. The gay and lesbian segment is estimated at $55 billion annual market as of 2007. Outside larger companies, LGBT tourists are offered other traditional tourism tools, such as LGBT hospitality networks of LGBT individuals who offer each other hospitality during their travels and even home swaps where people live in each others homes. Also available are social groups for resident and visiting gay, lesbian, bisexual and transgender expatriates and friends exist worldwide.

GAY TRAVEL DESTINATIONS

Gay travel destinations are popular among practitioners of gay tourism because they usually have permissive or liberal attitudes towards gays, feature a prominent gay infrastructure (bars, businesses, restaurants, hotels, nightlife, entertainment, media, organisations, etc.), the opportunity to socialize with other gays, and the feeling that one can relax safely among other gay people.

Gay travel destinations are often large cities, although not exclusively, and often coincide with the existence of gay neighborhoods. These municipalities and their tourism bureaus often work actively to develop their reputations as places for gays to travel to, commonly by aligning themselves to local gay organisations. Travel analysts state that the existence of a core gay friendly population is often the primary catalyst for the development of a gay-friendly tourist destination.

Gay tourism might also coincide with special gay events such as annual gay pride parades, gay neighborhood festivals and such gay community gatherings as gay chorus festivals and concerts, gay square dance conventions, gay sports meets such as Gay Games, World Outgames or Eurogames and conferences of national and international gay organisations. Gay tourism blossoms during these peak periods.

Gay tourism practitioners spend $64 billion a year on gay travel, according to Community Marketing Inc. The adult GLBT community has a total economic spending power of more than $600 billion per year, according to Wietck Combs. Philadelphia and Community Marketing found that for every one dollar invested in gay tourism marketing, $153 was returned in direct economic spending in shops, hotels, restaurants and attractions.

Since 2002, there has been a historic rise in gay tourism marketing. Destinations such as Philadelphia, Dallas and Ft. Lauderdale have engaged in gay tourism campaigns.

The gay cruise industry is experiencing a significant growth period. Community Marketing Inc. found in research studies that gay business travelers are 30% more likely to convert to a leisure visitor.

Philadelphia was the first destination in the world to create and air a television commercial specifically geared towards practitioners of gay tourism. Philadelphia was also the first destination to commission a research study aimed at a specific destination to learn about gay travel to a specific city.

Work is underway in conjunction with Israel's Ministry of Tourism to turn Tel Aviv into the international tourist destination for the gay-lesbian community in order to boost business in restaurants, hotels, city attraction sites and beaches. In an effort to boost gay tourism in Tel Aviv, the Gay and Lesbian Union has bid to host in Tel Aviv the 2009 Euro Pride, the largest annual gay parade in the world.

GAY TOURISM SPECIALISTS

The International Gay and Lesbian Travel Association (IGLTA) holds an annual world convention and four symposia in different tourism destinations around the world. Each symposium attracts over 100 representatives of tour agencies and travel publications that specialise in the gay and lesbian market. The association was founded in 1983, and it currently represents over 900 members. Its headquarters are in Fort Lauderdale, Florida.

The "14th International Gay & Lesbian World Travel Expo" in 2006 will visit six U.S. cities. The annual Expo series is produced by Community Marketing, a gay tourism research and travel marketing firm.

Out Traveler, from the publishers of *Out* and *The Advocate*, is a glossy magazine aimed at gay and lesbian travellers. It is published six times yearly. One of Europe's gay and lesbian travel marketing specialists is Out Now Consulting.

MEDICAL TOURISM

Medical tourism (also called **medical travel**, **health tourism** or global healthcare) is a term initially coined by travel agencies and the mass media to describe the rapidly-growing practice of traveling across international borders to obtain health care.

Such services typically include elective procedures as well as complex specialized surgeries such as joint replacement (knee/hip), cardiac surgery, dental surgery, and cosmetic surgeries. However, virtually every type of health care, including psychiatry, alternative treatments, convalescent care and even burial services are available. As a practical matter, providers and customers commonly use informal channels of communication-connection-contract, and in such cases this tends to mean less regulatory or legal oversight to assure quality and less formal recourse to reimbursement or redress, if needed.

Over 50 countries have identified medical tourism as a national industry. However, accreditation and other measures of quality vary widely across the globe, and there are risks and ethical issues that make this method of accessing medical care controversial. Also, some destinations may become hazardous or even dangerous for medical tourists to contemplate.

History

The concept of medical tourism is not a new one. The first recorded instance of medical tourism dates back thousands of years to when Greek pilgrims traveled from all over the Mediterranean to the small territory in the Saronic Gulf called Epidauria. This territory was the sanctuary of the healing god Asklepios. Epidauria became the original travel destination for medical tourism.

Spa towns and sanitariums may be considered an early form of medical tourism. In eighteenth century England, for example, medtrotters visited spas because they were places with supposedly health-giving mineral waters, treating diseases from gout to liver disorders and bronchitis.

Description

Factors that have led to the increasing popularity of medical travel include the high cost of health care, long wait times for certain procedures, the ease and affordability of international travel, and improvements in both technology and standards of care in many countries.

Medical tourists can come from anywhere in the world, including Europe, the UK, Middle East, Japan, the United States, and Canada. This is because of their large populations, comparatively high wealth, the high expense of health care or lack of health care options locally, and increasingly high expectations of their populations with respect to health care. An authority at the Harvard Business School recently stated that "medical tourism is promoted much more heavily in the United Kingdom than in the United States".

A forecast by Deloitte Consulting published in August 2008 projected that medical tourism originating in the US could jump by a factor of ten over the next decade. An estimated 750,000 Americans went abroad for health care in 2007, and the report estimated that a million and a half would seek health care outside the US in 2008. The growth in medical tourism has the potential to cost US health care providers billions of dollars in lost revenue.

A large draw to medical travel is convenience and speed. Countries that operate public health-care systems are often so taxed that it can take considerable time to get non-urgent medical care. The time spent waiting for a procedure such as a hip replacement can be a year or more in Britain and Canada; however, in New Zealand, Costa Rica, Singapore, Hong Kong, Thailand, Cuba, Colombia, Philippines or India, a patient could feasibly have an operation the day after their arrival. In Canada, the number of procedures in 2005 for which people were waiting was 782,936. Additionally, patients are finding that insurance either does not cover orthopedic surgery (such as knee/hip replacement) or imposes unreasonable restrictions on the choice of the facility, surgeon, or prosthetics to be used. Medical tourism for knee/hip replacements has emerged as one of the more widely accepted procedures because of the lower cost and minimal difficulties associated with the traveling to/from the surgery. Colombia provides a knee replacement for about $5,000 USD, including all associated fees, such as FDA-approved prosthetics and hospital stay-over expenses. However, many clinics quote prices that are not all inclusive and include only the surgeon fees associated with the procedure.

According to an article by the University of Delaware publication, UDaily:

> *"The cost of surgery in India, Thailand or South Africa can be one-tenth of what it is in the United States or Western Europe, and sometimes even less. A heart-valve replacement that would cost **$200,000** or more in the US, for example, goes for **$10,000** in India—and that includes round-trip airfare and a brief vacation package. Similarly, a metal-free dental bridge worth **$5,500** in the US costs **$500** in India, a knee replacement in Thailand with six days of physical therapy costs about one-fifth of what it would in the States, and Lasik eye surgery worth **$3,700** in the US is available in many other countries for only **$730**. Cosmetic surgery savings are even greater: A full facelift that would cost **$20,000** in the US runs about **$1,250** in South Africa."*

Popular **medical travel** worldwide destinations include: Argentina, Brunei, Cuba, Colombia, Costa Rica, Hong Kong, Hungary, India, Jordan, Lithuania, Malaysia, The Philippines, Singapore, South Africa, Thailand, and recently, Saudi Arabia, UAE, Tunisia and New Zealand.

Popular **cosmetic surgery travel** destinations include: Argentina, Bolivia, Brazil, Colombia, Costa Rica, Cuba, Mexico and Turkey. In South America, countries such as Argentina, Bolivia, Brazil and Colombia lead on plastic surgery medical skills relying on their experienced plastic surgeons. In Bolivia and Colombia, plastic surgery has also become quite common. According to the "Sociedad Boliviana de Cirugia Plastica y Reconstructiva", more than 70% of middle and upper class women in the country have had some form of plastic surgery. Colombia also provides advanced care in cardiovascular and transplant surgery.

In Europe Belgium, Poland and Slovakia are also breaking into the business. South Africa is taking the term "medical tourism" very literally by promoting their "medical safaris".

A specialized subset of medical tourism is **reproductive tourism** and **reproductive outsourcing**, which is the practice of traveling abroad to undergo in-vitro fertilization, surrogate pregnancy and other assisted reproductive technology treatments including freezing embryos for retro-production.

However, perceptions of medical tourism are not always positive. In places like the US, which has high standards of quality, medical tourism is viewed as risky. In some parts of the world, wider political issues can influence where medical tourists will choose to seek out health care.

Health tourism providers have developed as intermediaries to unite potential medical tourists with provider hospitals and other organisations. Companies are beginning to offer global health care options that will enable North American and European patients to access world health care at a fraction of the cost of domestic care. Companies that focus on medical value travel typically provide nurse case managers to assist patients with pre- and post-travel medical issues. They also help provide resources for follow-up care upon the patient's return.

Process

The typical process is as follows: the person seeking medical treatment abroad contacts a medical tourism provider. The provider usually requires the patient to provide a medical report, including the nature of ailment, local doctor's opinion, medical history, and diagnosis, and may request additional information. Certified medical doctors or consultants then advise on the medical treatment.

The approximate expenditure, choice of hospitals and tourist destinations, and duration of stay, etc., is discussed. After signing consent bonds and agreements, the patient is given recommendation letters for a medical visa, to be procured from the concerned embassy. The patient travels to the destination country, where the medical tourism provider assigns a case executive, who takes care of the patient's accommodation, treatment and any other form of care. Once the treatment is done, the patient can remain in the tourist destination or return home.

International Healthcare Accreditation

Because standards are important when it comes to health care, there are parallel issues around medical tourism, international healthcare accreditation, evidence-based medicine and quality assurance.

In the United States, the best known accreditation group is the Joint Commission International (JCI). They have been inspecting and accrediting health care facilities and hospitals outside of the United States since 1999 and are a trusted source for American medical tourists. Many international hospitals today see obtaining JCI accreditation as a way to attract American patients.

In the UK and Hong Kong, the Trent International Accreditation Scheme is a key player. The different international healthcare accreditation schemes vary in quality, size, cost, intent and the skill and intensity of their marketing. They also vary in terms of cost to hospitals and healthcare institutions making use of them. A forecast by Deloitte Consulting regarding medical tourism published in August 2008 noted the value of accreditation in ensuring quality of healthcare and specifically mentioned JCI, ISQUA and Trent.

Increasingly, some hospitals are looking towards dual international accreditation, perhaps having both JCI to cover potential US clientele and Trent for potential British and European clientele. As a result of competition between clinics for American medical tourists, there have been initiatives to rank hospitals based on patient-reported metrics

Other relevant organizations include:

- The Society for International Healthcare Accreditation (SOFIHA), a free-to-join group providing a forum for discussion and for the sharing of ideas and good practice by providers of international healthcare accreditation and users of the same.

  The primary role of this organisation is to promote a safe hospital environment for patients.

- HealthCare Tourism International, the first US-based non-profit to accredit the non-clinical aspects of health tourism, such as language issues, business practices, and false or misleading advertising prevention.

The group provides accreditation for all major groups involved in the health tourism industry including hotels, recovery facilities, and medical tourism booking agencies.

- The United Kingdom Accreditation Forum (UKAF) is an established network of accreditation organisations with the intention of sharing experience good practice and new ideas around the methodology for accreditation programmes, covering issues such as developing healthcare quality standards, implementation of standards within healthcare organisations, assessment by peer review and exploration of the peer review techniques to include the recruitment, training, monitoring and evaluation of peer reviewers and the mechanisms for awards of accredited status to organisations.
- The International Medical Travel Association, (IMTA) is the first nonprofit association formed to help address quality standards, liability issues, continuity of care, and other issues.
- Medical Tourism Association, is the second nonprofit association in the industry which focuses on transparency in quality and pricing.

Risks

Medical tourism carries some risks that locally-provided medical care does not. Some countries, such as India, Malaysia, or Thailand have very different infectious disease-related epidemiology to Europe and North America. Exposure to diseases without having built up natural immunity can be a hazard for weakened individuals, specifically with respect to gastrointestinal diseases (e.g. Hepatitis A, amoebic dysentery, paratyphoid) which could weaken progress, mosquito-transmitted diseases, influenza, and tuberculosis. However, because in poor tropical nations diseases run the gamut, doctors seem to be more open to the possibility of considering any infectious disease, including HIV, TB, and typhoid, while there are cases in the West where patients were consistently misdiagnosed for years because such diseases are perceived to be "rare" in the West.

The quality of post-operative care can also vary dramatically, depending on the hospital and country, and may be different from US or European standards. However, JCI and Trent fulfill the role of accreditation by assessing the standards in the healthcare in the countries like India, China and Thailand. Also, traveling long distances soon after surgery can increase the risk of complications.

Long flights and decreased mobility in a cramped airline cabin are a known risk factor for developing blood clots in the legs such as venous thrombosis or pulmonary embolus economy class syndrome. Other vacation activities can be problematic as well — for example, scars may become darker and more noticeable if they sunburn while healing. To minimise these problems, medical tourism patients often combine their medical trips with vacation time set aside for rest and recovery in the destination country.

Also, health facilities treating medical tourists may lack an adequate complaints policy to deal appropriately and fairly with complaints made by dissatisfied patients.

Differences in healthcare provider standards around the world have been recognised by the World Health Organization, and in 2004 it launched the World Alliance for Patient Safety. This body assists hospitals and government around the world in setting patient safety policy and practices that can become particularly relevant when providing medical tourism services.

Legal Issues

By traveling outside their home country for medical care, medical tourists may encounter unfamiliar ethical and legal issues. The limited nature of litigation in non-US countries is one reason for the lower cost of care overseas. While some countries currently presenting themselves as attractive medical tourism destinations provide some form of legal remedies for medical malpractice, these legal avenues may be unappealing to the medical tourist.

Should problems arise, patients might not be covered by adequate personal insurance or might be unable to seek compensation via malpractice lawsuits. Hospitals and/or doctors in some countries may be unable to pay the financial damages awarded by a court to a patient who has sued them, owing to the hospital and/or the doctor not possessing appropriate insurance cover and/or medical indemnity.

However new insurance products are available that protect the patient should an alleged medical malpractice occur overseas.

Ethical Issues

There can be major ethical issues around medical tourism. For example, the illegal purchase of organs and tissues for transplantation has been alleged in countries such as India and China.

Medical tourism may raise broader ethical issues for the countries in which it is promoted. For example in India, some argue that a "policy of 'medical tourism for the classes and health missions for the masses' will lead to a deepening of the inequities" already embedded in the health care system. In Thailand, in 2008 it was stated that, "Doctors in Thailand have become so busy with foreigners that Thai patients are having trouble getting care".

Employer-sponsored Health care in the US

More and more U.S. employers are looking into medical travel programs as a viable healthcare benefit option for their employees. The most compelling reasons for this include its promise of offering patients more quality healthcare options at a fraction of the cost of that within the U.S., the ability to compete better globally, ability to improve employee retention and satisfaction, and because it can be seamlessly integrated into the employer's existing health benefit plan design at no cost.

A few US employers have started offering incentives in their employee benefit packages, such as paying for air travel and waiving out-of-pocket expenses for care outside of the US. For example, in January 2008, Hannaford Bros., a supermarket chain based in Maine, began paying the entire medical bill for employees to travel to Singapore for hip and knee replacements, including travel for the patient and companion. Medical travel packages can integrate with all types of health insurance, including limited benefit plans, preferred provider organizations and high deductible health plans.

Insurers are beginning to establish partnerships with overseas health providers to treat their insureds as well. A 2008 article in *Fast Company* discusses the globalization of healthcare and describes how various players in the US healthcare market have begun to explore it.

Subfields

Dental

Dental tourism involves individuals seeking dental care outside of their local healthcare systems.

Fertility

Fertility tourism is the practice of traveling to another country for fertility treatments. The main reasons for fertility tourism are legal regulation of the sought procedure in the home country, or lower price. In-vitro fertilization, donor insemination and surrogacy are major procedures involved.

Destinations

Africa and Middle East

Countries in this region involved in medical tourism include Brunei, Saudi Arabia, South Africa, and Tunisia.

Israel

Israel is emerging as a popular destination for medical tourists. In 2006, 15,000 foreigners travelled to the country for medical·procedures, bringing in $40 million of revenue. Medical tourists choose Israel for several reasons. Some come from European nations such as Bulgaria where certain procedures are not available. Others come to Israel, perhaps most commonly from the US, because they can receive quality health care at a fraction of the cost it would be at home, for both surgeries and in-vitro fertilization treatments. Other medical tourists come to Israel to visit the Dead Sea, a world-famous therapeutic resort. The Israel Ministry of Tourism and several professional medical services providers have set out to generate awareness of Israel's medical capabilities.

Jordan

Jordan is an emerging medical tourism destination, with related revenues exceeding one billion dollars in 2007. More 250,000 patients from other countries sought treatment in Jordan that year. This included an estimated 45,000 Iraqis and approximately 25,000 patients each from Palestine and Sudan. An estimated 1,800 US citizens, 1,200 UK citizens, and 400 Canadians also sought treatment in Jordan that year. Treatment costs can be as low as 25 percent of costs in the US. The kingdom was rated as number one in the region and fifth in the world as a medical tourism hub in a study by the World Bank.

UAE

Hospitals in Dubai and other emirates have expressed an intent to develop in medical tourism. Some have American-sourced international healthcare accreditation, while others are looking towards the UK, Australia and Canada for accreditation services.

The Americas

Countries in the Americas that are treating foreign patients include Argentina, Bolivia, Colombia, Costa Rica, and the Dominican Republic.

Brazil

Brazil has long been known as a destination for cosmetic surgery. For non-cosmetic procedures, Brazil is only now entering the global market. However, Albert Einstein Jewish Hospital in São Paulo was the first JCI-accredited facility outside of the US, and more than a dozen Brazilian medical facilities have since been similarly accredited. Brazil requires visas for Americans based on a reciprocal arrangement since Brazilians are required to obtain a visa to visit the US.

Canada

Canada has entered the medical tourism field. In comparison to US health costs, medical tourism patients can save 30 to 60 percent on health costs in Canada. Canada's quality of healthcare is cited by the World Health Organization as equal to if not better than that of the US in most categories.

Cuba

Cuba has been a popular medical tourism destination for more than 40 years. Thousands of patients travel to Cuba, particularly from Latin America and Europe, attracted by the "fine reputation of Cuban doctors, the low prices and nearby beaches on which to recuperate." In 2006, Cuba attracted nearly 20,000 health tourists.

Medical treatments included joint replacement, cancer treatment, eye surgery, cosmetic surgery and addictions rehabilitation. Costs are about 60 to 80 percent less than US costs.

Cuba has hospitals for Cuban residents and others that focus on serving foreigners and diplomats. In the 2007 American documentary film, "Sicko," which criticizes the US healthcare system, producer Michael Moore leads a group of uninsured American patients to Cuba to obtain more affordable medical treatment. "Sicko" has greatly increased foreigners' interest in Cuban healthcare. A recent Miami Herald story focused on the high quality of health care that Canadian and American medical tourism patients receive in Cuba.

The Cuban government has developed Cuban medical tourism to generate income for the country. Residents of Canada, the UK and most other countries can travel to Cuba without any difficulty; a tourist visa is generally required. For Americans, however, because of the US trade policy towards Cuba, travelers must either obtain US government approval, or, more frequently, travel to Cuba from Canada, Mexico, the Bahamas, Jamaica or the Dominican Republic. Cuban immigration authorities do not stamp the passports of US visitors so that Americans can keep their travels a private matter.

To date no Cuban facility has achieved JCI Accreditation.

Mexico

Americans, particularly those living near the Mexican border, now routinely cross to Mexico for medical care. Popular specialties include dentristry and plastic surgery. Mexican dentists often charge one-fifth to one-fourth of US prices, while other procedures typically cost a third what they would in the US.

This trend has alarmed American healthcare providers who, fearing a loss of business, warn patients away from Mexico. "The phenomenon has unsettled US-based dentists who tell horror stories of rampant infections, undetected cases of oral cancer and shoddy work south of the border", claims hotly disputed by Mexican dentists. "In Texas, legislators explored the possibility of allowing health maintenance organizations to operate on both sides of the border. However, physicians in south Texas lobbied against the changes, arguing that local doctors could not compete with the lower costs in Mexico". US doctors point out that the Mexican legal system makes it almost impossible to sue Mexican doctors for malpractice.

However, many who travel to Mexico for care report that they are satisfied. According to a report commissioned by Families U.S.A., a Washington advocacy group for health-care issues, "About 90 percent feel the care they had received in Mexico had been good or excellent. About 80 percent rated the care they had received in the United States as good or excellent".

Indeed "some U.S. dentists ... have conceded to the competition and begun a 'reverse migration' opening offices in Mexico to take advantage of lower costs". More American insurers are providing coverage for travelers, as the out-of-pocket costs to them are much lower. "With healthcare costs in the United States continuing to rise, many employers in Southern California are turning to insurance plans that send their workers to Mexico for routine care, plans that are growing by nearly 3,000 people a year". In addition to dental and plastic surgery, Mexican hospitals are popular for bariatric surgery for weight loss, considered an elective procedure that is not covered by some US insurers. A popular bariatric procedure, lap band surgery, which was approved by the FDA in the US in 2001, has been performed for longer by Mexican surgeons.

Panama

In Panama, health and medical tourism is growing rapidly. Factors drawing medical tourists include Panama's tourist appeal, position as a hub for international travel, and use of the American dollar as the official currency. Many of Panama's doctors are bilingual, board certified, and accustomed to working with the same medical equipment and technology used in the United States and Europe. On most procedures, Panama offers savings of more than 50% compared to the US and Europe. No Panamanian hospitals currently have international healthcare accreditation, whether through US, British, Australian or Canadian sources.

United States

Much attention has been given to the growing trend of U.S. citizens seeking health care in other countries. But while the trend continues, and raises important questions about why so many Americans can't afford health care at home, a new report points out that the largest segment of medical travelers are headed stateside.

The availability of advanced medical technology and sophisticated training of physicians are cited as driving motivators for growth in foreigners traveling to the U.S. for medical care. Also, it has been noted that the decline in value of the U.S. dollar is offering additional incentive for foreign travel to the U.S. However, costs differences between the US and many locations in Asia far outweigh any currency fluctuations.

Several major medical centers and teaching hospitals offer international patient centers that cater to patients from foreign countries who seek medical treatment in the U.S. Many of these organizations offer service coordinators to assist international patients with arrangements for medical care, accommodations, finances and transportation including air ambulance services. It should be noted that many locations in the US that offer medical care comparable in price to foreign medical facilities are not Joint Commission Accredited.

Uruguay

Uruguay recently entered the medical tourism market. A private medical tourism initiative, Uruhealth, has been created with support from the Ministries of Tourism and Public Health. The initiative involves the infrastructure, human resources and experience of two healthcare companies: MP Personalized Medicine (Montevideo) and SEMM-Mautone Hospital (Punta del Este).

Asia/Pacific

Many Asian Pacific countries are medical tourism destinations. In addition to the countries listed here, New Zealand is an emerging player.

China

Although not necessarily considered a destination for such procedures as cancer treatment, hip replacement or treatment for heart disease; China is becoming a destination for Westerners who want to take advantage of stem cell treatments that are still considered experimental or have yet to be approved in their home country for conditions such as paralysis.

Hong Kong

As of 2006, Hong Kong had 12 private hospitals and 39 public hospitals, providing 3,124 and 27,755 beds respectively. A wide range of health care services are offered. All 12 of Hong Kong's private hospitals have been surveyed and accredited by the UK's Trent Accreditation Scheme since early 2001. This has been a major factor in the ascent of standards in Hong Kong's private hospitals. The Trent scheme works closely with the hospitals it assesses to generate standards appropriate to the locality (with respect to culture, geography, public health, primary care interfaces etc.), and always uses combinations of UK-sourced and Hong Kong-sourced surveyors. Some of Hong Kong's private hospitals have now gone on to obtain dual international accreditation, with both Trent and JCI (and have therefore attained a standard surpassing some of the best hospitals in Thailand and Singapore). Others are looking towards dual international accreditation with Trent and the Australian group. Hong Kong public hospitals have yet to commit to external accreditation.

India

India's medical tourism sector is expected to experience an annual growth rate of 30%, making it a Rs. 9,500-crore industry by 2015. Estimates of the value of medical tourism to India go as high as $2 billion a year by 2012. Advantages for medical tourists include reduced costs, the availability of latest medical technologies and a growing compliance on international quality standards, as well as the fact that foreigners are less likely to face a language barriers in India. The Indian government is taking steps to address infrastructure issues that hinder the country's growth in medical tourism.

Most estimates claim treatment costs in India start at around a tenth of the price of comparable treatment in America or Britain. The most popular treatments sought in India by medical tourists are alternative medicine, bone-marrow transplant, cardiac bypass, eye surgery and hip replacement. India is known in particular for heart surgery, hip resurfacing and other areas of advanced medicine.

Ministry of Tourism India(MoT) is planning to extend its Market Development Assistance (MDA) scheme to cover Joint Commission International (JCI) and National Accreditation Board of Hospitals (NABH) certified hospitals. A policy announcement of this effect is likely soon. Hospital groups like Apollo Hospitalsand Fortis Healthcare have increased their presence in international market for medical tourism. The south Indian city of Chennai has been declared India's Health Capital, as it nets in 45% of health tourists from abroad and 30-40% of domestic health tourists.

Malaysia

Malaysia has ambitions to develop itself as a medical tourism hub. The country has excellent hospitals, English is widely spoken, and many staff have been trained to a high level in the UK or in the US. There is a highly active Association for Private Hospitals of Malaysia working to develop medical tourism. However, while Malaysia has a national accreditation scheme (MSQH), few of Malaysia's hospitals currently hold international healthcare accreditation, whether British, American or Australian.

Philippines

The Philippines has been growing as a destination for medical tourism. The US Medical Tourism Association magazine reported that this services sub-sector grew 8.0% in 2007. The

Philippines is one of a few countries that sends qualified physicians and dentists to the US, a testament to its quality of medical education.

Procedures can be performed at a fraction of the amount that a patient would spend on the same procedure in the US or Europe. Some medical centers are accredited by the American accreditation group Joint Commission International (JCI).

Singapore

Singapore has a dozen hospitals and health centers with JCI accreditation. In 1997 (published 2000), the World Health Organization ranked Singapore's health care system sixth best in the world and the highest ranked system in Asia. Singapore has close political links to the USA.

"SingaporeMedicine" is a multi-agency government-industry partnership committed to strengthening Singapore's position as a medical hub and promoting Singapore as a destination for advanced patient care. Patients come from neighboring countries, such as Indonesia and Malaysia, and patient numbers from Indochina, South Asia, the Middle East and Greater China are growing.

Patients from developed countries such as the United States and the UK are also beginning to choose Singapore as their medical travel destination for relatively affordable health care services in a clean cosmopolitan city.

Taiwan

The Taiwanese government has declared its determination for the country to become a medical tourism center. It is estimated that the government will contribute NT$44.4 million to construct a platform for the collaboration of the government and the medical sector in promoting medical tourism.

Costs for procedures remain comparatively low. Taiwan is known for liver transplants, bone marrow transplants, and reconstructive and plastic surgery.

Thailand

Medical tourism has been a growing segment of Thailand's tourism and health-care sectors. In 2005, one Bangkok hospital took in 150,000 treatment seekers from abroad. In 2006, medical tourism was projected to earn the country 36.4 billion baht.

Treatments for medical tourists in Thailand range from cosmetic, organ transplants and orthopaedic treatments to dental and cardiac surgeries. Treatments also include spa, physical and mental therapies. Thailand offers everything from cardiac surgery to organ transplants at a price much lower than the US or Europe. Thai medicine also features a higher, more personalized level of nursing care than westerners are accustomed to receiving in hospitals at home. One patient who received a coronary artery bypass surgery at Bumrungrad International hospital in Bangkok said the operation cost him US$12,000 (8,200 euros), as opposed to the $100,000 (68,000 euros) he estimated the operation would have cost him at home. Bumrungrad treated approximately 55,000 American patients in 2005 alone, a 30% increase from the previous year.

Hospitals in Thailand are a popular destination for other Asians. Bangkok Hospital, which caters to medical tourists, has a Japanese wing, and Phyathai Hospitals Group has interpreters for over 22 languages, besides the English-speaking medical staff. When Nepal Prime Minister Girija Prasad Koirala needed medical care in 2006, he went to Bangkok.

Today many Thai physicians hold US or UK professional certification. One Thai hospital, Bumrungrad International, states that many of its doctors and staff are trained in the UK, Europe and the US. Bumrungrad International was accredited most recently in 2005 by an American group in order to ensure an international standard of medical services. Some of the country's major hospitals also have achieved other accreditations, and some have achieved certification by the International Organization for Standardization's ISO 9001:2000 (However, ISO not an accreditation scheme). The US consular information sheet gives the Thai health care system high marks for quality, particularly facilities in Bangkok, although the World Health Organization ranks the Thai healthcare system at number 47, below the USA's ranking at 37 and the United Kingdom's ranking at 18. The UK's Foreign and Commonwealth

Office web site states "There are excellent international hospitals in Bangkok but they can be expensive". Serious political problems during late 2008, including mass demonstrations and the complete closure of major airports, have made travel to Thailand less appealing than in the past, and the US State Department web site has expressed concerns about the country.

Europe

Countries in Europe that have active medical tourism sectors include Cyprus, Germany, Hungary, Lithuania, Malta, Poland, Portugal, Czech Republic, Slovakia, Spain, and Ukraine.

Poland

Since 2004, when Poland joined the European Union, it has become another locale for people seeking cheaper medical treatments. The quality of care in Poland must comply with EU standards. One well-known medical center in Poland is The Clinical Hospital No. 10 and Polyclinic in Bydgoszcz City.

Turkey

Turkey has attracted medical tourists from Europe and is seeking to build on its geothermal resources with expansion of therapeutic spas. German Hospital in Istanbul operates the country's first ISO-certified IVF center, while Memorial Hospital was the first private hospital to receive American JCI accreditation. Since then, over 15 hospitals have achieved Joint Commission International accreditation.

TOURISM DEVELOPMENT OVERVIEW

Advantages and Disadvantages of Tourism Development

The pros and cons of tourism development in rural America are varied. Tourism provides income and diversification to rural communities. Most of the dollars generated from outside visitors stay within the local economy.

In addition to gains from direct sales to visitors, many indirect benefits are realized from tourism. Visitors contribute to the tax revenues collected and can influence the quality of life by financing community facilities such as swimming pools, golf courses, restaurants, and shopping facilities.

Community events intended for tourists, also attract local residents. Many potential industries prefer locations that provide high quality services and recreational resources. If the community is a pleasant place, the visitors may become a permanent resident.

Tourism offers other indirect benefits. For example, the need to provide services to tourists creates new jobs in the community. Although they may not be high paying employment opportunities, these jobs satisfy the need of students and dual-earning families for part-time or seasonal employment.

On the other hand, developing and maintaining the tourist industry in a community requires added costs and puts pressure on public services. The cost of surveys, impact analysis, promotions, insurance, fund raising, and operations are some points to consider.

Managing Resources Requires Planning

Advanced planning maximizes the advantages and minimizes the disadvantages of developing rural tourism.

Tips and Technologies

Many communities can develop tourism into a major industry using these techniques:

- Understand the potential for tourism development
- Inform and educate the community to create support
- Secure investments for public and private sources
- Manage natural, human, and financial resources
- Build an image for the community

Where to Start

Leaders must first assess the potential for tourism in the community. What businesses serve travelers and how much additional revenue will it generate? Are these enough services to satisfy the potential demands? What are the goals and objectives of the community? Talk about tourism with other members of the community. Tourism requires support, and one way to gain support is by informing and educating the citizenry. Introduce the idea to the Chamber of Commerce, at civic clubs, at city council, or at other community organization meetings. The community and its leaders can broaden support for tourism by securing financial commitments from public and private sources.

Existing Resources

Managing natural, human and financial resources is an important component of tourism development. Most communities have existing resources and attractions that can draw visitors, such as:

Capitalize on Existing Resources

- natural settings
- scenery
- parks and recreations
- historical identity
- cultural identity
- ethnic identity
- volunteers
- students
- retirees
- events
- festivals
- fairs
- shops
- hotels
- local industries
- art galleries

What Does Your Community Have to Offer?

Conduct an inventory of the things that your community has to offer to tourists. Describe each type of attraction in terms of quality and quantity. Separate them by "core elements" (primary reasons tourist are attracted) and "secondary elements" (supporting resources; those that contribute positively to the tourists' travel experience). Look ahead at the resources that might be enhanced or used more fully.

Developing a Marketing Plan

An important step in tourism planning is determining target market segments. Experts begin by defining the market areas that will draw the most visitors. They then divide the market into trip length categories. Finally, they define the clientele that will be attracted to the community. Use the chart below as a guide: When the expert has determined the market segments, leaders of the community are ready to make a written marketing plan. This plan helps them to see the best combination of marketing strategies, prices, places and promotions to use. Which characteristics are unique to the community? Using the plan, the leaders are able to develop a theme that ties the community's businesses and services together.

It is important to involve all facets of the community in the decision making process. Remember that everyone and everything the visitor has contact with projects and promotes something about the community.

Keep your promotional messages short and targeted to the community theme. Use your theme to promote your community:

- on brochures, billboards, posters
- on t-shirts, hats, stickers, coupons
- at demonstrations, contests, the library
- for public announcements on television, radio or community calendars

Surveys and Models

Surveys and models are used in the process of tourism planning to determine:

- Community attitudes toward tourism
- Recreational use value and demand
- Tourism patterns
- Travel costs
- Economic impacts

Types of survey methods include telephone interviews, questionnaires, and mall interviews.

Telephone interview are low in cost, and provide a quick turn-around. In order to simplify the responses, the interviewer offers a minimum number of choices to each question in the survey. The interviewer also sends a letter before the call is made to state the date and time of the survey and ask the customer's cooperation.

Questionnaires can be used to identify the different types of tourists, or market segments. The surveyor lists responses that can be checked off by the visitor. This type of response is easy to tabulate. The survey may include questions that ask:

- Where does the visitor live?
- What attracts the visitor to the community?
- How does the visitor find out about tourist attractions?
- What type of businesses/facilities does the visitor use?
- What kinds of accommodations/services are needed?

The survey tests the questionnaire to determine the typical responses and to modify the questions.

Face-to-face interviews are useful if visual aids are necessary, for instance, in evaluating what promotional materials are pleasing to the consumer. These interviews are conducted at a central location, such as in a shopping mall.

9

Tourism Culture

INTRODUCTION

The inhabitants of the UK have been drinking ale since the Bronze Age, but it was with the arrival of the Romans and the establishment of the Roman road network that the first Inns called tabernae, in which the traveller could obtain refreshment, began to appear. By the time the Romans had left, the Anglo-Saxons had formed alehouses that grew out of domestic dwellings. The Saxon alewife would put a green bush up on a pole to let people know her brew was ready. These alehouses formed meeting houses for the locals to meet and gossip and arrange mutual help within their communities. Here lies the beginnings of the modern pub. They became so commonplace that in 965 King Edgar decreed that there should be no more than one alehouse per village.

A traveller in the early Middle Ages could obtain overnight accommodation in monasteries, but later a demand for hostelries grew with the popularity of pilgrimages and travel. The Hostellers of London were granted guild status in 1446 and in 1514 the guild became the Worshipful Company of Innholders.

Traditional English ale was made solely from fermented malt. The practice of adding hops to produce beer was introduced from the Netherlands in the early 15th century. Alehouses would each brew their own distinctive ale, but independent breweries began to appear in the late 17th century. By the end of the century almost all beer was brewed by commercial breweries.

The 18th century saw a huge growth in the number of drinking establishments, primarily due to the introduction of gin. Gin was brought to England by the Dutch after the Glorious Revolution of 1688 and started to become very popular after the government created a market for grain that was unfit to be used in brewing by allowing unlicensed gin production, whilst imposing a heavy duty on all imported spirits. As thousands of gin-shops sprang up all over England, brewers fought back by increasing the number of alehouses. By 1740 the production of gin had increased to six times that of beer and because of its cheapness it became popular with the poor, leading to the so-called Gin Craze. Over half of the 15,000 drinking establishments in London were gin-shops.

The drunkenness and lawlessness created by gin was seen to lead to ruination and degradation of the working classes. The distinction was illustrated by William Hogarth in his engravings *Beer Street* and *Gin Lane*. The Gin Act (1736) imposed high taxes on retailers but led to riots in the streets. The prohibitive duty was gradually reduced and finally abolished in 1742. The 1751 Gin Act however was more successful. It forced distillers to sell only to licensed retailers and brought gin-shops under the jurisdiction of local magistrates.

A pub that offers lodging may be called an inn or (more recently) hotel in the UK. Today many pubs in the UK, Canada and Australia with the word "inn" or "hotel" in their name no longer offer accommodation, or in some cases have never done so. Some pubs bear the name of "hotel" because they are in countries where stringent anti-drinking laws were once in force. In Scotland until 1976, only hotels could serve alcohol on Sundays.

Overview

There are approximately 57,500 public houses in the United Kingdom, with at least one in almost every city, town and village. In many places, especially in villages, a pub can be the focal point of the community, playing a complementary role to the local church in this respect. The writings of Samuel Pepys describe the pub as the heart of England and the church as its soul.

Public houses are culturally and socially different from places such as cafés, bars, bierkellers and brewpubs.

Pubs are social places based on the sale and consumption of alcoholic beverages, and most public houses offer a range of beers, wines, spirits, alcopops and soft drinks. Many pubs are controlled by breweries, so beer is often better value than wines and spirits, while soft drinks can be almost as expensive. Beer served in a pub may be cask ale or keg beer. All pubs also have a range of non-alcoholic beverages available. Traditionally the windows of town pubs are of smoked or frosted glass so that the clientèle is obscured from the street. In the last twenty years in the UK and other countries there has been a move away from frosted glass towards clear glass, a trend that fits in with brighter interior décors.

The owner, tenant or manager (licensee) of a public house is known as the publican or landlord. Each pub generally has "locals" or *regulars*; people who drink there regularly. The pub that people visit most often is called their *local*. In many cases, this will be the pub nearest to their home, but some people choose their *local* for other reasons: proximity to work, a venue for their friends, the availability of a particular cask ale, non-smoking or formerly as a place to smoke freely, or maybe a darts team or pool table.

Until the 1970s most of the larger public houses also featured an off-sales counter or attached shop for the sales of beers, wines and spirits for home consumption. In the 1970s the newly built supermarkets and high street chain stores or off-licences undercut the pub prices to such a degree that within ten short years all but a handful of pubs had closed their off-sale counters.

A society with a particular interest in British beers, ales and the preservation of the 'integrity' of the public house is Campaign for Real Ale, (CAMRA).

Another organisation, lauched in Dorset (initially) in 2009 is Community Alert on Pubs which seeks to prevent the closure of pubs which form part of the rural social fabric. A particular concern has been the practice of closing a pub and leaving it derelict as an eyesore until such time as the local authority may (or may not) grant a change of use e.g. for residential property development.

Beer Houses and the 1830 Beer Act

By the early 1800s and encouraged by a lowering of duties on gin, the gin houses or "Gin Palaces" had spread from London to most major cities and towns in Britain, with most of the new establishments illegal and unlicensed. These bawdy, loud and unruly drinking dens so often described by Charles Dickens in his Sketches by Boz (published 1835–6) increasingly came to be held as unbridled cesspits of immorality or crime and the source of much ill-health and alcoholism among the working classes.

The British government's eventual response to the problem seems strange now to modern eyes. Under a banner of "reducing public drunkenness" the Beer Act of 1830 introduced a new lower tier of premises permitted to sell alcohol, the **Beer Houses**. At the time beer was viewed as harmless, nutritious and even healthy. Young children were often given what was described as small beer, which was brewed to have a low alcohol content, to drink, as the local water was often unsafe. Even the evangelical church and temperance movements of the day viewed the drinking of beer very much as a secondary evil and a normal accompaniment to a meal. The freely available beer was thus intended to wean the drinkers off the evils of gin, or so the thinking went.

Under the 1830 Act any householder who paid rates could apply, with a one-off payment of two guineas, to sell beer or cider in his home (usually the front parlour) and even brew his own on his premises. The permission did not extend to the sale of spirits and fortified wines and any beer house discovered selling those items were closed down and the owner heavily fined. Beer houses were not permitted to open on Sundays. The beer was usually served in jugs or dispensed direct from tapped wooden barrels lying on a table in the corner of the room. Often profits were so high the owners were able to buy the house next door to live in, turning every room in their former home into bars and lounges for customers. In the first year four hundred beer houses opened but within eight years there were 46,000 opened across the country, far outnumbering the combined total of long established taverns, public houses, inns and hotels. Because it was so easy to obtain permission and the profits could be huge compared to the low cost of gaining permission, the number of beer houses was continuing to rise and in some towns nearly every other house in a street could be a Beer House. Finally in 1869 the growth had to be checked by magisterial control and new licensing laws were introduced. Only then was the ease by which permission could be obtained reduced and the licensing laws which operate today formulated.

Although the new licensing laws prevented any new beer houses from being created, those already in existence were allowed to continue and many did not fully die out until nearly the end of the 19th century. A vast majority of the beer houses applied for the new licences and became full public houses. These usually small establishments can still be identified in many towns, seemingly oddly located in the middle of otherwise terraced housing part way up a street, unlike purpose built pubs that are usually found on corners or road junctions. Many of today's respected real ale micro-brewers in the UK started as home based Beer House brewers under the 1830 Act.

The beer houses also tended to avoid the traditional public house names like *The Crown*, *The Red Lion*, *The Royal Oak* etc and, if they didn't simply name their place *Smith's Beer House*, they would apply topical pub names in an effort to reflect the mood of the times.

Licensing Laws

From the middle of the 19th century restrictions were placed on the opening hours of licensed premises in the UK. However licensing was gradually liberalised after the 1960s, until contested licensing applications became very rare, and the remaining administrative function was transferred to Local Authorities in 2005.

The Wine and Beerhouse Act 1869 reintroduced the stricter controls of the previous century. The sale of beers, wines or spirits required a licence for the premises from the local magistrates. Further provisions regulated gaming, drunkenness, prostitution and undesirable conduct on licensed premises, enforceable by prosecution or more effectively by the landlord under threat of forfeiting his licence. Licences were only granted, transferred or renewed at special Licensing Sessions courts, and were limited to respectable individuals. Often these were ex-servicemen or ex-policemen; retiring to run a pub was popular amongst military officers at the end of their service. Licence conditions varied widely, according to local practice. They would specify permitted hours, which might require Sunday closing, or conversely permit all-night opening near a market. Typically they might require opening throughout the permitted hours, and the provision of food or lavatories. Once obtained, licences were jealously protected by the licensees (always individuals expected to be generally present, not a remote owner or company), and even "Occasional Licences" to serve drinks at temporary premises such as fêtes would usually be granted only to existing licensees. Objections might be made by the police, rival landlords or anyone else on the grounds of infractions such as serving drunks, disorderly or dirty premises, or ignoring permitted hours.

Detailed records were kept on licensing, giving the Public House, its address, owner, licensee and misdemeanours of the licensees for periods often going back for hundreds of years. Many of these records survive and can be viewed, for example, at the London Metropolitan Archives centre.

These culminated in the Defence of the Realm Act of August 1914, which, along with the introduction of rationing and the censorship of the press for wartime purposes, also restricted the opening hours of public houses to 12noon–2.30pm and 6.30pm–9.30pm. Opening for the full licensed hours was compulsory, and closing time was equally firmly enforced by the police; a landlord might lose his licence for infractions. There was a special case established under the State Management Scheme where the brewery and licensed premises were bought and run by the state until 1973, most notably in the Carlisle District. During the 20th century elsewhere, both the licensing laws and enforcement were progressively relaxed, and there were differences between parishes; in the 1960s, at closing time in Kensington at 10.30 pm, drinkers would rush over the parish boundary to be in good time for "Last Orders" in Knightsbridge before 11 pm, a practice observed in many pubs adjoining licensing area boundaries. Some Scottish and Welsh parishes remained officially "dry" on Sundays (although often this merely required knocking at the back door of the pub).

However, closing times were increasingly disregarded in the country pubs. In England and Wales by 2000 pubs could legally open from 11am (12 noon on Sundays) through to 11pm (10.30pm on Sundays). That year was also the first to allow continuous opening for 36 hours from 11am on New Year's Eve to 11pm on New Year's Day. In addition, many cities had by-laws to allow some pubs to extend opening hours to midnight or 1am, whilst nightclubs had long been granted late licences to serve alcohol into the morning. Pubs in the immediate vicinity of London's Smithfield market, Billingsgate fish market and Covent Garden fruit and flower market were permitted to stay open 24 hours a day since Victorian era times to provide a service to the shift working employees of the markets. These restricted opening hours led to the tradition of lock-ins.

Scotland's and Northern Ireland's licensing laws have long been more flexible, allowing local authorities to set pub opening and closing times. In Scotland, this stemmed out of a late repeal of the wartime licensing laws, which stayed in force until 1976.

The Licensing Act 2003, which came into force on November 24, 2005, aimed to consolidate the many laws into a single act. This now allows pubs in England and Wales to apply to the local authority for opening hours of their choice. Supporters at the time argued that it would end the concentration of violence around half past 11, when people had to leave the pub, making policing easier. In practice, alcohol-related hospital admissions rose following the change in the law, with alcohol involved in 207,800 admissions in 2006/7. Critics claimed that these laws will lead to '24-hour drinking'. By the day before the law came into force, 60,326 establishments had applied for longer hours, and 1,121 had applied for a licence to sell alcohol 24 hours a day. However, nine months after the act many pubs had not changed their hours, although there is a growing tendency for some to be open longer at the weekend but rarely beyond 1:00 am.

Indoor Smoking Ban

In July 2007, a law was introduced to forbid smoking in all enclosed public places in England and Wales. Scotland had introduced the ban in April 2006. Concerns by publicans prior to the ban that a smoking ban would have a negative impact on sales appear to have come true with Wetherspoons reporting a 16% fall in profits, and Scottish & Newcastle's take over by Carlsberg and Heineken being reported as partly the result of its weakness following falling sales due to the ban.

To accommodate the remaining smokers most pubs, that have the space, have provided outdoor facilities. These can range from a simple picnic bench table with a parasol umbrella in the garden or carpark, to a purpose built brick lean-to with a tiled roof. The law states that the facility must be open on at least one side and cannot be in an area where nonsmokers have to pass while entering or leaving the pub premises. Country pubs with plenty of space and beer gardens have adapted to the changes reasonably easily, but smaller city centre pubs on the pavement edge and with no rear gardens have suffered significant losses of custom by not being able to provide a suitable smoking area.

PUB ARCHITECTURE

The Saloon or Lounge

By the end of the 18th century a new room in the pub was established: the saloon. Beer establishments had always provided entertainment of some sort — singing, gaming or a sport. Balls Pond Road in Islington was named after an establishment run by a Mr. Ball that had a pond at the rear filled with ducks, where drinkers could, for a certain fee, go out and take a potshot at shooting the fowl. More common, however, was a card room or a billiards room. The saloon was a room where for an admission fee or a higher price of drinks, singing, dancing, drama or comedy was performed and drinks would be served at your table. From this came the popular music hall form of entertainment—a show consisting of a variety of acts. A most famous London saloon was the Grecian Saloon in *The Eagle*, City Road, which is still famous these days because of an English nursery rhyme: "Up and down the City Road / In and out The Eagle / That's the way the money goes / Pop goes the weasel.". The implication being that, having frequented the Eagle public house, the customer spent all his money, and thus needed to 'pawn' his 'weasel' to get some more. The exact definition of the 'weasel' is unclear but the two most likely definitions are: that a weasel is a flat iron used for finishing clothing; or that 'weasel' is rhyming slang for a coat (*weasel and stoat*).

A few pubs have stage performances, such as serious drama, stand-up comedians, a musical band or striptease; however juke boxes and other forms pre-recorded music have otherwise replaced the musical tradition of a piano and singing.

The Public Bar

By the 20th century, the saloon, or lounge bar, had settled into a middle-class room — carpets on the floor, cushions on the seats, and a penny or two on the prices, while the public bar, or tap room, remained working class with bare boards, sometimes with sawdust to absorb the spitting and spillages, hard bench seats, and cheap beer.

Later, the public bars gradually improved until sometimes almost the only difference was in the prices, so that customers could choose between economy and exclusivity (or youth and age, or a jukebox or dartboard). During the blurring of the class divisions in the 1960s and 1970s, the distinction between the saloon and the public bar was often seen as archaic, and was frequently abolished, usually by the removal of the dividing wall or partition itself. While the names of saloon and public bar may still be seen on the doors of pubs, the prices (and often the standard of furnishings and decoration) are the same throughout the premises, and many pubs now comprise one large room. However, the modern importance of dining in pubs encourages some establishments to maintain distinct rooms or areas, especially where the building has the right characteristics for this. Yet, in a few pubs there still remain rooms or seats that, by local custom, "belong" to particular customers.

However there still remain a few, mainly city centre pubs, that retain a public bar mainly for working men that call in for a drink while still dressed in working clothes and dirty boots. They are now very much in a minority, but some landlords prefer to separate the manual workers from the more smartly dressed businessmen or diners in the lounge or restaurant.

The Snug

The "snug", also sometimes called the *Smoke room*, was typically a small, very private room with access to the bar that had a frosted glass external window, set above head height. You paid a higher price for your beer in the Snug, but nobody could look in and see you. It was not only the well off visitors who would use these rooms. The snug was for patrons who preferred not to be seen in the public bar. Ladies would often enjoy a private drink in the snug in a time when it was frowned upon for ladies to be in a pub. The local police officer would nip in for a quiet pint, the parish priest for his evening whisky, and lovers would use the snug for their clandestine visits.

The Counter

It was the public house that first introduced the concept of the bar counter being used to serve the beer. Until that time beer establishments used to bring the beer out to the table or benches. A bar might be provided for the manager to do his paperwork whilst keeping an eye on his customers, but the casks of ale were kept in a separate taproom. When the first public houses were built, the main room was the public room with a large serving bar copied from the gin houses, the idea being to serve the maximum amount of people in the shortest possible time. It became known as the public bar. The other, more private, rooms had no serving bar - they had the beer brought to them from the public bar. There are a number of pubs in the Midlands or the North which still retain this set up. But these days you fetch the beer yourself from the taproom or public bar. The most famous of these is The Vine, known locally as The Bull & Bladder, in Brierley Hill near Birmingham.

Isambard Kingdom Brunel, the British engineer and railway builder, introduced the idea of a circular bar into the Swindon station pub in order that customers were served quickly and didn't delay his trains. These island bars quickly became popular as they also allowed staff to serve customers in several different rooms surrounding the bar. In a modern renovated pub, where the partitions between rooms have been removed, the island can be clearly seen.

Beer engine

A "beer engine" is a device for pumping beer, originally manually operated and typically used to dispense beer from a cask or container in a pub's basement or cellar. It was invented by the locksmith and hydraulic engineer Joseph Bramah. Strictly the term refers to the pump itself, which is normally manually operated, though electrically powered and gas powered pumps are occasionally used; when manually powered, the term "handpump" is often used to refer to both the pump and the associated handle.

ENTERTAINMENT

Games and Sports

Traditional games are played in pubs, ranging from the well-known darts, skittles, dominoes, cards and bar billiards, to the more obscure Aunt Sally, Nine Men's Morris and ringing the bull. Betting is legally limited to certain games such as cribbage or dominoes, but these are now rarely seen. In recent decades the game of pool (both the British and American versions) has increased in popularity, other table based games such as snooker, Table Football are also common.

Increasingly, more modern games such as video games and slot machines are provided. Many pubs also hold special events, from tournaments of the aforementioned games to karaoke nights to pub quizzes. Some play pop music and hip-hop (dance bar), or show football and rugby union on big screen televisions (sports bar). Shove ha'penny and Bat and trap was also popular in pubs south of London.

Many pubs in the UK also have football teams composed of regular customers. Many of these teams are in leagues that play matches on Sundays, hence the term "Sunday League Football".

Music

While many pubs play piped pop music, the pub is often a venue for live song and live music. See:

- Pub rock - bands such as Kilburn and the High Roads, Dr. Feelgood or The Kursaal Flyers
- Pub songs from Skiffle to Danny Boy
- Folk music

The pub has also been celebrated in popular music. Examples are "Hurry Up Harry" by the 1970s punk rock act Sham 69, the chorus of which was the chant "We're going down the pub" repeated several times. Another such song is "Two Pints Of Lager and a Packet of Crisps Please!" by UK punk band Splodgenessabounds.

As a reaction against piped music, the Quiet Pub Guide was written, telling its readers where to go to avoid piped music.

Food

Traditionally pubs in England were drinking establishments and little emphasis was placed on the serving of food, usually called 'bar snacks', of which the usual fare consisted of specialised English snack food such as pork scratchings, pickled eggs, along with crisps and peanuts — salted snacks sold or given away to increase customers' thirst. If a pub served meals they were usually basic cold dishes such as a ploughman's lunch. In South East England (especially London) it was common until recent times for vendors selling cockles, whelks, mussels and other shellfish, to sell to customers during the evening and at closing time. Many mobile shellfish stalls would set up near to popular pubs, a practice that continues in London's East End.

In the 1950s most British pubs would offer "a pie and a pint", with hot individual steak and ale pies made easily on the premises by the landlord's wife. In the 1960s and 1970s this developed into the then fashionable and universal "chicken in a basket", a portion of roast chicken with chips, served on a napkin, in a small wicker basket.

The offering in Irish pubs has always been a hearty experience, with fresh local food being offered. In less well-off times this would have been a stew and some fresh soda bread but today all over the world you can enjoy the best of food locally supplied.

Since the 1990s food has become more important as part of a pub's trade and today most pubs serve lunches and dinners at the table (colloquially this is known in England as *pub grub*) in addition to (or instead of) snacks consumed at the bar. They may have a separate dining room. Some pubs serve excellent meals that can rival a good restaurant's. A pub that claims to focus on quality food (perhaps rather than necessarily on good beer) will now call itself a gastropub. The growth in importance of food, and the appeal of eating informally in a pub rather than with the formality expected in a restaurant, has led to some establishments giving all tables over to food and removing the bar stools (even though a visitor expecting a quick drink and a conversation at the bar is likely to receive short shrift at such places, there is no legal bar to such a licensed restaurant calling itself a pub).

PUB GRUB

"Pub grub" is food that is typically found in a pub. A British pub menu tends to include items such as beef and ale pie, steak and kidney pie, shepherd's pie, fish and chips, bangers and mash, hot pot, Sunday roast, ploughman's lunch, pasties. Some dishes that are quite specific to pubs include chicken or scampi in a basket, and meals served in plate-sized Yorkshire puddings. In addition, international dishes such as burgers, curry, lasagne and chilli con carne are often served.

Typically pub food is ordered at the bar and paid for in advance. Customers traditionally seat themselves, and are often given a number, or a unique table marker, to assist the barstaff in delivering their food.

Gastropub

A gastropub is a pub which specialises in high-quality food a step above the more basic "pub grub." The name is a combination of pub and gastronomy and was coined in 1991 when David Eyre and Mike Belben opened a pub called The Eagle in Clerkenwell, London. They placed emphasis on the quality of food served.

In 1393 King Richard II compelled landlords to erect signs outside their premises. The legislation stated "Whosoever shall brew ale in the town with intention of selling it must hang out a sign, otherwise he shall forfeit his ale."

This was in order to make them easily visible to passing inspectors, borough ale tasters, who would decide the quality of the ale they provided. William Shakespeare's father, John Shakespeare was one such inspector. Another important factor was that during the Middle Ages a large percentage of the population would have been illiterate and so pictures on a sign were more useful than words as a means of identifying a public house. For this reason there was often no reason to write the establishment's name on the sign and inns opened without a formal written name—the name being derived later from the illustration on the public house's sign. The earliest signs were often not painted but consisted, for example, of paraphernalia connected with the brewing process such as bunches of hops or brewing implements, which were suspended above the door of the public house. In some cases local nicknames, farming terms and puns were also used. Local events were also often commemorated in pub signs. Simple natural or religious symbols such as the 'The Sun', 'The Star' and 'The Cross' were also incorporated into pub signs, sometimes being adapted to incorporate elements of the heraldry (e.g. the coat of arms) of the local lords who owned the lands upon which the public house stood. Some pubs also have Latin inscriptions.

Other subjects that lent themselves to visual depiction included the name of battles (e.g. Trafalgar), explorers, local notables, discoveries, sporting heroes and members of the royal family. Some pub signs are in the form of a pictorial pun or rebus. For example, a pub in Crowborough, East Sussex called *The Crow and Gate* has an image of a crow with gates as wings. Most British pubs still have decorated signs hanging over their doors, and these retain their original function of enabling the identification of the public house. Today's pub signs almost always bear the name of the pub, both in words and in pictorial representation. The more remote country pubs often have stand-alone signs directing potential customers to their door.

Names

Pubs often have traditional names. A very common name is the "Marquis of Granby". These pubs were named after John

Manners, Marquess of Granby, who was the son of John Manners, 3rd Duke of Rutland) and a general in the 18th century British Army.

He showed a great concern for the welfare of his men, and on their retirement, provided funds for many of them to establish taverns, which were subsequently named after him. The name may also have gained popularity because of the novel The Pickwick Papers. In that much-loved book, Charles Dickens depicted a character, Tony Weller, who was owner (by marriage) of a pub named The Marquis of Granby.

Many names for pubs that appear nonsensical may have come from corruptions of old slogans or phrases, or of certain nobles' or politicians' names. Often, these corruptions evoke a visual image which comes to signify the pub; these images had particular importance for identifying a pub on signs and other media before literacy became widespread.

An example is the pub name *The Goat and Compasses*, which is said to be a corruption of the phrase "God encompasseth us". Another example of a mistaken pub name is the Oyster Reach pub in Ipswich, England. This pub spent several decades being called the Ostrich, before historians informed the owners of the original name.

More possible but uncorroborated corruptions include "The Bag o'Nails" (Bacchanals), "Elephant and Castle", (Infanta de Castile), "The Cat and the Fiddle" (Caton Fidele) and "The Bull and Bush", which purportedly celebrates the victory of Henry VIII at "Boulogne Bouche" or Boulogne-sur-Mer Harbour. While these corruptions are amusing there are usually more substantiated explanations available.

A too-obviously humorous name is likely to be a recent coining of a marketing executive, rather than traditional. This is especially true for names with unsubtle double-entendres or names that have elements common to all the pubs in a particular chain (eg "XXXX and Firkin").

TYPES OF PUBS

After the development of the large London Porter breweries in the 18th century, the trend grew for pubs to become tied houses which could only sell beer from one brewery (a pub not tied in this way was called a Free house). The usual arrangement for a tied house was that the pub was owned by the brewery but rented out to a private individual (landlord) who ran it as a separate business (even though contracted to buy the beer from the brewery). Another very common arrangement was (and is) for the landlord to own the premises (whether freehold or leasehold) independently of the brewer, but then to take a mortgage loan from a brewery, either to finance the purchase of the pub initially, or to refurbish it, and be required as a term of the loan to observe the solus tie. A growing trend in the late 20th century was for the brewery to run their pubs directly, employing a salaried manager (who perhaps could make extra money by commission, or by selling food).

Most such breweries, such as the regional brewery Shepherd Neame in Kent and Young's in London, control hundreds of pubs in a particular region of the UK, whilst a few, such as Greene King, are spread nationally. The landlord of a tied pub may be an employee of the brewery—in which case he would be a manager of a managed house, or a self-employed tenant who has entered into a lease agreement with a brewery, a condition of which is the legal obligation (trade tie) only to purchase that brewery's beer. This tied agreement provides tenants with trade premises at a below market rent providing people with a low-cost entry into self-employment. The beer selection is mainly limited to beers brewed by that particular company. A Supply of Beer law, passed in 1989, was aimed at getting tied houses to offer at least one alternative beer, known as a guest beer, from another brewery.This law has now been repealed but while in force it dramatically altered the industry.

The period since the 1980s saw many breweries absorbed by, or becoming by take-overs, larger companies in the food, hotel or property sectors. The low returns of a pub-owning business led to many breweries selling their pub estates, especially those in cities, often to a new generation of small chains, many of which have now grown considerably and have a national presence. Other pub chains, such as *All Bar One* and *Slug and Lettuce* offer youth-oriented atmospheres, often in premises larger than traditional pubs.

A free house is a pub that is free of the control of any one particular brewery. "Free" in this context does not necessarily mean "independent", and the view that "free house" on a pub sign is a guarantee of a quality, range or type of beer available is a mistake. Many free houses are *not* independent family businesses but are owned by large pub companies. In fact, these days there are very few *truly free* houses, either because a private pub owner has had to come to a financial arrangement with a brewer or other company in order to fund the purchase of the pub, or simply because the pub is owned by one of the large pub chains and pub companies (PubCos) which have sprung up in recent years. Some chains have rather uniform pubs and products, some allow managers some freedom. Wetherspoons, one of the largest pub chains does sell large amounts of a wide variety of real ale at low prices - but its pubs are not *specifically* "real ale pubs", being in the city centre to attract the Saturday night crowds and so also selling large quantities of alcopops and big-brand lager to large groups of young people.

Companies and Chains

Organisations such as Wetherspoons and the Eerie Pub Company, were formed in the UK since changes in legislation in the 1980s necessitated the break-up of many larger tied estates. A PubCo is a company involved in the retailing but not the manufacture of beverages, while a Pub chain may be run either by a PubCo or by a brewery. If the owning company is not a brewery, then the pub is technically a 'free house', however limited the manager is in his/her beer-buying choice.

Pubs within a chain will usually have items in common, such as fittings, promotions, ambience and range of food and drink on offer. A pub chain will position itself in the marketplace for a target audience. One company may run several pub chains aimed at different segments of the market. Pubs for use in a chain are bought and sold in large units, often from regional breweries which are then closed down. Newly acquired pubs are often renamed by the new owners, and many people resent the loss of traditional names, especially if their favourite regional beer disappears at the same time. A small number of pub chains (usually small ones) are noted for the independence they grant their managers, and hence the wide range of beers available.

Theme Pubs

Pubs that cater for a niche audience, such as sports fans or people of certain nationalities are known as **theme pubs**. Examples of theme pubs include sports bars, rock pubs, biker pubs, Goth pubs, strip pubs, and Irish pubs (see below).

In Canada the majority of theme pubs are referred to as bars, such as 'biker bar', 'sports bar', 'gay bar', 'strip bar', etc. Pubs centred on dance floors featuring DJ's or less often, live music, are usually referred to as 'dance clubs'.

In the U.S., almost all drinking establishments called "pubs" are simply bars with an Irish or British theme.

Country Pub

A "country pub" by tradition is a rural public house. However, the distinctive culture surrounding country pubs, that of functioning as a social centre for a village and countryside community, has been changing over the last thirty or so years. In the past, many rural pubs provided opportunities for country folk to meet and exchange (often local) news, while others - especially those away from village centres - existed for the general purpose, before the advent of motor transport, of serving travellers as coaching inns.

In more recent years, however, many country pubs have either closed down, or have been converted to establishments more intent on providing seating facilities for the consumption of food, than that of the local community meeting and convivially drinking. Organisations such as CAMRA (Campaign for Real Ale) show real concern that these trends be reverted before the inevitable disappearance of the country pub.

UK Pubs of Interest

Contenders for the smallest pub in the UK include:

- The Nutshell in Bury St Edmunds
- The Lakeside Inn, Southport
- The Little Gem, in Aylesford, Kent.

The largest pub in the UK is The Regal, Cambridge, converted from a former cinema.

Oldest pub contenders include:

- The Bingley Arms, Leeds
- Ye Olde Trip To Jerusalem, Nottingham
- Ye Olde Fighting Cocks, St Albans

PUBS OUTSIDE BRITAIN

Although "British" or "Irish" pubs found outside of Britain and its former areas of influence are, as previously mentioned, often themed bars owing little to the original British public house, a number of "true" pubs may be found around the world. In Denmark - a country, like Britain, with a long tradition of brewing - a number of pubs have opened which eschew "theming", and who instead focus on the business of providing carefully conditioned beer, often independent of any particular brewery or chain, in an environment which would not be unfamiliar to a British pub-goer. Some go to the considerable trouble of importing British cask ale, rather than kegs, in order to provide the full British real ale experience to their customers. This newly-established Danish interest in British cask beer and the British pub tradition is reflected by the fact that some 56 British cask beers were available at the 2008 European Beer Festival in Copenhagen, which was attended by more than 21,000 people.

In Popular Culture

Inns and taverns feature throughout English literature and poetry, from Chaucer onwards. All the major soap operas on British television feature a pub, with their 'pub' becoming a household name. The Rovers Return is the pub on *Coronation Street*, the British soap broadcast on ITV. The Queen Vić (short for the Queen Victoria) is the pub on *EastEnders*, the major soap on BBC One, while The Bull in *The Archers* and the Woolpack on *Emmerdale* are also central meeting points. The sets of each of the three major television soap operas have been visited by royalty, including Queen Elizabeth II. The centrepiece of each visit was a trip into the Rovers, the Vic or the Woolpack to be offered a drink.

Much of the plot-line in British film *Shaun of the Dead* involves the characters trying to reach their local public house, The Winchester, to escape a zombie invasion.

Another famous fictional pub is The Nag's Head featured in the BBC sitcom Only Fools and Horses. British comedian Al Murray's best-known character is a comic right-wing pub-owner, "The Pub Landlord", not necessarily a representation of the southern-English pub landlord. US president George W. Bush fulfilled his ambition of visiting a 'genuine English pub' during his November 2003 state visit to the UK when he had lunch and a pint of non-alcoholic lager with British Prime Minister Tony Blair at the Dun Cow pub in Sedgefield, County Durham.

Lock-in

A "lock-in"' is when the owner of a public house allows a number of patrons to continue staying in the pub after the legal closing time. The origin of the lock-in was a reaction to changes in the licensing laws in England and Wales in 1915, which curtailed opening hours to stop factory workers turning up drunk and harming the war effort. Since 1915 the licensing laws changed very little, leaving the United Kingdom with comparatively early closing times. The tradition of the lock in therefore remained and is on the whole a peculiarly British concept.

The attraction for many was that lock-ins were secret, a conspiracy between publican and patron. Also, they were exclusive, usually with only a few select regulars. The lock-in became a tradition. While publicans risked losing their licences by allowing them, police often turned a blind eye if things were kept low key.

As a result of the Licensing Act 2003 premises in England and Wales may apply to extend their opening hours beyond 11 pm, allowing round-the-clock drinking and removing much of the need for lock-ins.

In other areas, a "lock-in" occurs when a violent, or potentially-violent patron is removed from the premises, and the doors are deadlocked to prevent the individual(s) from re-entering, and to prevent patrons inside from leaving for a short duration so as to prevent contact with aggressors (as a measure of duty of care). During the lock-in period, it is often a traditional courtesy of the venue to provide free drinks and snacks. This practice depends on the local public liability laws and is far less common where bouncers are used.

TYPES OF RESTAURANTS

Restaurants range from unpretentious lunching or dining places catering to people working nearby, with simple food served in simple settings at low prices, to expensive establishments serving refined food and wines in a formal setting. In the former case, customers usually wear casual clothing. In the latter case, depending on culture and local traditions, customers might wear semi-casual, semi-formal, or even in rare cases formal wear.

Typically, customers sit at tables, their orders are taken by a waiter, who brings the food when it is ready, and the customers pay the bill before leaving. In finer restaurants there will be a host or hostess or even a maître d'hôtel to welcome customers and to seat them.

Other staff waiting on customers include busboys and sommeliers. Restaurants often specialize in certain types of food or present a certain unifying, and often entertaining, theme. For example, there are seafood restaurants, vegetarian restaurants or ethnic restaurants. Generally speaking, restaurants selling "local" food are simply called restaurants, while restaurants selling food of foreign origin are called accordingly, for example, a *Chinese restaurant* and a *French restaurant*.

Restaurant Regulations

Depending on local customs and the establishment, restaurants may or may not serve alcohol. Restaurants are often prohibited from selling alcohol without a meal by alcohol sale laws; such sale is considered to be activity for bars, which are meant to have more severe restrictions. Some restaurants are licensed to serve alcohol ("fully licensed"), and/or permit customers to "bring your own" alcohol (BYO / BYOB). In some places restaurant licenses may restrict service to beer, or wine and beer.

Restaurant Guides

Restaurant guides review restaurants, often ranking them or providing information for consumer decisions (type of food, handicap accessibility, facilities, etc). In 12th century Hanzhou (mentioned above as the location of the first restaurant,) signs could often be found posted in the city square listing the restaurants in the area and local customer's opinions of the quality of their food. This was an occasion for bribery and even violence. Today, restaurant review is carried out in a more civilized manner. One of the most famous contemporary guides, in Western Europe, is the Michelin series of guides which accord from 1 to 3 stars to restaurants they perceive to be of high culinary merit.

Restaurants with stars in the Michelin guide are formal, expensive establishments; in general the more stars awarded, the higher the prices. The main competitor to the Michelin guide in Europe is the guidebook series published by Gault Millau. Unlike the Michelin guide which takes the restaurant décor and service into consideration with its rating, Gault Millau only judges the quality of the food. Its ratings are on a scale of 1 to 20, with 20 being the highest.

In the United States, the Mobil Travel Guides and the AAA rate restaurants on a similar 1 to 5 star (Mobil) or diamond (AAA) scale. Three, four, and five star/diamond ratings are roughly equivalent to the Michelin one, two, and three star ratings while one and two star ratings typically indicate more casual places to eat. In 2005, Michelin released a New York City guide, its first for the United States. The popular Zagat Survey compiles individuals' comments about restaurants but does not pass an "official" critical assessment. In the United States Gault Millau is published as the *Gayot* guide, after founder Andre Gayot. Its restaurant ratings use the same 20 point system, and are all published online. The Good Food Guide, published by the Fairfax Newspaper Group in Australia, is the Australian guide listing the best places to eat. Chefs Hats are awarded for outstanding restaurants and range from one hat through three hats. The Good Food Guide also incorporates guides to bars, cafes and providers. *The Good Restaurant Guide* is another Australian restaurant guide that has reviews on the restaurants as experienced by the public and provides information on locations and contact details. Any member of the public can submit a review. Nearly all major American newspapers employ restaurant critics and publish online dining guides for the cities they serve. A few papers maintain a reputation for thorough and thoughtful review of restaurants to the standard of the good published guides, but others provide more of a listings service. More recently Internet sites have started up that publish both food critic reviews and popular reviews by the general public. This is a growing area and the market is still immature with no sites yet gaining dominant public or critical support. Several are gaining traction including Zagat.com, chowhound.com, and Fodors.com. Their major competition comes from bloggers and search engines since search engines often favor active bloggers over large somewhat static websites.

Economics

As of 2006, there are approximately 215,000 full-service restaurants in the United States, accounting for $298 billion, and approximately 250,000 limited-service (fast food) restaurants, accounting for $260 billion. There are 86,915 commercial foodservice units in Canada, or 26.4 units per 10,000 Canadians. By segment, there are:

- 38,797 full-service restaurants
- 34,629 limited-service restaurants
- 741 contract and social caterers
- 6,749 drinking places

Fully 63% of restaurants in Canada are independent brands. Chain restaurants account for the remaining 37%, and many of these are locally owned and operated franchises.

One study of new Cleveland, Ohio restaurants found that 1 in 4 changed ownership or went out of business after one year, and 6 out of 10 did so after three years. (Not all changes in ownership are indicative of financial failure.) The three-year failure rate for franchises was nearly the same.

INN

Inns are generally establishments or buildings where travelers can seek lodging and, usually, food and drink. They are typically located in the country or along a highway.

History & Origins

Found in Europe, they possibly first sprang up when the Romans built their system of Roman roads two millennia ago.

Some inns in Europe are several centuries old. In addition to providing for the needs of travellers, inns traditionally acted as community gathering places.

"Inn" in more recent times has often come to denote a business serving alcoholic beverages, especially in North America, where they are usually alcohol-serving restaurants that have never provided lodging or serviced the needs of travellers.

In Europe, it is the provision of accommodation, if anything, that now differentiates inns from taverns, alehouses and pubs. The latter tend only to supply alcohol (although in the UK the conditions of their licence sometimes require them to have a nominal supply of food and soft drinks). Inns tend to be grander and more long-lived establishments. Famous London examples include the George and The Tabard. There is however no longer a formal distinction between an inn and other kinds of establishment, and many pubs will use the name "inn", either simply because they are long established and maybe were once a Coaching inn, or to summon up a particular kind of image; however, originally an *Inn* had to provide not only food and lodging, but also stabling and fodder for the traveller's horse(s) and for fresh horses for the Mail coach.

The original functions of an inn are now usually split among separate establishments, such as hotels, lodges, and motels, all of which might provide the traditional functions of an inn but which focus more on lodging customers than on other services; public houses, which are primarily alcohol-serving establishments; and restaurants and taverns, which serve food and drink. (Hotels often contain restaurants and also often serve complimentary breakfast and meals, thus providing all of the functions of traditional inns.) In North America, the lodging aspect of the word "**inn**" lives on in hotel brand names like Holiday Inn, and in some state laws that refer to lodging operators as innkeepers.

German Language

The German words for "inn", "innkeeper", and "innkeeping" illustrate the historical importance of inns. An innkeeper is **Wirt** (a host), the inn itself is a **Wirtshaus** (a host's house), and innkeeping is **Wirtschaft**. This last word, *Wirtschaft*, has departed from its meaning as simple hospitality and is now the German term for business and the economy; the latter usage may have derived by analogy, as the word "economy" itself is the Greek term for housekeeping (from *oikos*, "house," and *nomos*, "law"). Taken one step further, economics is *Wirtschaftswissenschaft*, literally the "science of the economy," or (still more literally) the "science of innkeeping."

Inns of Court

The Inns of Court were originally ordinary inns where lawyers met to do business, but have become institutions of the legal profession in London.

TOURISM AND RESTAURANT

A **restaurant** prepares and serves food and drink to customers. Meals are generally served and eaten on premises, but many restaurants also offer take-out and food delivery services. Restaurants vary greatly in appearance and offerings, including a wide variety of cuisines and service models. A restaurant owner is called a *restaurateur*; both words derive from the French verb *restaurer*, meaning "to restore". Professional artisans of cooking are called chefs, while prep staff and line cooks prepare food items in a more systematic and less artistic fashion.

HISTORY

Islamic World

Restaurants came into existence throughout the medieval Islamic world before doing so in China. The Islamic world had "restaurants where one could purchase all sorts of prepared dishes." These restaurants were mentioned by Al-Muqaddasi (born 945) in the late 10th century.

Restaurants in medieval Islamic Spain served three-course meals, which was earlier introduced in the 9th century by Ziryab, who insisted that meals should be served in three separate courses consisting of soup, the main course, and dessert. The concept of the take-away restaurant was later developed by the Bengali Muslim entrepreneur Sake Dean Mahomed

(1759–1851). After migrating to England, he founded the Hindoostanee Coffee House in 1810. It was an Indian curry house that operated on George Street, Central London.

China

Food catering establishments which may be described as restaurants were known since the 11th century in Kaifeng, China's northern capital during the first half of the Song Dynasty (960–1279). With a population of over 1 million people, a culture of hospitality and a paper currency, Kaifeng was ripe for the development of restaurants.

Probably growing out of the tea houses and taverns that catered to travellers, Kaifeng's restaurants blossomed into an industry catering to locals as well as people from other regions of China. Stephen H. West argues that there was a direct correlation between the growth of restaurant businesses and institutions of theatrical stage drama, gambling, and prostitution which served the burgeoning merchant middle class during the Song. Restaurants catered to different styles of cuisine, price brackets, and religious requirements. Even within a single restaurant much choice was available, and people ordered the entree they wanted from written menus. An account from 1275 writes of Hangzhou, the capital city for the last half of the dynasty:

> *"The people of Hangzhou are very difficult to please. Hundreds of orders are given on all sides: this person wants something hot, another something cold, a third something tepid, a fourth something chilled; one wants cooked food, another raw, another chooses roast, another grill".*

The restaurants in Hangzhou also catered to many northern Chinese who had fled south from Kaifeng during the Jurchen invasion of the 1120s, while it is also known that many restaurants were run by families formerly from Kaifeng.

Ma Yu Ching's Bucket Chicken House was established in Kaifeng in 1153 AD during the Jurchen-controlled Jin Dynasty (though documentation does not exist to prove continuous service) and is still serving meals today.

Western World

In the West, while inns and taverns were known from antiquity, these were establishments aimed at travellers, and in general locals would rarely eat there. Restaurants, as businesses dedicated to the serving of food, and where specific dishes are ordered by the guest and generally prepared according to this order, emerged only in the 18th century. According to the Guinness Book of Records, the Sobrino de Botin in Madrid, Spain, is the oldest restaurant in existence today. It opened in 1725. Another claim to be the world's oldest restaurant is made by Stiftskeller St. Peter in Salzburg, which has been in existence since 803 AD, since the time of emperor Charlemagne.

The term *restaurant* (from the French *restaurer*, to restore) first appeared in the 16th century, meaning "a food which restores", and referred specifically to a rich, highly flavoured soup. It was first applied to an eating establishment in around 1765 founded by a Parisian soup-seller named Boulanger. The first restaurant in the form that became standard (customers sitting down with individual portions at individual tables, selecting food from menus, during fixed opening hours) was the Grand Taverne de Londres (the "Great Tavern of London"), founded in Paris in 1782 by a man named Antoine Beauvilliers, a leading culinary writer and gastronomic authority who achieved a reputation as a successful restaurateur. He later wrote what became a standard cookbook, *L'Art du cuisinier* (1814).

Restaurants became commonplace in France after the French Revolution broke up catering guilds and forced the aristocracy to flee, leaving a retinue of servants with the skills to cook excellent food; whilst at the same time numerous provincials arrived in Paris with no family to cook for them. Restaurants were the means by which these two could be brought together — and the French tradition of dining out was born.

A leading restaurant of the Napoleonic era was the Véry, which was lavishly decorated and boasted a menu with extensive choices of soups, fish and meat dishes, and scores of side dishes. Balzac often dined there. Although absorbed by a neighboring business in 1869, the resulting establishment Le Grand Véfour is still in business. The restaurant described by Britannica as the most illustrious of all those in Paris in the 19th century was the Café Anglais (the "English coffee-shop") on the Boulevard des Italiens, showing for a second time the high regard that Parisians evidently had for London, England, and the English — at least when it came to naming their restaurants.

Restaurants then spread rapidly across the world, with the first in the United States (*Jullien's Restarator*) opening in Boston in 1794. The oldest restaurant with contiguous operation in the United States, Union Oyster House is also in Boston and has been open since 1826. Most restaurants continued on the standard approach of providing a shared meal on the table to which customers would then help themselves (*Service à la française*, commonly called "family style" restaurants), something which encouraged them to eat rather quickly. Another formal style of dining, where waiters carry platters of food around the table and diners serve themselves, is known as *Service à la russe*, as it is said to have been introduced to France by the Russian Prince Kurakin in the 1810s, from where it spread rapidly to England and beyond. The familiar pattern of service where customers are given a plate with the food already arranged on it is called "American Service," though it surely did not originate in America...

HOTEL TOILET-PAPER FOLDING

Hotel toilet-paper folding is a common practice performed by hotels worldwide as a way of assuring guests that the bathroom has been cleaned, and sometimes, with more elaborate foldings, to impress or delight guests with the management's creativity and attention to detail.

The common fold normally involves creating an inverted triangle ▽ or "V" shape out of the first sheet or square on a toilet paper roll. Commonly, the two corners of the final sheet are tucked behind the paper symmetrically, forming a point at the end of the roll. More elaborate folding results in shapes like fans, sailboats, and even flowers.

Toilet-paper folding (also known as "Toilet paper origami") has attracted the attention of observers within the hotel industry and beyond it, involving both sober discussion of the practice as a marketing move as well as wry commentary with various degrees of seriousness.

Extent of Hotel Toilet-paper Folding

The practice is followed by hotels "the world over", according to Stephen Gill, a British photographer who published a book of pictures of folded hotel toilet paper from various nations. Dr. Susan Blackmore, who uses the example of hotel toilet-paper folding to illustrate the use of "memes", pointed out in the 2006 Darwin Day Lecture before the British Humanist Association that even a remote guesthouse she visited in rural Assam in India folded the first sheet on its rolls of toilet paper. Hotel toilet-paper folding is such an institution that in the horror movie *1408* it is used as one of the eerie happenings noticed by the main character — after using the toilet paper, he finds it mysteriously has been freshly folded over.

Reasons for Hotel Toilet-paper Folding

The practice is meant to assure customers that their hotel room has been cleaned, according to David Feldman, in his "Imponderables" syndicated newspaper column. Feldman reported that he had contacted "most of the largest chains of innkeepers in the country", asked why the toilet paper was folded, "and received the same answer from all". He quoted James P. McCauley, executive director of the International Association of Holiday Inns: Hotels want to give their guests the confidence that the bathroom has been cleaned since the last guest has used the room. To accomplish this, the maid will fold over the last piece of toilet paper to assure that no one has used the toilet paper since the room was cleaned. It is subtle but effective. Gill believes the practice is meant to please or impress customers: "But the neatly made bed, the folded toilet paper — all these things symbolise attention and love. Perhaps such finishing touches are also an attempt to suggest flawlessness or excellence, and so distract you from whatever failings the room may have. They create a moment of stillness."

Variations in Hotel Toilet-paper Folding

Gill found differences in the style and care of folding between hotels. One example from Tokyo, "with its tiny pleats, really stands out", according to the photographer. "Only in Japan did I find such minute attention to detail. ... The New York City example, on the other hand, is very poor quality, asymmetrical on rough, thin paper. And the Romania example is a great slab with a small, right-hand fold."

"Toilet Paper Origami" (also called "toilegami"), involves folding toilet paper, often in more elaborate shapes.

According to one hotel industry website, "Housekeepers at luxe lairs around the world are neatly folding the loose end of a partially used roll of toilet paper into a neat little bow or fan." Some hotels provide more elaborate flourishes: some apply a sticker attaching the folded end to the roll; others wrap spare rolls with a ribbon;

Thompson Hotels imprint their logo on the first square. The Eldorado Hotel in Santa Fe, New Mexico, also imprints its name and logo on the ends of its toilet paper — a practice done by supervisors checking the work of the housekeepers.

As part of a $1 billion renovation of the Fountainebleau Hotel in Miami Beach, Florida in 2006, the typical triangular fold practice was stopped as one of a number of changes in order to give customers an impression that the hotel was special. Other changes included setting policy in the way linen cocktail napkins would be folded and the shape of glass tumblers.

"We're not going to do the little pointy thing," rooms division chief Charlotte Rosenau told the *Miami Herald*. "Every hotel does that." The change in toilet-paper policy was made after Rosenau and several housekeepers crowded into a bathroom to experiment with different methods. They settled on "folding the first square in half, then resting the crease midway down the roll", according to the newspaper. "It just looks nice and clean," Rosenau explained.

The Tickle Pink Inn, a motel in Carmel Highlands, California, folds the ends of its toilet paper into fan-like designs, mirroring the folds of its bathroom washcloths. A review in the San Francisco Chronicle noted the practice as "a fancy touch".

One travel writer noted seeing toilet paper folded into flowers and sailboats at hotels in Costa Rica.

Elaborate Toilet-paper Folding Beyond Hotels

An automated toilet paper folding machine called "Meruboa" was invented in Japan. With the push of a lever, the device folds the first sheet of toilet paper into a triangle.

Elaborate wedding dresses have been made from folded toilet paper (also using glue).

Opinions on and Humor about Hotel Toilet-paper Folding

In a humorous opinion article at the Hotel Online website, Larry Mundy wrote in his "Room With a View" column, perhaps partly with seriousness: "In my experience, there are two basic types of hotels: those that have the housekeeper fold a cute little triangle into the unused end of the toilet paper, and those that don't. Call it silly, call it pointless, I call it a sure indicator of the service levels I can anticipate at the property." Mundy continued: "That tiny detail of carefully triangulated tissue tells me that someone cared, that another member of my own species was here, in this very room, within the past few hours and spared no effort to make the end of the roll both presentable and easier to grip in my time of need. I don't need to engage in frustrating roll-rotation exercises just to find the loose end. I don't need to contemplate the jagged tear-line from the last user's haste — in fact, it doesn't occur to me there was a 'last user' at all, because the roll looks neat and new." Comedian John Cleese has commented on the practice in a humorous speech: "Why? What is it for? Is it proof that your house-maid has studied origami? ... If you're a Mason, are you supposed to fold it again into some sort of rhomboid?"

A reviewer writing about the Walden Country Inn & Stables, a hotel in Aurora, Ohio, noted a "horsey theme" reflected throughout the hotel's decoration, "never overdone (except, perhaps, for the Walden horse-head logo crimped into the end of the toilet paper)".

An anonymous commentator at the Hotel Chatter website pooh-poohed the idea of elaborate toilet-paper folding, "Certainly, this is an experience that should give anyone pause. At least a moment or two to wonder what hotel industry executive dreamed up this idea (and if his colleagues laughed in the meeting where he presented it). We'd also like to know if they couldn't find something better for the housekeepers to do besides fold the toilet paper ends into clever little forms? Were they not happy with the existing hotel towel origami art?"

NIGHT AUDITOR

A **night auditor** is a hotel employee who typically handles both the duties of the front desk agent and some of the duties of the accounting department. This is necessitated by the fact that most fiscal days close at or around midnight, and the normal workday of the employees in the accounting department does not extend to cover this time of day.

In larger hotels, night auditors may work alongside other nighttime employees, such as security officers, telephone attendants, room service attendants, and bellhops. In smaller hotels and motels, the night auditor may work alone, and may even only be "on-call", meaning that once he or she completes running the daily reports, the auditor retires to an area away from the desk while remaining available to attend to unexpected requests from guests.

Qualifications

In the United States, applicants to the position of night auditor are usually required to be high school graduates who are able to communicate effectively in English. Formal training in accounting or bookkeeping is not necessary. The successful night audit candidate will be detail-oriented, have a good grasp of basic arithmetic, and have a customer service focus.

Compensation

In the United States, night auditors are usually hourly employees. The salary ranges from $7 to $20 per hour. A night auditor typically makes $0.50 to $1.00 more per hour than a front desk agent with similar experience. This pay differential is due to the shift worked (11PM-7AM) and the additional responsibilities if there is no manager on site during the shift.

Accounting Function

The night audit itself is an audit of the guest ledger. The guest ledger (or front office ledger or transient ledger) is the collection of all accounts receivable for currently registered guests.

It can also be defined as the collection of all guest folios. A folio is the account of an individual guest who is currently registered. The guest ledger is distinct from the city ledger, which a the collection of accounts receivable for non-registered guests (such as crcard companies).

One task of the night auditor is posting the day's room rate and room tax to each guest folio at the close of business (which usually occurs from midnight to 2AM). Second, the night auditor must ensure the accuracy of the charges to the guest folios. Ensuring that the sum of revenues due to accounts receivable from the various departments (ie. Food & Beverage, Rooms, gift shop) found on the department control sheets equals the sum of the charges made to the guest folios.

The closing balance of the guest folios is calculated using the night audit formula:

TODAY'S CLOSING GUEST LEDGER BALANCE = TODAY'S OPENING GUEST LEDGER BALANCE + TODAY'S CHARGES (ie. room rates, Food & Beverage, etc.) - TODAY'S CREDITS (ie. payments from guests in cash, or transfers to the city ledger)

The folios for guests who are scheduled to leave the next morning may be printed and delivered to the guests' rooms. Most hotels currently use computerized property management systems (PMS) to help perform the night audit. This has significantly reduced the amount of time required to perform the audit, as well as the arithmetic skill required of the auditor. An audit for a 1,000 room hotel can be completed in an hour with a PMS, whereas it would have taken an eight hour shift using previous generation of technology (the NCR 4200 mechanical system). Another duty of night auditors is to run daily management reports off of the PMS. These include occupancy reports and calculations of average daily rate (ADR) and revenue per available room (Revpar).

Front Desk Function

In addition to the accounting function, night auditors may also be required to perform the typical front desk functions during the graveyard shift. These functions include check-in, check-out, reservations, responding to guest complaints, coordinating housekeeping requests, and handling any emergencies that may arise.

Due to the nighttime shift, the clientele that the night auditor must deal with may be different than that of a typical front desk agent. At some properties, night auditors are known for frequent interactions with prostitutes, who tend to visit hotels at late hours for rendezvous with guests and the graveyard shift staff. Night Auditors usually work alongside a Security Officer to maintain a level of security during late-night hours for both night staff and guests.

APARTMENT HOTEL

An **Apartment Hotel** (also **ApartHotel**, **Apart Hotel** and **Apart-Hotel**) is a type of accommodation, described as "a serviced apartment complex that uses a hotel style booking system". It is similar to renting an apartment, but with no fixed contracts and occupants can 'check-out' whenever they wish.

Apartment hotels are flexible types of accommodation; instead of the rigid format of a hotel room, an apartment hotel complex usually offers a complete fully fitted apartment.

These complexes are usually custom built, and similar to a hotel complex containing a varied amount of apartments. The length of stay in these apartment hotels is varied with anywhere from a few days to months or even years. Prices tend to be cheaper than hotels. The people that stay in apartment hotels use them as a home away from home, therefore they are usually fitted with everything the average home would require.

Origins

Apartment hotels were first created in holiday destinations as accommodation for families that needed to 'live' in an apartment rather than 'stay' as they would in a hotel. The apartments would provide a 'holiday home' but generally be serviced.

Later on these apartments evolved to be complete homes, allowing occupants to do everything they would at home, such as cleaning, washing and cooking.

Services and Facilities

Essentially the apartment hotel combines the flexibility of apartment living with the service of a hotel. Many of the apartments take advantage of prime locations with panoramic views of cities seen through wall to ceiling windows. Suites usually include high quality finishes, broadband connection & interactive TV, servicing and integrated kitchen and bathroom.

High quality leather sofas in the living area and king size beds bring the hotel experience to a whole new level. Those are the luxuries, they also come with the basics: satellite or cable TV, washer, dryer, dishwasher, cooker, oven, fridge, freezer, sink, shower, bath, wardrobes, all the furnishings to be expected in a luxury home.

Extended Stay Hotels

Extended stay hotels are a type of lodging with features unavailable at standard hotels. These features are intended to provide more home-like amenities. There are currently 27 extended stay chains in North America with at least 7 hotels, representing over 2,000 properties. There is substantial variation among extended stay hotels with respect to quality and the amenities that are available. Some of the economy chains attract clientele who use the hotels as semi-permanent lodging.

Extended-stay hotels typically have self-serve laundry facilities and offer discounts for extended stays, beginning at 5 or 7 days. They also have guestrooms (or "suites") with kitchens. The kitchens include at a minimum usually: a sink, a refrigerator (usually full size), a microwave oven, and a stovetop. Some kitchens also have dishwashers and conventional ovens.

Extended stay hotels are popular with business travelers on extended assignments, families in the midst of a relocation, and anyone else in need of temporary housing. Extended stay hotels are also used by travelers who appreciate the larger space a typical suite provides.

Residence Inn is credited with popularizing the "extended stay" concept. The chain was launched in 1975 in Wichita, Kansas by Jack DeBoer, and acquired by Marriott Corporation in 1987. As of April 2005, there were over 450 Residence Inn hotels in the United States, Canada and Mexico. Jack DeBoer has jumped back in the Extended Stay market developing a concept called Value Place.

Other upscale brands of extended-stay hotels, such as Staybridge Suites which is part of the InterContinental Hotels Group, have made this segment of the lodging industry one of the fastest-growing.

One of today's most popular long term lodging brands came from the merger of Extended Stay America and Homestead Hotels. Both these chains were already well established when they combined in 2004 to become Extended Stay Hotels with over 670 owned and operated properties nationwide.

Another worldwide hotel chain, Choice Hotels International, franchisor for name brands such as Comfort Inn, Comfort Suites, Sleep Inn and Quality Inn, entered the extended stay market with their MainStay Suites brand. They proceeded to acquire the Suburban Extended Stay hotel chain in 2005, making them a sizeable extended stay system with over 150 hotels open and under development.

In the United States, a popular low-budget extended stay chain is Intown Suites. The chain, which was founded in 1988, now has nearly 140 locations in 21 states, and is distinguised for offering weekly rates much lower than many other chain lodging companies in North America. The company, however, has been criticized by many of its guests and reviewers for providing a sub-standard quality of service, poorly maintaining its properties, and treating its guests poorly.

Extended stay concept is steadily spreading throughout Europe due to increase in the number of travelers and business people visiting every year. The concept was organized by Belgium Housing and the chain of hotels covers 42 countries of Europe including all the major cities of the continent.

BOUTIQUE HOTEL

Boutique hotel is a term popularised in North America and the United Kingdom to describe intimate, usually luxurious or quirky hotel environments. Boutique hotels differentiate themselves from larger chain/branded hotels and motels by providing personalized accommodation and services / facilities. Sometimes known as "design hotels" or "lifestyle hotels", boutique hotels began appearing in the 1980s in major cities like London, New York, and San Francisco. Typically boutique hotels are furnished in a themed, stylish and/or aspirational manner. They usually are considerably smaller than mainstream hotels, often ranging from 3 to 50 guest rooms. Boutique hotels are always individual and are therefore extremely unlikely to be found amongst the homogeneity of large chain hotel groups. Guest rooms and suites may be fitted with telephony and Wi-Fi Internet, air-conditioning, honesty bars and often cable/pay TV, but equally may have none of these, focusing on quiet and comfort rather than gadgetry. Guest services are often attended to by 24-hour hotel staff. Many boutique hotels have on-site dining facilities, and the majority offer bars and lounges which may also be open to the general public. Despite this definition, the popularity of the boutique term and concept has led to some confusion about the term. Boutique hotels have typically been unique properties operated by individuals or companies with a small collection. However, their successes have prompted established multi-national hotel companies to usurp the term and/or try to establish their own brands in order to capture a market share. The most notable example is Starwood Hotels and Resorts Worldwide's W Hotels, ranging from large boutique hotels like the W Union Square NY to the W 'boutique resorts' in the Maldives to true luxury boutique hotel collections like the Bulgari collection, SLS Hotels, Thompson Hotels, Joie De Vie hotels, and The Keating Hotel, among many others.

There is some overlap between the concept of a small boutique hotel and a bed and breakfast.

In the United States, New York remains the centre of the boutique hotel phenomenon, as the original Schrager-era boutique hotels remain relevant and are joined by scores of independent and small-chain competitors, mainly clustered about Midtown and downtown Manhattan. The French Quarter and Garden District, New Orleans have several dozen boutique hotels, most of which are located in old homes or inns. These usually provide an ambience based on 19th-century antiques, artwork with New Orleans themes, vintage or reproduction furniture and decor and/or interesting historical associations. Miami and Miami Beach also have a large number of boutique hotels, mostly found along the beachfront streets Ocean Drive and Collins Drive. Most of these are in buildings from the heyday of the Art Deco period. Their attractions include the Art Deco ambiance, beach access, nouvelle and Latin cuisines and tropical-themes interior decor. Spain have boutique hotels distributed all around its geography.

The concept of boutique or design hotels has spread elsewhere outside the US. A good example is Thailand where many boutique or design hotels are sprouting, especially in resort locations, such as Phuket and Hua Hin. Boutique hotels are even now appearing in such places as Indonesia, Shanghai, Iceland, Peru and Turkey. Boutique and design hotels are becoming increasingly popular in Far Eastern cities such as Bangkok, Singapore, Hong Kong and even Beijing. Currently, there are a few publications dedicated to boutique hotels. One is boutique DESIGN magazine, which is published quarterly. Another is Deluxe Traveller Magazine, which is available in print and online. The online version can be downloaded for free at their website, www.deluxetraveller.com. Boutique hotel resources are more commonly available online. A number of sites are dedicated to boutique hotels such as Avantgarde Hotels, Chic Retreats, Epoque Hotels, Escapio, Tablet Hotels, and TemptingPlaces.com though some are purely a collection of online brochures with limited editorial content and review. There are also a number of stylized design and coffee table books highlighting various properties throughout the world.

An increasing number of hotels label themselves "boutique" nowadays forcing true boutique hotels to make focused choices to differentiate themselves. They typically promote local culture, ecology, cultural heritage, and art and choose to provide real experiences to their visitors. For example : swimming amidst Singapore's skyline (the Naumi in Singapore), sleeping in Francis Ford Coppola's villa in Belize (the Turtle Inn), releasing baby turtles in Malaysia's South-East China (Gem Island in Malaysia) sea, choosing the colour of your room in Hong Kong (the Cosmo), experiencing a carbon neutral hotel in Shanghai (the URBN), or taking Mexican cooking lessons in Peubla (Meson Sacristia de la Compania in Mexico)...

ECO HOTEL

Eco hotel is a term used to describe a hotel or accommodation that has made important environmental improvements to its structure in order to minimize its impact on the environment.

Traditionally these hotels were mostly presented as Eco Lodges because of their location, often in jungles, and their design inspired by the use of traditional building methods applied by skilled local craftsmen in areas such as Costa Rica and Indonesia. Today the term has developed to include properties in less "natural" locations that have invested in improving their "green" credentials.

An eco hotel should meet the following criterial:

- Dependence on the natural environment
- Ecological sustainability
- Proven contribution to conservation
- Provision of environmental training programs
- Incorporation of cultural considerations
- Provision of an economic return to the local community

The term is being used on a more regular basis as new websites devoted to the subject become more prominent and hotel owners are more interested in protecting the areas their guests have come to visit.

New properties are being built from sustainable resources – tropical hardwoods, local stone – and designed to better blend in with their environment. In addition they are also being run on eco-friendly principles, such as serving organic or locally grown food or using natural cooling as opposed to air conditioning, all of which is doing far more good than just asking guests to reuse their towels.

There are many ways of establishing the "green" credentials of your hotel and as there are more than 100 certification programs worldwide there is a certain amount of confusion on the subject. It is up to guests to check whether the hotel is being run on environmental principles and the best way of doing this is to research your hotel before booking.

Ecolabelling of hotels in Europe

Any tourism accommodation operator in the EU - from a large hotel chain to a small farmhouse has been able to apply for the European Eco-label since 2003. The operators must meet strict minimum standards with regard to environmental performance and health standards. These should include the use of renewable energy sources, an overall reduction in energy and water consumption, measures to reduce waste, environmental policy setting and the provision of non-smoking areas.

The first eco-labelled hotel in the European Union was the Sunwing Resort Kallithea, Rhodes Greece in 2003. **The first eco-labelled hotel on the Iberian Peninsula** (Spain and Portugal) was the Hotel Jardim Atlântico on the Portuguese island of Madeira. This hotel was built with major ecological concern and it was integrated with the landscape in order to minimize the impact of the infrastructure on the natural environment. For example, it has a biological wastewater treatment station. To build the hotel and meet the standards for eco-labelling certification was more than a challenge as the hotel is located on clifftops 480m above the Atlantic Ocean and surrounded by mountains in The Laurissilva forest which is UNESCO World Natural Heritage.

HOMESTAY

Homestay is a form of tourism and/or study abroad program that allows the visitor to rent a room from a local family to better learn the local lifestyle as well as improve their language ability. While homestays can occur in any destination worldwide, some countries do more to encourage homestay than others as a means of developing their tourism industry. Hosting a homestay participant also allows the local family to earn some additional, needed income. Having low profitability, as it is, homestay can not be regarded as strictly commercial activity, but more of cross cultural exchange. Students generally arrange a homestay with their school or educational institution, but can also informally arrange to stay with a family through social connections, and through a variety of private agencies. There are a number of online homestay agencies that connect students with hosts all over the world (usually for a nominal fee).

Types of Homestays

Homestay scenarios can range from a completely immersive family experience, to a very basic room rental. In the immersive family experience a homestay student lives, eats, and shares the majoritiy of their time in the host country with the hosts and their family. Family events such as dining out, amusement parks, camping, travel, etc. usually involve the host student who may or may not be expected to pay a portion for the participation (tickets, parking, gas, travel expenses, et al.) The student is invited to participate in Holiday festivities (Thanksgiving, Christmas, etc.) and family events (weddings, birthdays, etc.)

At the other end of the spectrum, students may simply be renting a room within a private home with minimal supervision from a host or family. Additionally, there are a working homestay agreements where a student is expected to perform duties such as yard work, farm work, babysitting, maid services - usually in exchange for accommodation fees or as part of.

Typical Contracts and Agreements

A clash of cultures can sometimes result between a homestay student and the host family. To mitigate any issues, most homestay arrangements involve a contract or written agreement between the host and student. A contract will outline what is expected of the homestay student and may include items such as;

- Chores to perform (cleaning, laundering)
- Curfews
- Use of the Internet, television
- Use of the telephone
- Guest visits
- Smoking/drinking rules

as well as the details of what is being provided by the host in terms of:

- Accommodations

- Furniture/facilities
- Meal provisions
- Transportation
- Communications (Internet, telephone)
- Entertainment (TV, radio)

Generally, a host must provide a private room for sleep and study that has a lock and a washroom must be available that is convenient for the student to use. Most other items are negotiable in terms of availability and price.

Risks for the Host

Typically, hosting a homestay student is a rich and rewarding experience that allows the sharing of cultures, information, and experience. However, studying abroad is often the first time the homestay student is away from the parents and home country. This may result in adjustment issues for the student. The host must be able to deal with separation issues, anxiety, and the like.

Scams on the internet are becoming fairly commonplace - when engaging in financial transactions that may require international payments, cheques, and money orders being sent there is always the possibility of making oneself vulnerable to scams and fraud. The host family is best to educate themselves on the issues, and protect themselves adequately through the use of a good contract.

A recent and common example of a scam perpetrated on host families plays as follows;

- Parents of a student email the host family to request a room - usually claiming to be from Europe/Asia.
- The host replies with availability and costs etc.
- The parent agrees to the fees, and offers to pay the fees up front.
- Usually some sort of family crisis arises, and the transaction must be handled with urgency.
- The parent sends payment with an overage, and aks the host to refund the excess payment.
- The host family refunds the payment.

- The initial payment (cheque, money order, etc.) bounces or is fraudulent.
- The host family has lost the money it has sent as a refund.

This scam can happen in any situation any time payment is required in the form of cheque/money order/cashiers cheque, etc. In-depth discussion on frauds of this type is beyond the scope of this article, but the host family is encouraged to exercise caution when dealing with overseas payments and transactions.

Risks for the Student/guest

There are two basic motivations for a family to engage in the operation of a homestay:

1. The family is looking to assist students, inject culture, and better understand the world and its people through a mutual exchange of traditions, knowledge and culture.
2. The family is looking to augment their income.

Usually, a family bears a healthy mix of these two reasons in opening their home to students and international visitors.

Occasionally, however, there are instances where a family, or individual, is looking only to capitalize on the financial opportunity and has little or no concern for the interests of the student. A student is encouraged to look at the history of students and guests that the family has hosted, and to ask for a reference from a student who has recently attended their homestay. If a family refuses to give a reference, a student is advised to stay away. Also, look for a contract that not only protects the interests of the homestay host, but also the interests of the student. There should be a clear listing of the obligations of both the student and host family.

VACATION RENTAL

Vacation rental is a term in the travel industry meaning renting out a furnished apartment or house on a temporary basis to tourists as an alternative to a hotel. Vacation rentals have long been a popular travel option in Europe (especially in the UK) as well as in Canada and are becoming increasingly popular across the world. They are often referred to as self-catering rentals or villa rentals. In some cities, like Barcelona, local authorities determined that vacation rentals were becoming a threat to the hotel industry and passed some legislation placing regulations and limits on the industry, while in others, such as England, Ireland, France and Spain, the government promotes and certifies holiday rentals, even offering its own program of holiday/vacation rentals.

A **vacation rental** is a fully furnished property, such as a condominium, townhome or single-family-style home, often referred to as villa rentals in Europe. The client/traveler arranges to rent the vacation rental property for a designated period of time, many rent on nightly basis similar to hotel rooms, although the more prevalent vacation rental industry practice is typically weekly rentals. A true vacation rental is not for sale to the guest; rather, the owner of the vacation rental merely allows the guest to rent the property for a predetermined length of time.

Differences between Villa/vacation Rentals and Timeshares

Consumers unfamiliar with the concept of a vacation rental may confuse it with the seemingly similar, but distinctly different, timeshare. A timeshare can still be rented as a vacation rental should an owner decide to put his owned week(s) on a vacation rental program. Many timeshare resorts offer quarter-ownership which offers the owner 13-weeks of ownership and, therefore, more weeks to offer for rental.

A timeshare is a piece of real estate—often a fully furnished condominium—that is jointly shared by multiple owners. While different types of timeshare ownerships exist, in general, each owner bears a portion of the responsibility, along with the right to a segment of time in which he or she is granted sole use of the property. Timeshare resorts allow financially qualified guests to rent and tour their unowned properties and then make those properties available to the guest for purchase. Timeshare owners can also choose to bank their week with and exchange company such as RCI, or rent the unit

Although lower rents for vacation rentals by owner were once the norm, this is not always the primary benefit. Quite often a vacation rental will feature more amenities and features, such as more space, fully-equipped kitchens, sports and beach equipment, games, DVD libraries, books, etc. Owners managing their own properties tend to be more aware of wear and tear and have better cash flow to use to maintain and upgrade the property. Perhaps the primary difference is that vacation rentals tend to offer more space and the advantage of sampling what life in one's destination is truly like for the locals.

Pros and Cons of Vacation Rentals

Vacation and villa rentals are generally appealing for many reasons, some of the foremost being cost savings, more space, and no tips, taxes or service charges that are associated with hotel rooms. Villa and vacation rentals have kitchens for cooking, living rooms for gathering together and offer the appeal of living in a real neighborhood and soaking up the rhythm of the locals. In the United States, hotels often enjoy the advantages of brand recognition, familiar reservation processes, and on-site staff for problem resolution. For a guest, booking a vacation rental may mean stepping out of that comfort zone in order to garner some of the advantages they offer. Perceived cons of vacation rentals can include having to communicate directly with the property owner, being unfamiliar with the property, lack of on-site staff, and concerns about quality or cleanliness — however, these are most often mitigated by dealing with villa or vacation rental agencies that manage vacation properties for owners and they offer many of the same services hotels offer to their guests, e.g., front desk check-in, 24-hour maintenance, in-house housekeeping, concierge service.

The benefits generally outweigh the potential negatives, with many vacation rentals offering more space (multiple bedrooms and bathrooms, separate living areas), more amenities (fully equipped kitchens, fireplaces, private hot tubs), convenient locations (on the beach, ski-in/ski-out, city centers in real neighborhoods) and greater privacy than a hotel, including the fact that many villa/vacation rentals give travelers the option of inhabiting real neighborhoods in their destination and living like the locals. As of 2006, vacation rental management has become a $10 billion industry and continues to become more popular. Vacation rentals can range from budget studio apartments to lavish, expensive private villas in the world's most desirable locations, some with pricetags of many thousands per night and all the amenities you would find in any luxury accommodation (fully staffed, private beaches, boats, chefs, cooking lessons, etc) to cater to the guests.

Vacation rentals are available in most states of the US and very prevalent in major tourist areas such as Hawaii, California, and Florida. The vacation rental market is much larger in Europe than it is in the United States as it has long been a common travel option for European travellers.

Management Companies

Many property owners contract a vacation rental management company to manage the business of their vacation rentals. These management companies market the vacation rental property, providing information and photos to guests and handling reservations and billing in the homeowner's stead. These companies also handle details such as guest check-in, housekeeping and property maintenance.

The largest vacation rental property management company in the United States represents nearly 17,000 vacation rental properties and there are many such specialty agencies throughout the world. Guests who book through vacation rental management companies may experience benefits including quality control, housekeeping services, professional reservations agents and on-site or on-call staff.

Many such companies are members of the Vacation Rental Managers Association and there are additionally many rental property management companies that deal only with vacation rental brokers/agencies that specialize in the villa/vacation rental industry.

Listing Services and Aggregators

There are numerous agencies that specialize in villa/ vacation rentals and most can be booked via the internet. Reputable vacation rental agencies will have familiarity with the regions and properties they represent as well as official booking/rental agreements and generally standardized booking procedures, cancellation policies, key collection, etc.

Additionally, vacation rentals may be offered through aggregation portals. Aggregators typically display property information and photos provided by the homeowner, however the listing services bear no legal responsibility for the accuracy of the information. Also, because the listing services do not verify the information guests are encouraged to request references from past renters and to procure a lease agreement prior to sending money directly to a homeowner.

A vacation rental may not be booked directly with a listing service. Because each property owner has his or her own deposit and payment requirements, cancellation policies, key-pick-up procedures, etc., a guest must contact the property owner or owner's agent directly in order to book. A guest who books through a listing service or direct from owner may experience the benefit of lower rental rates.

CONCIERGE

A **concierge** is an employee who lives on the premises of apartment buildings and serves as a general property caretaker; while the phenomenon and the term are most common in France, they can be seen elsewhere, for example in the French-influenced neighborhood of Heliopolis in Cairo, Egypt. A similar position, known as the *portera*, exists in Spanish-speaking regions. In medieval times, the concierge was an officer of the King who was charged with executing justice, with the help of his bailiffs. The term concierge evolved from the French *Comte Des Cierges*, The Keeper of the Candles, who tended to visiting nobles in castles of the medieval era.

In 19th century and early 20th century apartment buildings, particularly in Paris, the concierge often had a small apartment on the ground floor and was able to monitor all comings and goings. However, such settings are now extremely rare; most concierges in small or middle-sized buildings have been replaced by the part-time services of door-staff. These are less costly and less intrusive. Some larger apartment buildings or groups of buildings retain the use of a concierge. The concierge may, for instance, keep the mail of absented dwellers; be entrusted with the keys of apartments in cases of emergencies in the absence of the inhabitant; and perform other tasks.

In hotels, a concierge assists guests with various tasks like making restaurant reservations, arranging for spa services, recommending nightclubs, finding escorts, procurement of tickets to special events and assisting with various travel arrangements and tours of interesting places to visit. In upscale establishments, a concierge is often expected to "achieve the impossible", dealing with any request a guest may have, no matter how strange, relying on an extensive list of personal contacts with various local merchants and service providers.

Hotel concierge staff have their own professional association, called Les Clefs d'Or ("The Golden Keys"). It was formed in France in October 1929. It now reaches over 3000 members in over 50 countries. Members can be distinguished by the gold keys they display on their lapels.

In hospitals, concierge services are becoming more and more available. A concierge in hospital will provide similar services to those of a concierge in a hotel, however rather than just serving a guest, they are serving patients and employees as well. This adds a huge benefit to the employees of hospitals who work long shifts, and helps to provide work-life balance.

Personal concierge services are also available that allow clients to "buy back" their precious time. A personal concierge works on the most basic of premise: people want things done and just don't have the time to do them.

Today there are numerous independently owned and operated concierge companies. Many of these companies provide errand services, as well as informational services for their members. Services include informational requests, setting dinner reservations, making telephone calls, researching travel arrangements and more.

Typically, concierge companies will bill on an hourly rate, and depending upon the type of task at hand fees can fluctuate drastically. Other companies bill a flat monthly fee based upon the number of requests a member is allowed to place each month. This service offering is also know as lifestyle management. The number of independently owned concierge companies has skyrocketed as the start up costs and barriers of entry are quite feasible for many entrepreneurs. Concierges also entertain their clients.

The owners and operators of concierge and errand service businesses are supported and advocated by the non-profit International Concierge and Errand Association and the National Concierge Association. These associations serve their members through essential resources, continuing education, networking opportunities and other professional endeavors.

CATERING

Catering is the business of providing foodservice at a remote site.

Catering Officers on Ships

Merchant ships often carry Catering Officers - especially ferries, cruise liners and large cargo ships. In fact, the term "catering" was in use in the world of the merchant marine long before it became established as a land-bound business. The "Careers Scotland" website 1 gives the following definition of a Catering Officer's duties:

Merchant Navy catering officers oversee the purchase, preparation and serving of food and drink to crew members and passengers. They are also responsible for accommodation services, including the provision of linen, bedding and laundry. They may be in overall charge of administration, organising record keeping, wage payment, and the interpretation of customs and immigration records that apply while the ship is in port.

On larger ships, responsibilities may be shared with the purser, who looks after passengers' comfort and facilities such as banking and shopping, while the catering officer concentrates on organising stores, overseeing the preparation of menus and meals and generally managing dining rooms and services. On a cruise liner, catering officers may be known as 'hotel services managers'.

Merchant Navy officers sometimes work in difficult and uncomfortable conditions. They spend long periods of time away from family and friends.

Mobile Catering

A mobile caterer serves food directly from a vehicle or cart that is designed for the purpose. Mobile catering is common at outdoor events (such as concerts), workplaces, and downtown business districts.

Event Catering

Event ranges from box-lunch drop-off to full-service catering. Caterers and their staff are part of the food service industry.

When most people refer to a "caterer", they are referring to an event caterer who serves food with waiting staff at dining tables or sets up a self-serve buffet. The food may be prepared on site, i.e., made completely at the event, or the caterer may choose to bring prepared food and put the finishing touches on once it arrives.

The event caterer staff are not responsible for preparing the food but often help set up the dining area. This service is typically provided at banquets, conventions, and weddings. Any event where all who attend are provided with food and drinks or sometimes only hors d'oeuvres is often called a *catered event*.

Many events require working with an entire theme or color scheme. A catering company or specialist is expected to know how to prepare food and to make it attractive. As such, certain catering companies have moved toward a full-service business model commonly associated with event planners. They take charge of not only food preparation but also decorations, such as table settings and lighting.

The trend is towards satisfying all the clients senses with food as a focal point. With the correct atmosphere, professional event caterers with experience can make an event special and memorable.

Beautifully prepared food alone can appeal to the senses of taste, smell, and sight - perhaps even touch, but the decorations and ambiance can play a significant part in a successfully catered event.

Bibliography

Bryson, McDowell: *Concierge: Key to Hospitality: A Training Manual*, New York, Wiley, 1992.

Clark, Mona: *Interpersonal Skills for Hospitality Managers*, London, Chapman Hill, 1995.

Dennis, J.: *How Consumers Pick a Hotel: Strategic Segmentation and Target Marketing*, New York, Haworth Press, 1997.

Donald, M.: *Customer Service in the Hospitality and Tourism Industry*, Englewood Cliffs, Prentice Hall, 1994.

Eberts, Marjorie: *Careers in Travel, Tourism, and Hospitality*, Lincolnwood, VGM Career Horizons, 1997.

Elio, C.: *The Hospitality Law Desk Reference*, Miami, Southern Beverage Journal, 1994.

Hubert, B.: *A Host of Opportunities: An Introduction to Hospitality Management*, Chicago, Irwin, 1996.

James, M. : *The Meeting Planner's Legal Handbook*, Washington, D.C.: Goldberg & Associates, 1996.

Koontz, H.: *Management: A Global Perspective*, New York, McGraw Hill, 1993.

Medlik, S.: *Managing Tourism*, Oxford, Butterworth-Heinemann Ltd., 1991.

Michael, John: *Principles of Hospitality Law*, London, Cassell, 1999.

Nancy, N.: *Choosing a Career in Hotels, Motels, and Resorts*, New York, Rosen Pub. Group, 1997.

Norman, G.: *Hotel, Restaurant, and Travel Law: A Preventive Approach*, Albany, Delmar Publishers, 1993.

Pender, Lesley: *Marketing Management for Travel and Tourism*, Cheltenham, Stanley Thornes Publishers, 1999.

Robert, H.: *Managing Hospitality Human Resources,* East Lansing, Educational Institute of the American Hotel & Motel Association, 1997.

Rocco, M.: *An Introduction to Hospitality Today,* Orlando, Educational Institute, 1998.

Rosemary, E.: *Managing Employee Relations in the Hotel and Catering Industry,* London, Cassell, 1995.

Swarbrooke, J.: *Marketing Tourism, Hospitality and Leisure in Europe,* London, International Thomson Business Press, 1996.

Thomas, F. : *Introduction to the Hospitality Industry,* New York, Wiley, 1995.

Thomas, F.: *Introduction to Management in the Hospitality Industry,* New York, Wiley, 1995.

Timothy, R.: *Cases in Hospitality Management: A Critical Incident Approach,* New York, Wiley, 1995.

Waller, Keith: *Improving Food and Beverage Performance,* Oxford, Butterworth-Heinemann, 1996.

Index

I

L

M

N

O

P

R

S

T

W